Robert Harbinson was born in Belfas there and in Enniskillen, Co. Fermana
as a cabin boy on a dredger in Belfast
medical missionary. He left Belfast in
South Wales Bible College and he we
Canada and Venezuela. He took up o
and South America and his hunting a
and Stony Indians began a long inte........................ ....
feature in his many travel books which were published in the 1960s under the name of Robin Bryans.

In more recent years he has become involved in music, concentrating on his work as an opera librettist from his London home/music studio.

Song of Erne is the second volume of his four-part autobiography which begins with *No Surrender*, and continues with *Up Spake the Cabin Boy* and *The Protégé*. In addition to these and his travel books he has also published *Tattoo Lily and Other Ulster Stories*, the novel *Lucio*, and his collection of poems *Songs Out of Oriel*.

SONG OF ERNE

Robert Harbinson

THE
BLACKSTAFF
PRESS
BELFAST AND WOLFEBORO, NEW HAMPSHIRE

First published in 1960 by
Faber and Faber Limited
This Blackstaff Press edition is a photolithographic facsimile
of the first edition printed by Latimer Trend & Co. Limited

This edition published in 1987 by
The Blackstaff Press
3 Galway Park, Dundonald, Belfast BT16 0AN, Northern Ireland
and
27 South Main Street, Wolfeboro, New Hampshire 03894 USA
with the assistance of
The Arts Council of Northern Ireland

Printed in Northern Ireland by
The Universities Press Limited

British Library Cataloguing in Publication Data
Harbinson, Robert
Song of Erne. — 2nd ed.
1. Harbinson, Robert   2. Northern Ireland
— Biography
I. Title
941.6082'2'0924   CT808.H3/

Library of Congress Cataloging-in-Publication Data
Harbinson, Robert, 1928–
Song of Erne.
Reprint. Originally published: London : Faber and
Faber, 1960.
1. Harbinson, Robert, 1928–   — Biography — Youth.
2. Authors, Irish — 20th century — Biography.
3. Fermanagh (Northern Ireland) — Social life and
customs.   I. Title.
PR6058.A617Z47   1987   828'.91409 [B]   87–27848

ISBN 0-85640-394-6

FOR
SALLY AND CHRISTOPHER
WITH LOVE

Contents

	LOCAL TERMS	*page* 9
1.	EXODUS	13
2.	STRANGE NEW WORLD	20
3.	LAKE DWELLINGS	38
4.	GENTRY INDEED!	55
5.	A BLACK SNOUT	67
6.	THE MASTER'S TENANTS	78
7.	HERDSMEN OF THE SCILLIES	95
8.	LOST HORIZON	110
9.	THE PROMISED LAND	118
10.	MEADOWSWEET SUMMER	134
11.	SUNDAY POSH	147
12.	THOSE ENDEARING OLD CHARMS	165
13.	WINTER PRELUDE	181
14.	HERE COMES I . . .	199
15.	THE LINNET OF BOHO	219
16.	NO LONGER A CUB	231

LOCAL TERMS

BAD TIMES 1916–23
BARONY A territorial division
BLACK HEADS Knapweed
BLACKMOUTHS Presbyterians
BLACK PIG'S DYKE, THE Fortification mound
BLACK SCOTER Common scoter
BOUR-TREE Elder
BOXTY Potato cake
CEILI (pronounced kaylee) An evening gathering
CUBS Boys
CUTTIES Girls
DEVIL'S CHURNSTAFF Sun spurge
DEVIL'S GARTERS Bindweed
DRUMLINS Rounded hills
FENIANS Roman Catholics
GREAT HUNGER, THE The Famine 1845–48
HALSE Hazel
JACK-IN-THE-BOX Lords and Ladies
JAMES THE FLEEING James II
LINT-HOLE Flax dam
MARIGOLD-GOLDINS Corn marigolds
MITCHING SCHOOL Playing truant
PLOUGHLAND As much land as a plough could
    turn in a year
QUICKBEAM Rowan tree
QUICKEN-BERRY Fruit of rowan

RED SERVING-BOYS   Gillaroo trout
RISING, THE   Easter 1916
RUCKS   Ricks
SOUPERS   Catholics who became Protestants in
    the Famine in order to obtain soup and work
STRINGS OF SOVEREIGNS   Creeping jenny
TURF   Peat
WEASELS   Stoats
WEATHER-BLADE   Snipe
WILD GEESE, THE   The Irish soldiers who went
    to France after the defeat of James II

AUTHOR'S NOTE

Over a few events in the latter part of this book,
I have taken an author's privilege of telescoping
time. Some things which, in fact, occurred up to
1946, have been regarded as happening during
1940–42.

Chapter One

Exodus

Ballinamallard—what a place!

My mother moved her lips, trying to master the name of my destination as an evacuee. It proved quite intractable. In the end she picked up the buff label, with the one word BALLINAMALLARD printed in spidery letters, and went over to Mrs. Murray. She was my friend Dizzy's mother.

'Look where my fella's goin',' said my mother in disgust, pointing at the impossible word.

But Mrs. Murray was equally nonplussed. In fact, her own son had a similar label for Lisbellaw, and who, she demanded indignantly, had ever heard of *that* place either!

The school in Belfast, which I had attended for two years, swarmed with people. Not only were the usual pupils there, but their infant brothers and sisters from other schools, to say nothing of parents, aunts, uncles, neighbours and friends all come to witness the great exodus. The like, indeed, had never been seen before.

A farewell crowd gathered round me and everyone confirmed with a single voice my mother's opinion, that the word on my label was perfectly outrageous. Not one could pronounce it. Eventually, somebody with initiative succeeded in swapping my label for another Lisbellaw one. Though also unpronounceable, it would at least ensure that I would have

Dizzy for company. This clever manœuvre did not, however, mean the end of Ballinamallard in my life.

Two years in class together had welded Dizzy and me into an inseparable pair. We had sat huddled in the same desk, in the very room where now the buff labels had been given out. We were the two biggest in our class, and joined in this latest escapade, we would be fit to face anything—even the imminent unknown.

No one remembered it was Sunday. Until we began to move out to the buses waiting importantly outside, laughter and bedlam had occupied our attention. As the children filed in two by two as if going into the ark, friends and relations milled round the windows to say good-bye. Now that panes of glass separated them, the parting became reality. The first tears leaked out. Being infectious, the weeping began to weaken the stoutest hearts. I was twelve years old, almost a man and seldom cried. But at the sign of collapse, my mother told me to 'play the man', despite the last-minute brimming of her own eyes.

The engine chugged into life, and the desperate tears and shouts grew frantic. Then the bus edged forward, and the distress of those left behind was painful to see. But we only managed a few yards, before a woman stood in the way, waving her arms. Our driver pulled up, and she got in, to enquire if any members of the Church of Ireland were aboard. A few, including myself, put up their hands and were given postcards. These were for sending to the bishop with the address of our new homes in the west, homes we already referred to as 'billets'. Our souls were not to be forgotten. While this shepherding of the ninety-and-nine was in progress, one lost sheep, a little girl, was struggling to escape. Throwing aside all control she tried to get out through the windows. All the way to the school gates, her parents pulled and tugged, and finally out she went. Her mother proclaimed that for all she cared, the Jerries could come, bombs and all, she and the child would rather die together than live apart. And so we lost the first of our number.

Sentiments of that sort never occurred in my mother. She faced every situation in life with a practical outlook. I was going because I loved the country. On being discharged in that very month from the tuberculosis clinic, the doctors had instructed that I was to get all the fresh air possible. Besides, I would not be away very long, for in just over a year I would be fourteen, and would return to Belfast to become an apprentice in the shipyard.

My mother's last words, flung through the window as the bus gathered speed, were—'An' keep yer snout clean up there.' For her, the country was always 'up there', and she was anxious I should forsake the evil ways I had picked up in the city. She wanted me to come back sobered and settled, prepared to face a steady life in the docks. Wild escapades must be at an end, new leaves must be turned, my snout, in fact, kept in an impeccable condition.

Evacuation promised to be an exceedingly novel affair. Who, for instance, had ever driven out of the school gates in a bus before? Familiar streets slid by as though seen in a dream, real but beyond reach. Then they changed to unfamiliar ones and finally gave way to the station with its grand entrance which seemed such a suitable prelude to our journey. Either the motion of the bus, or the emotion of parting, had overcome many of the passengers, and when we poured into the concourse, they dashed to the lavatories. After much counting and marshalling, we somehow got on the train. But another check revealed that two more of our party had absconded, presumably away off to their homes. So far, within half an hour, the score was three.

After interminable delays, while the station roof echoed the rows of escaping steam, and important-looking organizers peered at us through the smoky glass, the train gave a jolt. We were off! Realizing that escape was over for the rest of the day, we settled to various occupations. Mine was to sit in a corner and gaze at Belfast flitting by.

Rows of mean houses flashed past in succession. Besides festoons of plumbing, the back walls gave a complete exhibition of Orangemen's art. Rude slogans against the Pope appeared in many different patterns, some scrawled hastily in whitewash, other painted elegantly with a rococo flourish on the bricks. Whole gables were filled with elaborate murals in honour of William III's glorious victory at Boyne Water. 'Remember 1690' said other notices, as if we were likely to forget the famous date that seemed nearer than last week. I might be one of the episcopalian minority, but even the Presbyterian blackmouths were staunch Protestants and full of the Orange cause.

Clearing a larger hole in the compartment window, I could glimpse long stretches of the sally-bush verges. How derelict they looked. Once I had roamed their shady paths and haunted their hidden places with a gang of older boys. We had sat in secret enclaves, with potatoes roasting in the campfire aisles, and our hearts burning with rebellion.

The train tore me relentlessly away, over the same rails on which I tried once to flatten a halfpenny into a penny. We sped on, the wheels singing now with a more steady, metallic music. Shrieking like all the banshees in Ulster, it dashed urgently into the maw of tunnels, and out again into the blinding light. Not having travelled previously in a train, many of the children were excited as never before in their lives. At every tunnel, or steep cutting or mere bridge, our general idea was to shout or scream as loudly as possible, matching our voices against the entombed booming of wheels in the black abyss, where sparks flew by like demons. It was terrifying, exhilarating, even for me, who had lived all my life by the railway. Before we had cleared the suburbs, the schoolteacher in charge of us, had despaired of dampening the noise. Triumphant, we rolled westwards.

Our cases, or parcels done up in newspaper and hairy string, contained sandwiches, meant to last a whole day. We also had great bagfuls of our favourite dulse seaweed, and this produced an unsuspected source of torment—thirst. A strict ban had been put on drinking the train's water, and the supply of oranges out of the cases and parcels soon dwindled.

Outside, the country unrolled as an endless tapestry, gently patterned with willow brooks, grey stone villages, and meadows ripe with high summer. Boglands passed, and mountains loved by merlin and peregrine.

At signals or junctions our splendid train stopped, panting for breath, hissing plumes of steam, like the bread-server's horse on frosty mornings at home. At one such stop, longer than the others, somebody told us that we were about to cross the border. Of course, none of us believed it. A train-load of us Protestant children being taken across the border into the Free State to be massacred? Things had not *quite* come to that, even if all the German spies that ever existed were hiding down in Dublin.

My alarm over this was not so intense as in some other children. I thought myself widely travelled. Had I not already been in four of Ulster's six counties? Had I not seen the razor-bills on Rathlin, and climbed the hump of Slemish, where St. Patrick's visions came to him as he herded Milchu's pigs? On several twelfths of July, I had walked with the loyal Orangemen to Finaghy's Field. I had concealed myself many times in lorries and vans and empty cattle-trucks going out of Belfast. But I had to admit to myself that none of these adventures had actually taken me to the border.

Being so worldly-wise, I gave it as my considered opinion that despite authority's announcement we were *not* at the border. Where, I asked, were the battlemented walls, the moats and the vast palings with cruel iron spikes which must separate the dirty Free State from our clean and righteous Ulster? It could

B   17

not be. Nevertheless, just in case we should be in the danger zone, we determined to show the rascally Fenians the stoutness of our Orange hearts, and sang 'Dolly's Brae':

And when we came to that great hill they were ranked on every side
And offering up their Papish prayers for help to stem the tide.
But we loosed our guns upon them and quickly won the day.
And we knocked five hundred Papishes right over Dolly's Brae.

Without so much as seeing the shadow of a Catholic gunman, the train ground away again. Morning departures lapsed into the past. A long afternoon began and wore on, with nothing to beguile it. The wheel music of steel gripping steel drilled itself into our ears. Surely it was the longest journey in all Ireland.

Hungry for amusement Dizzy Murray and I joined some other boys in daring each other to touch the communication cord. As though charged with lethal electricity, the red chain's brief appearance out of its tubing exerted an irresistible influence. We reached up as though the faintest touch would kill us instantly. Making the slightest contact with the awful chain we whipped our hands away like lightning. Becoming elated at this success, an elation tinged with disappointment that the train was not slowing to a standstill, a bolder move was made. The chain was pressed to see what tension was on it.

My turn at this had not come, before one of the schoolmasters had been summoned from an adjoining carriage. Pulling a cane from his sleeve, like a sword from its scabbard, he sliced the air with the stinging swish of authority. This monstrous abuse of his privilege was not taken lightly, for it was, despite Germans and evacuation, still Sunday—and even the most tyrannical knew that pedagogic power ceased from Friday till Monday. To express our strongest disapproval of his mean advantage, we retired as a mob about to riot, into the lavatories, where we stayed sulking and plotting revenge.

But at last began the long *rallentando*, a slow but prescient drop in speed, while the wheel's roar faded to a hiss, and then to a sigh. Down came the cases and what remained of the newspaper parcels, and hugging these few precious possessions, the only link with all the things of home, we swarmed on to the platform. We had come to a country town—Enniskillen. It was late afternoon, and the sun, like our train, would soon be at the end of its journey. Already it drooped a little and made long shadows.

We had no time to take stock of our surroundings, for more buses waited in the station yard, and whisked us off to another school. There we were sorted out and crammed into yet more buses for the final distribution over the countryside. By a smart move, Dizzy and I contrived to get into the wrong bus, and so never saw Lisbellaw. We wanted to evade those who knew us, and who might write home about our bad behaviour.

For an hour we drove beside lakes, and under dappled naves of beeches, pulling up at a small village school. All sorts of good-works matrons milled and fussed about us, organizing transport to the scattered farm billets. Because of my wrong label which did not correspond with the organizer's list, I was left until last. A long time passed before anything happened. Then a horsey woman, who impressed herself on me solely because of a goitre throat and a fine range of la-de-da that it filtered, plonked me in the front seat of a battered car, and drove me away. We were going to a country rectory. The horsey woman chattered away in her posh voice in quite a friendly manner, but said that as the rector's wife was in poor health I must be on my best behaviour. After all, she reasoned, it was an unusual honour to be billeted in the rectory.

Chapter Two

Strange New World

The sun had gone, and bats shivered through the gloaming. From the little car I saw huge gateposts of rotting wood that leaned over a drive, dense with evening-dark foliage. And it curved round to a mansion that loomed up and dissolved into the sky. After the close and sickly atmosphere of trains and buses, the country air, sweet and velvety, blew as though I had come to heaven. The rich headiness of roses weighed the breezes down with mingled luscious scents. Along a nearby garden wall, waves of cream roses washed as though breaking on a shore, and as though the petals, showered on to the lawn beneath, were foam, held by a spell from dissolution.

The horsey woman pulled a handle and somewhere deep inside the building a friendly bell clanged. We stood on the top step, both silent and listening for footsteps inside. At last they came. A maid opened the door and stood aside, while the horsey woman hawked me in as though familiar with the place. I acquiesced in everything and clutched my case, scarcely believing that this great strong house and its enchanted garden were going to be my home.

The rector was old, and sat by a diminutive fire in his study. He talked chirpily to the woman who had brought me. Then he chuckled, patted me on the head like a dog, and called me 'boy'. Then he seated himself by the fireplace again and withdrew to a remote world of his own making. Fortunately the appearance of the maid saved me from trying to renew contact with the old man. My supper, she announced, as if I were a duke, was ready. Down we trailed, along dark musty corridors, she in front, I following behind in a miniature procession. She opened a door and stood aside to allow my entry. The maid then signalled that I should occupy the sole place laid at a polished table as big as a skating-rink.

I didn't know what to do. Before me, beautiful silver was laid out, smiling and winking in the warm light of a paraffin lamp. But there were so many pieces in so many rows and in such strange positions, I might as well have been back in the operating theatre confronted with the surgeon's instruments. Nostalgically I recalled the brown-handled, iron-bladed knife I used at home and the bent fork that did duty for everything. And my self-confidence began to ebb away. I had never sat in a room like that before, with a maid showing me a little bell on the table, which I should ring when I was ready for the next course. The lamp created a ball of amber showing me the meal's splendour. It was all too removed from the little kitchen of my own working-class home, with its black-leaded hob, from which the food was lifted on to the newspaper that covered the deal table. I did not dare produce the tin mug and plate that had gone in my case as part of our equipment. And when the pudding came in, my fears were confirmed.

A gooseberry-pie lay in a fine china dish. I loved gooseberries but had never had them cooked before. A taste convinced me that treated in this way, they were inferior to their sharp rawness on coming straight from the greengrocer's box. I could not, of course, leave them for fear of being punished. At home if we did not eat anything served up, we were either forced, or the hated food was set aside until the next meal, by which time we should be so hungry as to devour anything. No, the only answer was to hide the pie. Up the chimney, or in one of the numerous cupboards? These were useless ideas. And then in a corner I spied a *jardinière* supporting a robust aspidistra, and I tipped the unwanted pie beneath its sheltering leaves until morning.

I had hardly regained my seat when the door opened. A figure stood there, and I thought it was a righteous spirit come to take vengeance for wasting food—such high-class stuff too from the rector's kitchen. The figure advanced and I saw it was a small woman, whose pale wrinkled face was sprung with a nervous twitch. Tiny corkscrew curls surrounded her head with an aura whose colour varied from patch to patch. We eyed each other apprehensively like two cats on a backyard wall. She quizzed the new member of the household through steel-rimmed glasses, and this preliminary sniffing done, she announced shyly that she was the rector's wife. Kindness modulated her voice. Seeing my empty plate, from which every vestige of gooseberry had been swept, the rector's wife said I must be so hungry after my long journey. Thereupon she went herself into the kitchen and brought back more of the gooseberry pie. With another chat she glided away as she had come, like a ghost. For the second time I paid a swift and furtive visit to the *jardinière*.

Before going to bed I was shown into the bathroom on the ground floor. It too was exceedingly grand, as shiningly magnificent in terms of tiles and porcelain as the dining-room was in mahogany and silver. On one wall was a huge mirror. Below it on shelves was such a collection of bottles and tubes of perfumes and powders and lotions and vivid bath crystals as I had never dreamt could exist in one house. I tried to decide what places of the body all the coloured liquids were intended for. The whole collection seemed rather immoral for a rectory. The w.c. had a separate room, long, high and narrow, with the pan at one end, as though in a throne-room. Here to my joy, I discovered unlimited quantities of toilet paper. I filled my pockets with dozens of sheets, so that I could have music wherever I went, by humming through the paper wrapped over my comb.

And so to bed, without having used the bathroom in spite of a thorough exploration. But if the dining-table was an ice-rink and the bath a swimming pool, what could I make of the vast chamber which was to be my bedroom? True, I had long been used to a room of my own—the back one of our little house, with its gas bracket minus a mantle, and a view of the trains that shook the house every time they thundered by. Did these people now expect me to sleep in a castle? The big room seemed the most enormous I had ever been in. I went along the windows pulling out the shutters. These were also new to me, and I thought they must be connected in some way with sieges and the repelling of attackers. The big iron bar which fastened across them, made the place into a real castle.

The bed surpassed what could reasonably be demanded of a bed. It was nearly as big as my whole room at home. Frilly curtains and valances hung to the floor and filled the bottom and head panels. Its wide headboard ended in two winged brackets filled with more chintz. Surely no ordinary mortal was expected to sleep in the bed alone. Undressed, I flung myself into the centre of it and sank into the feather tick's soft depths. To my surprise the rector's wife came in to ask what kind of book I would like her to read me. This was the end! No one had ever read to me in bed at night, and though only twelve, I was unusually developed for my age. I did quick mental calculations—was the woman quite barmy or merely trying to be fresh?

She gave extracts from something which seemed to have a religious flavour. I could not but think of one of my mother's sayings, 'The bigger the Bible, the bigger the rogue.' She got up from the bedside chair, 'Nan will bring you your hot water at eight.' In reply I grunted, not understanding what she meant. At home I always washed at the kitchen sink from the cold tap. The rector's wife came round to the other side of the bed. 'I do believe that water hasn't been changed today,' she said, picking up a carafe from the small table. Such things had only come my way before in the mission-halls of Belfast where they stood on green baize, for the refreshment of long-winded preachers. Surely she did not think I would get up in the night to drink water. Strange new world, it was very perplexing. Half the things they did, possessed no rhyme or reason, certainly my mother would have thought it queer and daft. Replenished with fresh water, the carafe was put back by the rector's wife. I tried to appear natural and at ease, as though accustomed to these odd rituals. When bidden good-night I gave a cheery 'Sleep tight, missus' which I thought very polite.

Of course I had not the faintest intention of sleeping. Every corner of the room would have to be inspected to make sure that I was quite safe. I blockaded the door, for it had no key in the lock. If anyone came prowling in the night, I would want to know, so I placed a chair by the door and a glass oil lamp on top. He would have to be a clever intruder to get in without making an almighty crash. Although the rector's Roman collar lent an air of righteousness to the place, the house was after all a mansion, and must be full of ghosts, to say nothing of burglars breaking in for a load of that silver, left for the taking down in the dining-room.

I swung the shutters open again. The summer night flowed in with a grating vesper of corncrake and the unmistakable churring of nightjars. Owls hooted wierdly, piercing the velvety darkness with uncanny messages. Some sounded softly from distant woods with long waverings and a distinct final yap. Others sat pontifically in trees that edged the lawn, and taught their young how to screech and hiss. The dense silhouettes of the tall beeches seemed immensely greater than any I had ever seen.

Having direct contact with the open air strengthened my feeling of security. I finished my defence inspection, by peeping under the bed valances, into the sad empty wardrobes, and even into a hatbox on top. I tried a door that led from another part of the room, thinking it must give on to a haunted closet, but it was firmly locked. In a box I found some bars of soap. Mice had delicately eaten the edges, leaving them like one of my mother's apple tarts, when she had pressed the edges to keep the juice in. There was a gun cartridge too. Till then, I had only seen empty ones, but never one with the live shot. Was it likely to blow up in the night—perhaps the little teeth of the mice would set it off.

At last, knowing that nothing more could be gained, I blew out my light and tried to sleep. But the corncrake's cry was so persistent, the owls' screeches turned to an eerie human snoring, and my home was so very far away that all I could do was to start up at every movement along the corridor and landing outside. I believed that only the rector, his wife, and Nan the maid lived in the house, though the amount of coming and going sounded now as if the house was full. Perhaps more evacuees had come and were eating gooseberry pie downstairs.

I suddenly remembered my card for the bishop. I had been told to fill it in, immediately on arrival at the billet, and then post it. It was essential for the church people at home to know my address. Not only did I belong to their denomination, but I was also an orphan living on the poor box. The clergy would be certain to contact my mother if the card did not go at once. I got up and took my barricade from the door. I had no matches for the lamp, but a tiny light burned on the landing. The opening of my door brought the rector from his room. Without his false teeth, and in ordinary pyjamas, he looked quite different from the old man I had seen by the study fire. Somehow, I expected him to sleep in a weird ecclesiastical garment. I explained about the postcard, and his deep old eyes kindled sympathetically. The card, he said, would do very well if posted in the morning, he was sure the bishop would be pleased enough.

My fears allayed, I went back to bed, first rebuilding the barricade. Out of the depths of my feathers I said my prayers a second time as a safeguard. I was almost asleep when an owl launched out of the ivy, uttering a terrible cry which scattered my dreams as if a maniac were laughing by my bed. There could be no sleep now. I lay plucking up enough courage to make a search, and could not be satisfied until I had crawled through the valances and right under the bed to ensure that nobody was hiding. The wardrobes fortunately had keys, which I put under my pillow. I shut the windows and folded the shutters in, sealing myself against owls and ghouls alike. Then to secure my soul against perdition, I got out my sacred sash of the Orange Order, and wore it under my shirt.

A swelling diapason at dawn woke me. Not even the bars and bolts of the shutters could keep out the thrilling, rising, singing of birds, which ran in an endless rhapsody to meet the sun. I lay still a long time trying to distinguish individual voices in the general music. For years now I had loved birds. Stealing out of Belfast on cattle-wagons or lorries, mitching from school to do so, I had followed birds' ways through the sky or at the water's edge and knew their calls. But from the rectory garden and surrounding trees came many notes strange to me. As the music explored every note on the keyboard, and as the invisible organist pulled out more stops, I realized that here were many pipes whose flowing melodies would need to be learnt. I wanted to get up and run down the garden, climb the rose wall and go off on exploration of the countryside. But there was no need to be impetuous, because mornings from now on, for more than a year, would be country mornings.

Then the sun played through chinks in the shutters and laid strokes of light across the high ceiling. The night of fantasies and fear vanished like a wreath of mist. I felt not altogether displeased at being the rector's boy. I dropped into an easy sleep from which a tap at the door woke me. I uncurled from the feather tick, took down my defences, and opened the door. There was nobody there. But on the mat stood a beautiful brass watering-can, or what I thought was a watering-can. It looked exactly like those used in the cemetery at home, except for its gleaming sides.

As I splashed about in the willow-pattern basin, I wondered why they had not allowed me to wash in the bathroom downstairs. Could it really be that the old rector and his wife were foxing about in the bath? In our Belfast streets there were no bathrooms, only a tin tub in front of the fire on Saturday nights. Full-length baths were associated by a vague sense with immorality, deriving from pictures of film stars reclining nude in them, lasciviously bowered in drifts of foaming soapsuds. Film stars were all right on the screen, but off it, well, everybody knew about their private lives. Full-length baths hinted at the luxury which was the reward of the ungodly.

Being widely travelled I had, of course, actually been in such a bath myself. The sitting-up soak that I had in front of our fire the night before leaving Belfast, was not the only thing I knew about baths. The summer holiday-home by the sea for poor children, where I went, possessed baths. But there the joy of luxuriating at full-length was impossible for we always bathed two boys at a time. And in any case, the matrons stood over us watching with righteous eyes to see that we behaved ourselves. And with baths in the hospital, the story of too much attention and treatment, and too little enjoyment, repeated itself. I so hoped they would let me have a bath all on my own at the rectory. Surely the old woman would not insist on coming in to scrub my back, as she had insisted on reading to me.

For that morning the brass ewer and willow-pattern basin had to suffice. When I went downstairs, I was surprised to see that my breakfast would be another solitary meal in the awesome dining-room. Afterwards I was summoned to family prayers in the study. Dutifully I closed my eyes and put my hand over them. But the prayers were so long and boring, mostly about foreign missions, that I made a slit between my fingers and peeped through. An old gardener, as well as Nan, attended with the rector and his wife. The gardener was not very intent on praying either and kept stroking the dog with his square, black hand. I noticed two of his flybuttons were undone and quickly turned to see if anyone else was looking through their fingers at this ungodly omission in the sacred study. The gardener remained sufficiently alert, however, to give forth a fruity 'Amen' at the end of each prayer. He said it in such a way as to imply 'Well prayed, rector—just what I would have prayed myself'. Nan had taken off her spectacles to pray, as though the glass clouded her view of heaven, but she spoilt the effect by yawning. Missionaries over and done with, there followed a little prayer for me. I felt very important—the same as when one of our neighbours back home had her name read on the wireless, as they played a request record for her son in the army.

Almost as though he knew better than to disturb the prayers, the postman arrived as soon as we finished. Nan went off along the hall to fetch the letters. It was an important-looking bundle, and even the maid got one of them. Never before, in my whole life, had I anticipated a letter, but now the postman became a vital person in my existence. The others started to read their mail, the rector at his study desk where I could see him through the open door, and his wife on the very edge of the drawing-room settee, and Nan where she stood in the hall.

I was crestfallen that the packet had contained nothing for me. I wondered why my mother had not made my elder sister, who was the family scribe, write to me. Of post office workings I knew nothing. A pillar-box stood near our house at home, and the man who came to empty it, seemed to do so at all hours of day and night. In spite of not yet letting my family know where I was, I somehow expected them to send a nice rude postcard, like some of the other boys used to get in hospital, or a taste of my mother's own potato-bread. Surely the evacuation authorities must know my whereabouts and had told her?

While the others scanned their mail, I stood opposite a big heavily-framed engraving hanging on chains in the hall. It was St. Patrick's Cathedral, Dublin. Beneath the glass I tried to disentangle the architectural details from the damp spots. The little wife coughed behind me then and said how much she loved Dublin and its cathedrals. In fact, she added, Belfast hardly appealed to her at all. This bewildered me. I had never heard anyone make such disparaging remarks about our Protestant capital. Everybody knew it was a finer city than dirty Dublin. Could this woman be a bit of a Papish as well as being barmy?

It made me feel lonelier than ever, and I went out into the village. Family parting gifts, presented the previous day (was it only one day I had been away—it seemed longer than anything else I could remember) amounted to two whole shillings, all in pennies. I turned my steps towards the telephone box. The woman who kept the baby-wear shop near my home had a telephone. I would ring her, and she would gallop away down the street for my mother. How surprised and delighted they would be. Telephone kiosks were familiar to me. I knew all about them, or so I thought. In Belfast, we boys never passed one without going in to press Button B to see if anyone had left two pennies.

The village kiosk stood near the shop. Full of confidence I picked up the receiver and even got 'Enquiries' to find me the number. Then the operator told me to insert two shillings and a sixpence. What a blow! Could it be true then that not all calls cost twopence? Sadly I put the receiver back. My pile of pennies which had seemed such a fortune, would not be enough. The loneliness was complete now, it cut deep, like acid on glass, leaving a pattern of misery.

Before I got out of the box, the horsey woman with the goitre hurried over from the other side of the street. The previous evening's la-de-da tone was still there, but this time tinged with vindictiveness. Had I seen my friend Dizzy Murray, she demanded. I said no, but she gave me an odd look, and clearly disbelieved me. Then I was taken over to the policeman. Dizzy had vanished. The people in his billet reported his disappearance, saying that he had got up long before them and left the house. Everyone presumed he had gone back to Belfast, though by what means no one could imagine. Being seen in the telephone kiosk, brought my own behaviour under suspicion now, and the woman insisted on driving me back to the rectory.

This time she placed me like a prisoner on the back seat, along with a box of groceries. While she stood gossiping about evacuees with various locals in a not-too-kindly voice, I had a look in the box. And there, to my delight, rested a large bag of dried figs. My pockets were soon stuffed and I had a good fill of raisins too. Then the car owner got in with another woman who, completely ignoring me, began to tell Mrs. Goitre about some terrible 'Belfast brats'. My gorge began to rise. Before reaching the rectory we were stopped by a fat country woman pedalling slowly along. Mrs. Goitre wound down the window and leaned out in her coarse way.

'Our lot', the cyclist began, 'is still over the fire doing breakfast.' And the calves weren't fed because the evacuees had finished every drop of the milk. She sounded really irate. 'You must take them away,' the woman next to the driver concurred sympathetically and retailed more outrages committed during the first day of evacuation. Robbing the hens of their eggs was already a common crime, and the evacuees made the grievance worse by sucking the eggs there and then. My depression deepened. I felt very small indeed sitting behind and wished I had taken more of the figs.

Once again the car turned into the drive, and while Mrs.

Goitre conversed secretively with the rector, I went up to my room and consumed the figs. This done, I opened the window, and tried to see if the owls really had nests in the smothering creeper. From my room, I discovered that the roof was easily accessible, and climbed out to a landscape of slate, full of wonderful chimney-perches for sitting on. From such eminence, the lakes we had driven by the night before, came into view, and beyond them, hills, and further out still, blue mountains. Silvery clouds, shaded like the palest breasts of doves, drifted in loose ridges across a wide sky of intense blue—kingfisher blue. Over the serrated land, and the mirrors of the lakes, soft shadows crept followed by lines of brilliant colour where the sunlight fell.

From that moment, in my stone roof-top eyrie, I knew how much I loved Fermanagh. Any vague plan I had of fleeing, and tracing Dizzy's footsteps back to Belfast, fell into abeyance, though were not entirely dismissed. For weeks before leaving the city I had lived in delirium. My fever was a love of the country so great that familiar streets, the Bog Meadows beyond the city, and even the railway's sally verges became intolerable. Real country, and only real country, away from factories and shipyards, could satisfy. Despite the strangeness of the rectory, and the loneliness for companionship, I was not going to run away, so soon after getting out to the country I wanted. Because the tobacco for my stump of pipe had run out, I pulled a stick of cinnamon from my pocket and began to smoke it in lieu of the pipe.

As I sat innocently happy, with the ardour of Fermanagh's summer lapping around me, a voice came up from the drive. The fat woman who had stopped the car, was telling me to come down. Involuntarily I put my tongue out and gave her the devil-rape-you sign. I then clambered down by way of some outhouse roofs and went off into a meadow. I lay and dreamed, watching the breezes brush the golden mane of long grass-

31

tops, and carry sheet lightning of movement across the broad acres.

When I went back to the house, not only was I very late for lunch, but found that the whole atmosphere had changed. The meddlesome women had done their worst, and now everybody concluded that I too had tried to run off. The meal was painful, taken together in the dining-room. The rector looked stern despite the blood-clotted piece of lavatory paper on his chin from shaving. His wife was tearful, the twitch in her face jerking up and down more than ever. Not a word passed, but afterwards the rector took me into his study and said that next morning I would be going to a new billet. He himself would write to Dr. MacNeice, our bishop in Belfast, and inform him of the change.

What now of my mother's warning to keep my snout clean up there? Already I had fallen from favour. Even if I wanted to, there could be no point in running away home for my mother would be far from pleased. I was worried now lest the clergy at home should stop the precious five shillings a week orphan allowance, which they gave towards my upkeep. Having the orphan funds stopped by the clergy because of my bad behaviour was always a dread, worse than them seeing my mother down town with a boy-friend.

Sullenly I went upstairs, and sat by the window. Why was I being sent away, had they discovered the gooseberry pie? Had Mrs. Goitre missed her few wretched figs, or did the silly old cow on the bicycle think I intended to burn the house down with my cinnamon stick? My motives in using the village telephone kiosk were easy to misinterpret, especially as the rectory itself possessed a telephone. I hated them, every single one. Instead of treating us as good Orange brethren, they thought us social outcasts. Indeed one woman in the village described her evacuees to Mrs. Goitre as 'so dirty'—just as if we were Catholics and had come from the Free State.

Yes, I hate them, I said to the birds on the lawn below. All except Nan, for she came up later and asked at what time I wanted my bath. The excitement of this put everything else out of mind. My first private bath! I was going to do it properly the way Mrs. Simpson or Mae West would. With visions of wallowing in the rich foam I went down to the bathroom, and locked the door. Choosing which of the coloured crystals to begin with, presented a great difficulty, but I decided to try bright mauve ones—just a small handful to start.

Standing naked, I admired myself in the large mirror, wondering if the rector and the others did the same. Never before had I seen my body reflected so well. There was more of it than I had imagined, and it seemed to move in so many places at once. I put on all sorts of comic and lecherous attitudes, and tried to frighten myself with grotesque faces. Then I stepped into the heavenly pool. The first disappointment was that the crystals had not filled the air with alluring incense. I began to whip up the water to make the clouds of suds that were the main attraction of the bath, but nothing happened. I beat and beat the water as though whipping eggs for an omelet. Still the fabulous suds failed to rise from the water. Perhaps more of the crystals were needed, so I emptied more than half the mauve ones in. And because the water remained unperturbed without so much as a bubble, I tried the green ones, but with similar results. In desperation I seized the bottles of oils and lotions, thinking that a combination could not fail to produce the lovely deep froth, film actress fashion, for which I so longed. The water became murkier, greasier, and did give off an incense, but hardly of the desired kind.

Feeling completely cheated, and my arms tired from smacking and stirring, I gave up the idea altogether of having a bath, and stepped out and dried myself. At least I could still experiment with the powders and perfumes, and find which were for the feet and which for the bottom. This proved to be quite an engaging occupation, and I became so absorbed that time slipped

C

away quickly, bringing a timid knock on the door and an anxious 'Are you quite safe?'

Dressed and reeking of perfume like a millgirl on a Saturday night, I slipped back to the bedroom, but not without some mementoes. Goodness knows how long it might be before I ever used a bathroom as wonderful as that again, so I loaded up with plenty of booty. And the things would serve to remind me of the curious household which expelled me for ill-defined reasons. Hardest to conceal of my haul was a whole new roll of toilet paper from a cupboard full of such treasure. The little closets in the backyards of our streets at home had never known such grandeur, there we used newspaper if we were lucky. I would be the very first to carry such a marvel back, and would ask privileged friends to come and share the honour. Two handkerchiefs, bought specially for my new life as an evacuee, were drenched with perfume. I was Narcissus-minded, and filled envelopes with powder, and took bars of scented soap.

In themselves these things were of little interest—I merely wanted to see what living as a lord or a film star was like. Only one thing I took for its intrinsic value—the pot-pourri. It stood in a large wooden bowl on the landing, displaying a score of gorgeous colours like a stained-glass window. Lifting its dry petals up, a heavenly scent flew out in the disturbed dust. Summers long past seemed to linger languidly in the dead roses. I found a paper bag and filled it with the late harvest. When I had moved away, I could bury my nose in the bag and be reminded of the evening arrival, when the rectory garden was saturated with the roses' heavy, cloying scent.

The practical part of me had also to be satisfied. In one of the outbuildings I found a toffee-tin full of elaborate brass clasps for holding stair-rods. They were just what we needed at home. Those bought in my grandmother's day for our oilcloth (we were not sufficiently upgraded to call it linoleum) were nearly all broken or missing. It was obvious that the full box of clips could not be wanted in the crammed rectory, for why had it been put into an old glory-hole full of cobwebs and mouse-dirt?

Before going up to my castle bedroom again that night, I also became familiar with the orchard. Gnarled apple and pear trees twisted about laden with fruit, and there were also plums and damsons and many kinds of soft fruit bushes. Not much of it was ripe except for red currants, but that did not prevent me from sampling everything. I could do nothing about the fruit's hard and green qualities, but its sourness I combated by taking more than a week's sugar rations from the dining-room.

Perhaps the rector's conscience pricked him because he had listened to silly gossip of Mrs. Goitre and her cronies, for when saying good-night, he invited me into his study. He thought perhaps I would like to hear some music. And so saying he opened a small glass-fronted cupboard standing on top of his desk, and lifted up a small lever. A round steel disc like a gramophone record, only fixed up on end, began to revolve, and there fell out of the box a sparkling waterfall of clear sounds.

I had not heard a musical box before. The rector said his was called a polyphon and when the disc stopped, he took it off and showed me the works behind it. Next to the church organ, I thought this the most beautiful instrument in the world. There was a pile of discs, one jolly tune on each, and I heard the lot through. In the twilight room the elaborate runs and trills of the music which echoed in the box like bells across vast fields, cheered me up.

When the old man said he would take me to Enniskillen in the morning, I understood it to be something of an apology. I would like it better he said, for a young family was going to look after me, and there would be lots of children and evacuees for me to play with. I made mental comparisons between creeping alone about the huge silent rectory and the fun I might be missing elsewhere. The old cleric was undoubtedly right, and because of the music and his concern over my loneliness, the hard core of hate inside me melted.

In atonement I allowed him to see my nature diary, and showed him specimens of the flowers I had pressed earlier in the day. This so pleased the old boy, that he rummaged in his bookshelves, and produced a well-used, but ever-to-be-treasured copy of *Flowers of the Field*. This he solemnly presented to me and then led the way upstairs himself. I almost regretted now having to go. But the prospect of living on the island-town of Enniskillen surrounded by all its lakes, and the possibility of more rooms to explore in another house, filled me with excitement.

Hardly had I settled into the rectory feathers, for the last time, when the pains began. A vice in my stomach tightened relentlessly. Three at a time the stairs flew beneath me, and fortunately the w.c. was vacant. This performance repeated itself at intervals for hours. And in spite of the urgency and the agony, I felt the rector's nightly apparition watching from his door. When the combined efforts of stolen figs and a dozen unripe fruits had rushed through and emptied my burning bowels, I fell back in the tick, wondering if it was all divine retribution for an innocent bit of pinchin'. And then my solitude was broken by the now familiar knock at the door. Nan and the water! Could it be tomorrow already, another morning of departure? I opened the door but instead of the brass can, Nan herself stood there, as though expecting a lion to spring out at her. Rightly discerning the cause of my excursions, she had prepared a glass of milk mixed with soothing herbs. I gulped it down, gasping at the bitter taste. Nan being so human had also brought a piece of chocolate to take the taste away. Then she hoped I would sleep well.

I did, and dreamlessly. After what I thought were only a few minutes, Nan knocked again and left the hot water. Then a scramble followed, to get into Enniskillen. The rector's wife was ill, they said, and I must move quietly about the house. Perhaps my advent into their stillness had upset her. Getting into the rector's car, for he was to drive me into the town, I saw his wife at the window in her nightdress. Imagining that she had got up to say good-bye, I waved. But she seemed not to notice. Then the old woman appeared at another window and I saw that she was trying to catch a bird in the room. As the car trundled away down the drive, I took a last look at the house. Was the bird a robin, come to herald the old woman's death?

We passed through a small town and pulled up for petrol. Before getting in again, the rector stopped to talk with another clergyman. Not a word of what they said reached my ears, but I could tell the all-consuming topic of evacuees filled the air, for the other divine bent down to peer into the car at me. And it was not Nan's nervous look, but that of a good judge of men shrewdly summing me up.

Chapter Three

Lake Dwellings

Mrs. Morsett loved coffee.

Swept off my feet by the current of genuine welcome, I could not take in everything at once. My eyes lit on a little blue and white machine fixed on the kitchen cupboard. I did not know what it was for, and wondered if in my whole life as an evacuee, I would ever discover the end of this strange new world. Already in my second home I had found a new gadget. I went closer to examine it, and tentatively turned its handle. Mrs. Morsett came back from seeing the rector off at the front door. Finding me absorbed in the machine, she exclaimed brightly, 'I hope you like coffee'.

Completely confused, I said, 'Yes'. Of course, I had never had coffee in my whole life. Had anyone who lived in Belfast districts like ours? Mrs. Morsett did not seem to be aware of this. For us, coffee belonged to film stars and suchlike, along with full-length baths. And we knew also that Frenchmen drank large quantities to make themselves 'hot', but being foreign, they were bound to do queer things. Coffee—what would I know of it, except for the coffee-iced sponge cake my sister had on her birthday from our dreaded great-aunts. I had liked that.

Pleased by my answer, Mrs. Morsett smiled as if I were a dog which had just learnt a new trick. 'I'm sure we shall get on like a house on fire.' Then I was shown how to put beans into the machine and grind them. 'We'll have a cup before Teddy comes.' I thought her husband must be very grand to own a home like this and be able to afford coffee to drink. But her familiar way of referring him to me, made me feel that here must be the ideal billet.

Despite pure white hair and an inclination to stoutness, my new foster-mother was a lively person, and felt she could not do enough for me. Her son's old room was to become mine, for he was married, living away in England. In a more subdued, sadder voice she said she had never expected to see his place filled ever again. To impress on me that I was to be a second son and not just an evacuee, Mrs. Morsett brought out all the discarded remnants of the son's playthings, and left me with them.

Such toys and books had never come my way before, and while sorting through them I heard her voice calling from the kitchen—would I prefer pineapples or peaches when we ate? The question confused me again, as the coffee had done. Did they also have afters here as at the rectory? And pineapples indeed, as if I was back in the hospital at Christmas and getting a special treat. Pineapples! Now the letter to my mother would have to be unsealed, and a note added to the effect that I was having pineapples for dinner. How my sisters' mouths would water!

Surfeit being the enemy of pleasure, within a week I was taking all these things for granted, and mention even of pineapples did not appear in my letters. But now meal-times, instead of being a drudge and the only way of ending hunger, became an active pleasure. I anticipated meals eagerly, meals heralded by wonderful smells. I ate enormously, and needed no threats or bullying for the plate to be scraped until it shone. Sometimes I caught Mrs. Morsett watching in a determined-not-to-be-shocked way, as I busily went round my plate mopping up every last drop of gravy. Everything she produced was devoured at top speed. But not the stuffing, for that was a difficulty greater than the gooseberry pie at the rectory. Pork had its apple sauce and I could eat that up on its own, but with her strong herbal stuffings, I could do nothing.

However, circumstances were good to me. Having learnt very early that a main grievance against evacuees was their fads about food, I determined not to upset Mrs. Morsett. I had heard her talking with other women from the semi-detached houses that stood just outside the bridge to Enniskillen island. The mania of their evacuees was for endless fry-ups of bacon and eggs and dipped bread. After listening to tirades from these frustrated women, whose cooking was despised, Mrs. Morsett would praise the unfailing emptiness of my plate. Little did she know how skilfully I arranged it. She and I started our dinner promptly at one o'clock 'While it's nice and hot' which she said every day as if for the first time. Her husband invariably came home late. While she got up and went into the kitchen on hearing him at the door, there were a few lightning seconds in which to whip my stuffing on a piece of newspaper, and into my pocket for disposal afterwards. Only once did she come near to finding out the truth, when the dog sniffed a large grease stain that appeared through my trousers pocket.

A self-effacing man, Mr. Morsett found time to be kind, and even to amuse me. Through him, London became not just the place where our king lived, but a romantic city, clearly very much finer than Belfast. Amongst his son's possessions which I inherited was a collection of London bus tickets. Mr. Morsett produced a large map and some pins and together we made ticket-flags and placed them in their respective positions. In a short time I had grasped the main areas of London and the position of districts with romantic names, Golders Green, the Angel, Piccadilly Circus, Shepherd's Bush, Blackfriars, the Elephant and Castle.

Lake Dwellings

My 'lady' was not possessive. As long as I was happy, she was content and left me free to come and go as I pleased. As the rector had foreseen, a need for companions of my own age soon made itself felt. I did not look amongst fellow-evacuees for new mates, somehow I sensed that trying to reconstruct the back-street and railway-verge life, out here in the far west, would not work. For me there could never be another gang like the one that broke up before I left home. Enniskillen showed me another world, I liked it, and in order to belong, a friend would have to be found from amongst its ranks.

John lived two doors away. His father was a policeman—man's natural enemy. Not until he told me that his father shaved the hair under his mother's arms, did I think that even a policeman could be human. That his father was more or less like other people brought friendship with John within possibility. First overtures concluded we developed a liking for one another, and ended by spending all our spare time together.

The houses were built at the edge of a large wooded estate and John knew of a short cut into the dark forest. He was an expert climber and knew the best trees. Reaching nimbly from branch to branch he would be up in the topmost, nestled in a comfortable crook. I went after him and together we sang our limited repertoire of songs over and over. Though I sometimes grew tired of prehensile exercise, I never did of John's other love in life—swimming. Twice a day we went to a pool by Lough Erne. It was good for swimming, and on the bank stood a wooden hut for changing.

One day a mob of police cadets invaded the hut, and our sole possession of the pool came to an end. I bundled up my clothes and scrambled into a corner, for as potential natural enemies these strapping youths were to be despised. For as long as I could remember, the Ulster police with their menacing revolvers and phallic truncheons, loomed in my life as monsters. At any time of day or night they waited to pounce cat-like on the unwary drunk or indiscreet courting couple, and, as I thought, any child who pee'd in the entry. Belonging to the notorious street gang did not improve my regard for policemen. For years they had hunted our gang for petty thieving and trespassing, and I knew as well as any how to dodge the law. When the crowd of big fresh-faced cadets entered the hut, I was like a cat hissing and arching its back at a pack of dogs.

Laughing and carefree the cadets began to change too. Off came the heavy boots with a clatter, then they were throwing off shirts and singlets. I was surprised to see that these were not made from steel to protect them from stray I.R.A. bullets. Standing about without the slightest sign of modesty, the cadets began looking for costumes. Some of them fooled about, flicking towels at each other, or hiding bathing trunks. Could it be that they liked their bodies, looked at them in mirrors as I had looked at mine in the rectory bathroom, and even indulged in wicked thoughts? But there was no time for moral philosophy, with a roar and rush they were out of the hut and into the pool. I glanced at John. The fact that these boys would soon be policemen did not seem to upset him—how could it as his own father was one?

Perhaps . . . perhaps after all, to be in the police did not necessarily mean that you were a bad man.

After that first day the cadets were always down at the pool. And when I found that they did not bully me, or arrest me, or ask questions about my city life, I came to accept them. In my new world, with afters every day for dinner and ground coffee, no doubt the police were different too. I decided to trust them. Soon I was calling them by their Christian names and began to select special ones as friends. And to see these I went purposely to the pool when I knew they would be there. Sometimes I would be hoisted on to a cadet's brawny shoulders, and John on another's, for water-fights, while the woods around rang with our shrieks and laughter.

The cadets expressed the opinion that being such a tall boy for my age, I had all the makings of a policeman. And they proved their point by making me stand back to back to measure my height against theirs. Me a copper—never! What a horror if ever the gang at home heard of such a thing! And yet during the long summer that year by Lough Erne, the desire grew in me to become one. Prophetically my mother's statement that 'my wee fella's tall enough for a peeler' looked as if it might come true. In Enniskillen the cadets strode through the town like young gods, or marched out of the garrison barracks with all the precision and elegance of Guardsmen. To drill in the morning, and then to make for the lake in afternoons to cool off in the mysterious depths like mermen, to be a constant object of admiration and hero-worship in the town, and to finish each perfect day with a lazy sculling about on the lakes, appeared as the ideal life. No dockyards for me—I was going to be a policeman.

Seldom a day went now without some new breaking free from the past. The young plant was shooting out new tendrils which gripped ever more firmly on other stems around it. Fears and superstitions that dogged in the city shadows dispersed as I found new horizons, new friends, new ambitions, and new longings to please people and be loved in return. I wanted desperately to belong, and be absorbed by the life I found in the west. Never for a moment now was the escape route back to Belfast contemplated. I still felt sorry that Dizzy Murray had gone, but I had no intention of following him. More than anything I wanted to grow over the six feet necessary for a policeman. Tom, my special friend among the cadets, taught me exercises that would cure my stooping. And every Saturday I spent a penny in the chemist's weighing machine, to see what effects Mrs. Morsett's great feeding produced.

The parish orphan of Belfast was beginning to change out of all recognition.

I lost many things of the old life, but not my love of birds, and the collecting and pressing of wild flowers. John took me in search of grey-lag geese, and one day when I was out fishing, and the rain stopped, I noticed the grass in places was suddenly speckled with blue eyes—Canadian blue-eyed grass for my collection. We had rows of bottled caterpillars all over the house, and on wet days had snail races up and down the window-panes. Together we watched hypnotized, as dragonflies emerged with kaleidoscope wings from indolent nymphs, and darted about like shooting stars.

The transports of delight at Lough Erne were literal as well as metaphorical, for the Morsetts' neighbours owned a boat with an outboard motor. And because I spent a number of dull afternoons at a desk in their shop filling in numbers and names on ration cards, they invited me out for trips on the lakes. A tiny man with a walrus moustache captained the expeditions. Besides the whiskers, he wore a cloth cap, and a once-white scarf, knotted several times as though to choke him, and then crossed over his chest in priestly fashion. He was a retired water-bailiff, but never spoke to me while the others were there. But if we were alone together he confided his most daring exploits to me.

Falling silent, and champing at his tobacco, he conjured up some event from the past. Then between shots of dark brown saliva aimed at nothing in particular I heard that his were the biggest pike, the finest sonaghan, the best brown trout. The tales fascinated me, though despite the elaborate fishing gear nothing spectacular ever came out of the lakes. But I was always given a share of whatever wriggled on the end of the lines, and however small, Mrs. Morsett fried it for my break-fast. Sometimes only a few pathetic little fingers of perch ended up on the plate. When the catch diminished beyond even culinary size, I appealed to the anglers, and bore the tiny fish home alive to add to my window-sill aquarium, which was a greater interest than a bony, tasteless breakfast.

Lake Dwellings

My joy in these trips on the lake did not come from fishing, but from merely sailing in and out of the creeks and inlets. Fermanagh spread out before me in a jigsaw of islands. At sundown, the lakes became millponds of shining ormolu-varnish, enriched with sparkling inlaid patterns where the engine frothed the wake behind us. We touched at many of the islands, pulling our small boat just out of the water, while we went to explore the tangled forests, crammed with oak and aspen, spindle-tree and willow, blackthorn and guelder-rose. There was never· an outing when the women did not alight first and make off in a group for the bushes. We knew what they went for, yet they brazenly returned declaring that they had been looking for wild flowers.

They had not to look far. Nobody inhabited these small humps of land, each flung on the water's surface like a brilliant arras woven with purple loosestrife and marigold-goldins, strings of sovereigns and the majestic standard-bearers of golden-rod. A sweet scent suffused from hemp agrimony, an irresistible lure to the gaudiest butterflies, who fluttered as though drawn by magnets to the raspberry-and-cream groves. There were reed labyrinths where the black scoter went to breed, and desert island shores turned by sandpipers into excited playgrounds. Birdsong sounded like the music of paradise and wings whirred on glissando flights from sunshine to shadow, in and out of the woods. From surrounding drumlins the wood-pigeon let fall his billing notes, and as we made for home, the throbbing of the nightjar filled the air with a mechanical, insistent purr.

Among this maze of islands where time stood still, I found the perfect contrast to my city life, led with the clashing cymbal accompaniment of trams and traffic. I wondered why nobody lived in those Elysian Fields. Later I learnt that the ambience of the islands' peace had fostered the building of abbeys and hermitages in the early years of Christianity—St. Molaisse to the Island of the Oxen, St. Ninny to the Island of the Plain of Sorrel.

Although not native to Fermanagh, Mr. Morsett had soaked himself in its legends and history, and knew its geography, as his wife used to say, 'backwards'. On Sunday evenings we often took long walks over the drumlins, and as we roamed farther away from the house, Mr. Morsett's shyness slid from him as he grew excited over some tale of the locality. Of course, I already knew about Enniskillen for it enjoyed a place in the Protestant heritage almost as great as besieged Derry itself. Five thousand Jacobite soldiers had stormed the town, and nobody had expected Enniskillen's two thousand to survive. But of the Catholic royalists two thousand were slain, half a thousand taken prisoner, and all this for only twenty dead Protestants. This was resounding victory for William of Orange, our beloved King Billy, and ignominy for the Jacobite cause.

This success pleased King Billy so much that at the battle of Boyne Water he said to the Enniskilleners, 'Gentlemen, you shall be my guards this day, I have heard much of you. Let me see something of you." Ever since, those words had echoed in Enniskillen's ears, and the little town wedged between the lakes had followed the success of its Dragoons and Fusiliers in their battles, in every part of the world. Never would the memory of glorious names fade from the streets of soft-grey architecture—Namur, The Netherlands, the Seven Years' War, American Independence, Waterloo, Balaclava, Sevastopol, South Africa, the Peninsular War, India and the Great War. I was twelve years old and thought it all wonderful.

I seemed to catch the greatest gleams of glory from the Inniskillings on Sunday mornings. Then Mr. Morsett and I sat in the cathedral gallery. The chancel was decked with musty old pieces of muslin, proud remains of regimental colours. They were quite transparent, and gauzy like the dragonflies' wings. Their air of venerated victory lent the whole place a military distinction. Below them, on the walls, and round the aisles, many brass memorials shone, and these also recorded the soldiers' noble victories and sacrifices. So highly and lovingly polished were these brasses that I often saw a woman surreptitiously adjusting a hat in their reflection. It was a church where war, not peace, was honoured. But I too had long treasured a battle trophy of the Inniskillings. My mother's brother, Our Danny, had been in the Fusiliers. He ran away from home as a mere boy, successfully lied about his age, and signed on. Brown-toned photographs of him, grouped with other young soldiers, stood on our mantelpiece. He had been a romantic, dare-devil figure in our life, and I was terribly proud at having his knapsack for a schoolbag.

But over all this glittering radiance a sinister shadow fell. The clergy, the schoolmasters, the history books, the Orange songbooks, and as we thought, the Holy Bible itself, pointed conclusively to the fact that the Protestant way was the only way. It was pumped into us so that our schooling had four R's—the usual three plus religion. Sums and the Orange Order went quite as naturally together as did history and *Foxe's Book of Martyrs.* A shock awaited me in the very centre of the good Protestant town of Enniskillen. There, sure enough, stood our own cathedral. But immediately opposite, with all the cheek in the world, as if it owned the place, was another—the Catholic one! Going to and fro past its door, the farmer in his ass-cart, the car-driver and the country girls going home on the buses, crossed themselves openly and shamelessly, and not one Orangeman tried to stop them. What would King Billy have said to discover such a canker at the rose's heart? What a different attitude the townspeople must have from our staunch Protestants of Sandy Row!

It took a long time to recover from the effects of this discovery on my first outing in the town. But before I got home for tea at Mrs. Morsett's, yet more surprises were in store.

Hearing the clap-clap of hooves on the road, I turned and saw a magnificent horse pulling a splendid carriage. And on the dickey sat a very regal-looking groom in livery, his top hat ending in a flourish with a cockade. I had seen similar things at funerals, and equipages like that passed our door in Belfast. But this was different. The cattle-drovers and cyclists touched their caps to an old man sitting inside. He wore a fresh straw boater and nodded condescendingly in response. Then I found John and he too was giving his Scout salute. That, he said seriously, was his lordship, the Earl of Belmore. He sounded indignant that I did not already know, and went on to explain that the old man owned the forest where we roamed, and that I must always salute him. And sure enough, a few days later when I was in the post office, the great lord came in. I had never seen a lord before, except in photographs in the Coronation book at home. It was disappointing that he wore no crimson robe trimmed with ermine as lords should. Indeed, despite the grandeur of his baronial carriage, the earl's shoes were in a decidedly shabby state.

Lords were all forgotten on the day I was awoken early by the lowing of cattle. Dawn had barely broken. Leaping from bed to the window I saw herds and herds of cattle passing slowly like a roan stream into the town. Along the surface of meaty backs was a rippling of muscle, and occasionally, like a leaf floating on a stream, a head and horns would be tossed up, and a wild eye roll despairingly. Traps and spring-carts edged their way through the crush, and driving on the right side of the road was impossible. For hours already the cattle, horses, droves of donkeys and jennets down from the mountains, and orange-painted carts full of piglets, had poured over the lake bridges. It was the fair—unforgettable day!

I dressed and flew out like a shot. The roads were green and golden with manure and cow-claps, filling the air with a sour-sweet stench. Excited and confused animals broke ranks and ran amok in gardens, and later when the pubs opened, even crashed into the bars and courtyards. Cows jumped each other, and farmers' sticks broke over runaways' backs. The morning mêlée exhilarated and bewildered me. Lads ran up and down with horses for inspection, and prospective buyers passed capable, experienced hands over the horses' legs and forced open their mouths to find teeth with tell-tale defects. Farmers were stopped in the street, their cows patted by the dealers who settled on their haunches and tested for a blind teat there and then, leaving squirts of milk behind on the pavement. No bargain concluded without a 'luck penny', a pound note or so, which went on rounds of drinks in the pub. But before any deal was made, horny, knotted hands clasped, and the buyer spat on his palm and brought it down with a smack on the seller's for another assurance of luck.

Of all the dealers, the most remarkable was a woman, an enormously broad creature in heavy boots and black woollen stockings. A suggestion of beard grew on her treble chins. She traded mostly in the pig markets. Horses and donkeys were taken out of the shafts and the piglets left in the cart for inspection. Along she came, surrounded by a group of men, and arguing with them in her hoarse voice, she threw back the cover. Squealing in terror, the piglets crowded into a corner with heads together. In went the woman-dealer's beefy arm, caught a pig by the tail and brought it out to be judged, quite indifferent to the heart-rending cries. And when she spat on her broad hand and took the owner's, there was no escaping the strong grip and her miraculous powers of bargaining.

Above the continual moan of cattle, the broken dirge of donkeys, and the screams of panicking pigs, the cry of an ancient evangelist soared. A vast silver beard spread from his chin like an upside-down halo, and in a stern voice he warned the country people of the wrath to come. He had been born into the Church of Ireland, somebody told me, but had forsaken that and a family fortune to found a religion of his own. I was often to see him afterwards, riding his bicycle on the coldest days of winter without an overcoat, in spite of advanced age.

Not far from him a lorry was parked, from which a high pile of second-hand clothes was being auctioned. The auctioneer's tone rivalled that of the evangelist, and in strident terms he wheedled the farmers into parting with five shillings for a pair of trousers. When an offer was acceptable, without further ado, he aimed the garment at the farmer in the crowd, accompanied by suitable remarks. Seductively he displayed a bunch of bright ties, which caught my eye, and made my heart thump, for no one called a bid. The ties had silver bars, and red stripes, some were yellow, and some were sky-blue. The auctioneer shook the bundle, so that the ties quivered like a peacock's tail. 'Come along now.' But not a voice was heard.

Already in my mind, I was pulling the ties through my fingers, holding them against my chest to see the effect in the mirror, and deciding which of them would go best with the Sunday suit I had inherited from a lodger at home. With consummate art, the auctioneer passed a despising eye over his audience. A series of grimaces expressed his disgust at their ignorance when confronted with real value, and he prepared to throw the ties back on the heap. At the very last minute I yelled, 'A tanner!' All the gaudy lot was mine!

I wanted to run straight home and try them on, but escaping from the crowds was not easy. Another attraction delayed me, a quack doctor selling powders. He held everyone spellbound by sticking hatpins through his arm muscles. Taking my fill of this marvel, I pushed through the buying and selling of pigs and jennets, the feeling of udders and the pacing of horses, the spitting and the sharing of luck pennies all still going on at fever pitch. Feeling that I had enjoyed the most fabulous morning of my life, I tore myself away and went home for the midday feast at Mrs. Morsett's, and the careful knotting of my ties.

Lake Dwellings

The first rumbling of storm-clouds which piled up on the horizon of my Arcadian world were heard at the swimming pool. Conspicuous always, but this time by absence, were the sisters. An indefinable something was added to life at the pool by these three sophisticated girls, aged eight to twelve. They came from my own district of Belfast, and Marie, the eldest, had attended the tuberculosis clinic with me. But they preferred city to country, and were highly distrustful of country people. And rightly so, I thought, after Marie appealed for my help one day. She vibrated with indignant sorrow, and pleaded with me to light a fire of sticks so that she could heat the curling tongs for their hair. The woman in their billet had forbidden her to use the fire at the house. An inordinate pride possessed the girls over their blonde hair. At the swimming pool, they covered it with silk scarves, as they had no bathing caps, and took to the water looking like three fortune-tellers.

Marie and her sisters so loved the pool that invariably they were the first to arrive and the last to leave. Their ritual of undressing was an involved affair. One held the towel up, while another stood modestly behind and disrobed, emerging like a water-nymph. And then the roles were exchanged. It was all very ladylike. Except, that is, when the defender's attention wandered, and a corner of the towel dropped below the point of common decency, when her sister would give a sharp reminder of duty, 'Hold it up, ya lazy bugger'.

The exquisite edge to this coquetry did not go unnoticed by the boys, even though the three sisters' ages were such a handicap. With equal interest we watched their descent into the water. Provided a sufficient number of admirers surrounded them, they might put a foot in. Then they would dash away, screaming, and protesting with high-pitched voices about the water being 'bloody cold', or some other quality which they felt outraged their delicate female constitutions. We loved it, of course, and flinging ourselves in with entirely unnecessary

51

splashings, shouted out that the water was *boiling*, just to show how manly we were. Which was what they wanted. Once, and only once, did they advance far in, and on that occasion the water actually reached their small pigeon-breasted hams. After the bathing, a protracted period of dressing followed. This hour-long process was often better attended than the bathing itself. With shrieks and a fearsome vocabulary, they warned off anyone who tried to glimpse the struggle with the combinations.

But that day, the sisters were not at the pool.

They were the first to go. Having removed us from the area of concentration in the city, the evacuation authorities now began to spread us thinly over the whole countryside. Even Enniskillen was thought too good a target for the raiders' bombs. We heard rumours about people leaving whom we didn't know, and then about the ones we did. Then the Milking Machine went, leaving a bad name behind herself. She was a woman who had come with her children, and given birth to a seventh child unexpectedly and in a most unconventional place. Further violence was done to the innocent world of the semi-detached villas, when she repeatedly sat at the side of the avenue sunning herself while the children took turns at both sides of a well-blessed breast with robust, wet sounds of relish, hardly heard in the best suburban circles. Motives other than fear of German bombs may have been responsible for her prompt dispatch into the country round about.

Every day a group of us went. I guessed my turn would come. When Mrs. Morsett called me into the kitchen, for a quick coffee, her nervous manner told me that something was in the air. She spilt some of the coffee beans, which I had never known her do before, and went on turning the handle long after the beans were ground. I was leaving next morning. My happy life tumbled about me like a house of cards. I could do nothing except go and mope with John.

Lake Dwellings

He suggested going across the lake, but there were no boats handy. The railway bridge offered the only alternative, and a forbidden one. It cheered me up immensely to realize that the dare-devil in me had survived the softening influence of a comfortable life. Kind but solemn warnings were frequently issued about going on the railway bridge, making its attraction even greater. We climbed through the railway fence where the line passed through a wood and crept warily towards the vast girders. From below it looked solid enough, but walking on it was another matter. Between the steels, enormous gaps gave terrifying views of the lake moving far below, and the countryside stretching away for miles into the distance. I did not dare to think of the one false step. We crossed on a wooden catwalk used by the railway-men, but its planks were rotten, or fallen through into the lake altogether.

Suddenly, the signal wires sang, jangled, and were quiet again. John held up his hand straining to catch a sound. I could hear nothing except the wind blowing in the girders. Then John said, 'Quick, in.' I stood hesitating a moment and then heard the train coming. And all at once it seemed to burst from the wooded bank and rush on to the bridge. Even as I stood, I could feel the structure trembling and from the corner of my eye saw the waters swirling threateningly below. Panic paralysed me. The worst fears of my childhood rushed to possess me—the terrible fatal fall my father had while out at his job as a window-cleaner. Our life at home had crashed with him; was my mother to lose me in the same way?

The engine thundered on, and John's voice calling brought life to my frozen muscles. I leapt and crept down beside him as he crouched in the hollow of the steelwork underneath. He grinned and after that it seemed ages before the grinding train came up, shuddering on the rails over our heads, shaking the great spans as if they were so many old tin cans. It went quite slowly and by the time the guard's van clattered by, my fear had gone, and I found the place where we nestled quite exciting. We sat on. Vistas of terror changed to beauty, and the lake smiled with a friendly blue. I fancied we were floating on a cloud, and that shadows skimming the water belonged to us. Twilight steeped the world in its inky dyes, and the birds winged homewards, etched as black shapes against the sky.

Being the last time together John and I swore eternal friendship. No matter how far away I was sent, I would hitch-hike back into Enniskillen, so that we could go exploring for goldeneye and scaup. One day, when I had amassed a hundred pounds, I would buy one of the lake islands. And to seal the bid, I promised to marry John's sister, though I did not really like her, as she had sties in her eyes.

We clung to the bridge and sang our songs, the old Orange ones, Scouting ditties that John had taught me. And then, of course, it had to be:

Fare ye well Enniskillen, I leave you awhile,
And all your fair waters and every green isle,
When the wars they are over we'll return in full bloom,
And we'll all welcome home the Inniskilling Dragoon.

Chapter Four

Gentry Indeed!

'We're the only gentry that have taken in evacuees,' I was grandly told. The woman led me from a musty, seldom-used sitting-room to the dark kitchen where the family lived. I had heard of the 'quality' and even the 'tofties', but never of the 'gentry'. Accordingly in my next letter home to my mother, I wrote that I was now living with the 'gentree but the house doesn't half smell'.

The smell pervaded everything, not only the house, but the people in it and the clothes they wore. It was compounded not so much of sour dirt and lack of ventilation, as from the animal food which simmered perpetually in the great open fireplace. Although they styled themselves gentry because their house was larger than the other farmers' round about, the Fenhills were nevertheless obliged to win their bread by the sweat of their own brow.

After that day, when the billeting-officer drove his car away down the steep boulder-strewn lane, I was never allowed to use either the musty sitting-room or the front door again. I must go in and out by the side door. Hens used this door also, for two of the downstairs rooms served as henhouses.

From the very first I knew that the Fenhills and I were not going to get on together. The real welcome and affection of the Morsetts was still too fresh in my mind for me to respond to a stranger's love, even had it been offered. I felt not the slightest gratitude that the house of the only gentry to take in 'likes of us', was now my home. When they set a very rough tea before me, I could only think of all the tasty things Mrs. Morsett had cooked, and of the careful way she inquired beforehand to see what I would like. And that night, when I went out and climbed a dike, to drop my trousers before going to bed, I could only think of the comfort and cleanliness of the Morsetts' shining blue bathroom. My new place actually had a bath that lived on the landing, and was only used once after I had spent an afternoon pumping water.

For me, nothing was right. In a few days I had changed into the typical evacuee, full of complaining and bitterness. And yet the Fenhill farm embodied everything I had dreamt of country life while still cooped up in Belfast. The house was built on the ridge of a hill. I thought all the west of Ireland could be seen from the top, for the distant turquoise hills folded into one another for miles and miles until they melted into a vague horizon. To right and left their gentle slopes leaped and gambolled, like a school of porpoises playing in a shallow green sea, where instead of waves, trees tossed, and grassy banks rippled in the wind. There was no sound here except the rustle of leaves and the birds' cries. When luminous clouds sailed over, their silver edges lit up the lake below, leaving a dark smudge where reeds grew in straight lines through the water.

The window from my own room overlooked this panorama. On the first night, I was lured to the window by the wildfowl which mingled their liquid twitterings and trilling clamour with the faint lapping of the lake. But I sensed that the house could never make me happy, nor become a proper home. The Fenhills had sired four sons and an equal number of daughters, who all lived and worked at the farm, except for the eldest now away working in a shop. With such a crowd which laboured so long and hard, more work could always be found. That anyone should live in the house and not contribute effort to keep the farm going, never entered their heads.

I ate a soda farl, and drank my tea from the tin mug brought from Belfast. The Fenhills did not let me use one of the cups hanging on the dresser, the first and last billet to refuse this hospitality. Then I was asked to take two of the dented buckets from the many grouped round the fire, and go out to feed the calves. A dozen calves turned large soft eyes when I entered the shed, clanking the two buckets. But half of them had to wait for only six buckets were available at a time. The poor creatures, within sight and smell of their feed, went frantic with anticipation, slobbered at the mouth and butted the wooden rail with their blunt bony heads. Two of the daughters came with me, and belaboured their way through the animals by means of great sticks, and kept the unlucky half away by blows.

Though I had often imagined myself handling farm animals, it had never actually happened before. One of the dancing calves, pushing with surprising strength to get the remains of his drink, slipped the bucket handle over its budding horns and consequently went into a panic. When the calamity was put right and order restored, I was given to understand in plain terms that in spite of my size and love of animals, I was useless and just what could be expected of an evacuee.

Nevertheless, having got me on their hands, it was inconceivable for me to be idle, though I could do little to lessen the fourteen hours, six days a week they spent themselves. A gentle rain sprayed the fields when I went out to my next job, and I wondered whether I should go back to the house. But the four brothers, seeing my hesitation, called to me, eager to see what Belfast horror had been dumped on them. Rain apparently did not stop these busy country workers, and they went on thinning cabbages. They chucked two sacks at me, and tying them round my legs, I got down on all fours and crawled along the planted furrows, quite unable to keep up with the others. Then the drizzle turned to hard, piercing needles, and we bolted to a high hedge for shelter. On the other side was an orchard belonging to the next farm. Some damson trees grew temptingly near. And with a glint of boyhood in their eyes, the brothers asked if I would like some fruit. Within a week I was bitterly to recall the orchard raid.

Milking time had come round already when I got back to the house. The farm lived on the monthly cheque from the creamery. The byres were filled with the sound of hot milk jets pinging into the pails. As all the buckets were out, I took a white basin from the dairy. My job as a beginner was to strip the cows already milked—a mere quarter of a pint that the cows released after the full milking. No electricity or milking machines helped out the work of dealing with three large byres crammed with cows, it had to be done twice a day by hand.

Lush summer grass made the animals almost burst with their milk. It surprised me to see some of the cows, unable to wait longer, letting their milk fall unaided to the ground. Only one cow was ready for stripping and I went over to the Friesian, white basin in hand. But it sensed danger from the newcomer, and its bulbous eye discerned terrors in the basin so unlike its usual bucket. I reached out for its udder, and a hoof gave a kick. I sprawled in the aisle and one of the boys directed a stream of milk at me, like a hose, amid the other's laughter.

But I would not be laughed at and determined to learn how to milk, as well or better than any of them. At the end of one byre I found an old red cow with a crumpled horn turned like a dagger to its eye as though with suicidal intentions. She stood against the wooden planking that shut off the hayshed. There was a gap through this which allowed me enough space to milk her from the other side. Her hoofs would hit nothing but the planks if she decided to dance, I would be secure behind something like a bullring palisade. After a more or less successful attempt, using my tin mug, I tried milking her from a three-legged stool—on her side of the planking.

Her teats were enormous and full of warts. But she was patient, even when they were cracked and teased by flies crawling over the sore places, and never made the slightest sign of a kick. And so Mabel the red cow was the first I ever milked, and became my first friend at the farm. I stroked her all over in search of blood-bloated ticks or the tell-tale lumps of warbles.

My second friend was Sam, the bull. I had come to Fermanagh with all the usual beliefs of a city child about bulls, the horrors of its charging at the slightest sign of red, and terrible gorings. It was through red Mabel I met Sam. As I sat behind the wooden planks milking, I looked round and found two vast eyes staring at me, and a nose-ring catching dim light from a crack in the door. My heart stopped, for I knew they belonged to a bull. I would have dashed out, but could not. Fortunately, one of the daughters came in by the door, and as I saw the bull's massive hulk taking shape in the gloom, and saw its silky flanks gleam, she rebuked it softly. Without a moan the trespassing bull retreated. No goring, no bloodshed.

Sam led a serene existence with his harem, down at the lake. It gradually became my job to fetch the cows into the byres for their evening milking. Never once did Sam show spleen at my leading his ladies away, and we became vast friends. When farmers with no bulls brought their cows to be serviced, I was often sent in search of Sam. In the heat of the day he would be standing knee-deep in the lake chewing his cud. Or if the clegs bit unmercifully, he would lead the cows away to the dark, cool tunnels among the bramble thickets. A tiny fox terrier assisted in the rounding-up of Sam by nipping the tender skin behind his hoofs.

The bull knew instinctively whether I had come for him or for the cows, perhaps because it was not milking time. Realizing that it was himself in demand, he made a beeline for the Methodist preaching-house. It was, however, not holy matrimony he had in mind, but merely that the preaching-house avenue was the usual appointed place. The farmers found it easier to bring their cows to be mated there, than all the way up the farm lane. Sometimes a 'saved' brother or sister, or the small woman who did the cleaning, would come across these operations on their way up to the conventicle. Then they would discreetly retire behind a tree, or find some other way of blending, unobserved, into the landscape.

Milk went off to town in the churns that sat up in the pony-cart like mummified cats. Responsibility for delivery rested with the youngest son, and he often took me with him. The pony was a favourite on the farm, where it trotted and fretted round with the hair of its golden tail trailing to the ground. He covered the five miles into town at lightning speed. And when we tacked on to the end of the donkey-carts queuing outside the creamery, our pony looked positively disdainful. Our milk was delivered in one side of the building, and a similar amount, devoid of its butter fat, picked up at the other. This thin milk was used for feeding the pigs and calves, and for baking the bread.

The little town was none other than 'the ford of the horse loads'—Ballinamallard! I had come, at last, to the impossible place. Only now, I could pronounce it.

Friendship with the pony did not develop as it had with Sam the bull. Why did the pony run about the field without anybody trying to ride him cowboy fashion? Why, I asked. 'That's why,' the brothers replied and told me, with a laugh, to try it myself. The eldest held the pony for me, and I climbed on using the mane as reins. He trotted off in his usual sprightly way, tearing towards the lake. Then suddenly he threw me, without either stopping or giving warning. I was winded, and disillusioned about riding the range.

My name was already blackened at the farm by this time, because I sucked eggs. The first time I swallowed the slimy mess still warm from the hen I was almost sick. But because it was the second eldest daughter, supposedly in charge of me, who collected the eggs, I persisted. The sale of the eggs provided the sisters with money and since I loathed this one in particular, I got through an enormous number in a week. I came to enjoy cracking the shells on my teeth, and it was little wonder I was bursting with energy.

None of these distractions changed my mind about the billet. I did not like it, and regretted leaving the Morsetts more as each day passed. Resorting to the escape route back to Belfast became a possibility again. I hitch-hiked into Enniskillen twice without the farm people knowing, and enjoyed a few hours at my former foster-home. A return to the city could not be undertaken, however, until the golden autumn departed, for I hated the dead Belfast streets in warm weather. Should conditions reach breaking point at the farm, there was a possibility that the billeting-officer would move me again.

From other evacuees at the village school I learnt that frequent migration from house to house was by no means uncommon. Some of the children decamped once a week. Such experts advised me on the nefarious ways of making the authorities bend over to one's will. Leaving the farm early in the morning, left plenty of time for speculation. Climbing over hedges and dikes, making my way through the wooded drumlins and leafy lanes that stretched between farm and school, I devised various schemes of escape.

But events precipitated themselves, and the first major skirmish at the farm took place soon after I started school. On my way home one afternoon I had gone into an orchard belonging to a 'gentleman's residence'. Other evacuees came too, and we certainly did no harm other than to take the excessive weight of apples from a few leaning branches. On entering our smelly kitchen that night, after bringing the cows home, I saw the policeman sitting by the fire. The fine attitude towards policemen that I developed in Enniskillen left me. I felt like a circus tiger that suddenly loses its tame habits and mauls its trainer. With all the old hostility burning inside, I glared at him, as he gave me a solemn warning not to break into other people's property. Pompously he got on his bicycle and departed. Then the jawing started again from the Fenhills, and nothing I could say about their own son conducting me into their neighbour's orchard was of the slightest avail. The damson trees, they insisted, weren't the same thing at all. The gravity of my crime rested in the fact that I had desecrated a 'gentleman's residence'. Tail between legs, I was sent off to apologize to the said 'gentleman'. They doubtless thought they would never live down the scandal of the police having to call on them, the local gentry, because of me.

Gentility obsessed the Fenhills, and entered the most mundane of their affairs—even when a neighbour came to borrow a cart. 'You're a born lady' he announced suavely when Mrs. Fenhill said he might have it. Such blandishments made her smile like a cat in the sun. Her men were away from the house just now, she said, and the cart was in pieces, to be sure, being painted. The wheels and axle lay about, still a vivid, tacky orange. But the man's need of a horse and cart was so urgent, that Mrs. Fenhill said that in default of her family, I would help him to put the wheels on. 'You're a real lady, now' commented the man. In return for the loan, he promised to bring it back loaded with gravel to help fill the potholes in the lane. Now Mrs. Fenhill felt obliged to evince the fact that she *was* a lady, and began, 'You're a real gent yourself, Tom, a real gent.' Over and over they exchanged flatteries until the cart went wobbling down the lane, with old Tom still shouting, 'I shan't never forget ya—ya born lady.'

Qualities other than her supposed social superiority, made

me prefer Mrs. Fenhill to any of them on the farm. I almost came to trust in her. Her husband seldom spoke to me, for responsibility of running the place without hired labour weighed him down. Anything he had to say was communicated in grunts rather than words, and only when he wanted me to help him, perhaps to turn the handle of a hook to make ropes of hay. I was reluctant to work in the fields, because tempers frayed, and they were so serious and harassed.

At the rival farmer's it was different. Harvesting in his fields gave me delightful freedom from the Fenhills. He had owned the Fenhills' farm before them, and in spite of their pretensionss looked down on them. Nothing was actually said, but I knew, from the way I was questioned about intimate details of goings-on at our farm, that he did not approve. On going back to the Fenhills, they in turn catechized me about the rival.

I had gone over in the first place to see two evacuees from my street in Belfast. But the big man, with a laugh like a gale, and a jovial friendly way with him, soon had me eating out of his hand. He gave the impression that even if all the children from the whole of Belfast had landed on his farm, he would have loved it. With no fuss at all, we were out in his fields working away, 'like blacks' as his wife used to say to him reprovingly. But we enjoyed it immensely, working in the sweet-smelling meadows, or stooking wheat and barley on the dry, stubbled earth. He paid us a shilling an hour for working on a great hill used as grazing pasture. Ragwort sprang up over the hill like a yellow leprosy, and the weeds in turn were alive with millions of caterpillars, looking like miniature footballers in black and orange striped jerseys. We earned our shillings by pulling up the ragwort, caterpillars and all, by its powerful roots. Within a week, the weed had vanished from the hill.

The Fenhills watched my activities over there with jealous eyes. But since they would never let my friends call to see me, there was no alternative but for me to go elsewhere. I grew to loathe five o'clock and going back from school for by then all the day's misdeeds had reached their ears with mysterious speed. I endeavoured to be secretive and to keep my affairs private, and this aggravated them sorely. In retaliation, they tried to sever my sense of connection with home, by intercepting my mother's letters. Until then the postman had always handed them to me, when I met him on the way to school. This must stop, I was told. In future all letters must be delivered to the house, and the daughter detailed to look after me, would attend to mine. Such isolation was unbearable, and I attempted to bribe the postman, and get him to tell me if there was a letter, so that I would not go the whole day through in an agony of suspense.

The lake ought to have provided another means of staying away from the farm for it fascinated me. Apart from the birds that teemed among quivering reeds, the water tempted restless young limbs. But I was not allowed to go swimming, unless one of the daughters came and paddled out to a rock. She sat on the top knitting and I was expected to splash about in the shallows between her boulder and the shore. And since she could not spare time for this from collecting and washing eggs, and helping to win the hay, it only occurred twice.

But the lake was large, and the farm occupied a good stretch of the shore. Nothing could bar me from these forbidden depths, the cool amber plain where the sun doused its embers. A wild wood ran by part of the shore, with a spongy carpet of sphagnum moss. Here, I could fling off my clothes and plunge into the lake unobserved. While I swam, the worry of being at the farm was lifted. I could dream undisturbed of being a mythical underwater creature in the regions beneath me. Then I would strike out for the wood again, and dry myself on great hummocks of the greeny-yellow moss. This was swimming— not trying to shield my buff from the knitting daughter, or waiting for her to say my ten-minute ration was up.

Things obviously could not last. The end, when it came, was swift.

One Friday I swam and then I went to help with harvesting at the rival farmer's, and arrived home late, long after my supper time. I was dismissed curtly for the night. Before going up I told them about a cow I had seen on the way in. She was in difficulty, being heavy with calf and stuck in a steep-banked stream, with water already lapping her back. She would certainly drown before the morning rounding-up. Ropes were brought and neighbours (not the rivals) roused to help in the rescue. Quite a crowd set off, and in rapidly deepening twilight I headed the procession. I went to the stream, but could not find the hole or the cow, and wandered up and down peering into the dense shadows. As the minutes went by, suspicion grew that this was just another evacuee hoax, and I was taken roughly by the arm, and threatened with a thrashing. A low moan reached us then. The fingers on my arm slackened, and fell away as the moan came again. 'Here she is,' someone yelled, and we stampeded to the spot.

It took hours in the darkness to get the unfortunate beast safely out. Finally it was led away, still moaning. And while the neighbours dispersed and were being thanked for helping in the emergency, I too had my thanks. Why was I still up at that time of night, I was asked harshly. I ought to have been in bed hours ago. Smarting under their ingratitude, I went behind the hedge for my usual last-night office. I would see no more of them until morning, thank goodness. I lingered, breathing deeply at the tang of harvest in the air. How wonderful the treacly night felt. Yet, in my heart, the decision was already made.

I would wait until morning before running away, but back to Belfast I must go. I loved the lakeside country, but could not live with resentment and go hungry for affection.

I woke early and looked over the dawn-filled land for the last time. Tomorrow at the same time, it would be the familiar bricks and chimneys of home. At breakfast I managed to wrap up some bread unobserved, and when the milk cart went off for the creamery, I went out to join it. If you were intending to run away, other evacuees had said, the best place to start from was the main Ballinamallard road. Lorries going right into Belfast could easily be picked up from there. This suited my purpose well, for when the cart got there, I could wander, as I often did, into the town, while it waited in the long queue. But this time there would be no coming back.

I told the son who was driving in, that I was going with him. He said 'No you're not'. Had he struck me, I could not have been more dazed. Indignation mingled with anger and frustration. 'Yes I am,' I shouted and demanded my thanks for having found the cow in the stream. He tossed his head back, and I saw his throat swell out with laughter. We were standing by the door, and he pushed me inside, pulled it behind him and locked it in my face. I hammered on it with my fists, pouring after him all the foul abuse I had ever heard. But above the noise I could hear the cart rattling away down the lane. The women came behind me, and my hatred fell on them with terrible force. I kicked and lashed out, and poured venom on them.

Then my fury spent itself, and within an hour I was being marched down the lane by Mrs. Fenhill, whose shins displayed some vicious blue swellings from my kicks. I wanted then to sing. They could not even wait until the billeting-officer came out to take me away to another house, but were conducting me to him there and then.

I clutched my case, enjoying the taste of well-earned freedom.

Chapter Five

A Black Snout

In those days the workhouse was still called a workhouse, and the big, grey building loomed up before me. I recognized it at once. The Fenhills could not even wait until the billeting-officer came back into the town, and so I was set down outside the workhouse. It had a door like a prison's, a maw that waited to swallow Fermanagh's unwanted human driftwood.

A dried-up-looking man in a sagging uniform wrote down my particulars and I was taken, free at last of the farm people, down dreary passages to a large room. There, women of all descriptions, but generally senile, were sorting laundry. Somebody handed me a pile of clothes for me to change into. But before I could undress, a plump little man came in. I felt relieved to see Tom Kirlan's beaming face, a red uncut Edam cheese, which I already knew from the Enniskillen fair. He served as henchman to a big cattle-dealer, but did many odd jobs also, including the running of semi-official errands. Everyone acknowledged him as one of the town's characters.

Tom took charge. He told me to leave my case and go back with him across the lake to Enniskillen. A rowing-boat did duty as ferry, and besides myself the passenger-list included two women who, whispered Tom, were full of the head-sickness. They wore odd, butcher-striped uniforms, and sang 'Nearer my God to Thee'. This did not strike Tom as peculiar, for they always sang it when crossing, just in case the rowing boat should sink, like the *Titanic*. Having commended themselves to the Almighty while the oars squeaked from the ferryman's prodigious efforts, one of the women brought out a tin of snuff from between her breasts. Her eyes fastened on me, but remained in focus with the fantasy-world in which she lived. Would I be taking a pinch she asked, proffering the tin. I would indeed, for snuff was an old weakness of mine.

Providence brought us safely to land, the women disappeared on some mysterious workhouse business, while Tom and I went in search of the billeting-officer. We hung about for him all the afternoon, but he did not appear. I gained some encouragement from the fact that business in evacuee-changing must be brisk. By evening he had not come and so we had to row back again to the workhouse. I would have made my planned escape to Belfast from the town, if Tom had not kept reassuring me, by saying that he knew just the right farm for me and that the officer would arrange it. As the building reared up again, I was trapped. The dark and nauseating corridors closed round me and I was alone. Another woman appeared and brought me to the old men's ward, where I would have to sleep that night. Though I looked more than my age and was very tall, I had never before been classified along with grown men. The room towered over me and lost itself in gloom above the feeble glitter of a few electric bulbs. Bare severity leered inhumanly from the walls. The whole thing was a perfect setting for a touching scene in a sentimental Victorian novel.

As if I were a tramp, or helpless, the woman stripped me, put me in a bath, and scrubbed me from head to foot with a hard-bristled brush that almost took my skin off. Then I was enveloped in a coarse grey nightgown. Worst of all, she removed my own clothes, taking away my last chances of escape. I resented this enforced retirement at such an early hour. It was not even my usual supper time, yet all the old men were inert beneath their blankets. The one next to me had a flowing beard, and a toothless mouth through which he took stentorian draughts of air. His bedpan, shaped like a crouched rabbit, caught my eye. I stood staring at it and the nurse asked if I was a bed-wetter. I said no, and got into bed. Wide awake, I propped myself on an elbow, quite bewildered by the coughing, moaning, snoring, and talking-to-themselves of the old men.

My case and clothes had been put at the far end of the ward near a screen. When all was as quiet as the veterans' nocturnal noises would permit, I slipped out of bed, thinking to make my escape there and then. Suspicions about everyone's motives, even Tom Kirlan's, were now beyond doubt. A plot had been made to imprison me. If a good farm-billet awaited me, as Tom had said, why hadn't the usual good-works matron appeared to take me there? We evacuees were forever encountering them. Why had I been scrubbed and given a workhouse nightshirt, if I was only to stay a few hours in the place? I felt the Fenhills were behind it all, and that at their suggestion, I had been shut up in the grey building, perhaps for ever. My poor great-aunt Beatrice, I recalled, had been decoyed into going to the workhouse for a 'rest' when she was quite a young girl, but had spent and ended her long life within its walls.

Without my own clothes I would be helpless. An escape in the nightdress could not be considered for a moment, as I would certainly be stared and laughed at as a dafty, before being caught and taken back. Carefully, I crept down the ward, and my hand was on the case, when from the old man next to my bed, came alarming bubbling, choking sounds. Quick, precise steps clicked along the passage, and I fled back to bed, waiting for a second chance.

The nurse attended to my ancient neighbour, explaining to me that his water-works were worn out, and should the scene re-occur, I was to put the crouched rabbit into his hand, as the poor old thing was almost blind. Comparative peace fell again until a clergyman, black and anonymous, passed through the ward. From the lateness of his visit I gathered someone must be at death's door. As if by instinct, the old men began to wake, like dogs sensing danger.

One by one the frail figures got out of the beds, and crept or crawled along to the lavatory, holding their crouched rabbits like candles. Met in congregation amongst the tiles, they held a whispered meeting. Since more were deaf than not, the whispers were in fact distinctly audible, and I heard every word of their confidences. A man like the symbol of Father Time came, bent at right-angles over two knobbly sticks, and stood at the end of my bed. His unshorn grey locks quivered with age, and when I failed to answer his questions, he prodded the foot of my bed with one of the sticks. None of the men, seen now shambling in the dim room, looked a day under eighty, and yet they behaved exactly as we boys had done in the Belfast hospital after lights-out. By the same instinct, that warned them of the clergyman's approach, they detected the nurse's step, sounding once more along the passage. Like mist dispersing, they vanished in their grey nightgowns to bed. The last pair of spindly legs had hardly been drawn up beneath the covers, when the nurse appeared.

This time she advanced straight to my bed. Had she guessed my escape intentions? I lay prone with a thumping heart, and feigned sleep. But pretended innocence availed nothing, for in a trice the bedclothes were whipped off, as though the nurse expected to surprise me at some forbidden pastime. 'Here's yer clothes,' she said. 'Get up and dress.' What now? A dungeon perhaps beneath the lake. As I fumbled with buttons, a man walked into the room. I could hardly believe, but it was the billeting-officer. He told me to hurry up. Having spent the whole evening hunting out a new place for me, he wanted to get me installed and go home. No encouragement was needed. Anything would be better than the gruesome workhouse.

A Black Snout

Around midnight we reached a small farmhouse. Twice, on the way, we had been stopped and asked for identity cards, as we were close to the Free State border. After the least of formalities the officer drove away to his deserved rest. Taking a candle, Harald, the farmer, led the way upstairs to the loft under the thick thatch. For him, too, it was long past his usual bedtime. I liked him at once. His face was kind, and before I would let him leave me, I poured out my heart to him. The past weeks of tension at the Fenhills had built up a dam of misery, and now it flooded out. I told him all about the cow and how I had saved it and how unkind they were and how they wouldn't let me get my letters from the postman and how . . . and how. . . .

Harald listened, with deep concern in his eyes. 'Didn't they even give you five bob?' he asked about the cow rescue. I shook my head, and he made a clucking sound in his mouth. 'Well,' he said, 'if ya ever find one of *my* beasties in a shuck, I'll see ya right.' His sympathy filled me with such happiness, that I wanted to go out that minute, to see if I could find a wounded or lost animal. And not for the reward, but because I wanted to please Harald, and make him understand how overjoyed I was that he had delivered me from the Fenhills and from workhouse horrors.

He looked so distressed at my tale that I would have done anything in gratitude. But all he wanted, was for me to get into an iron bedstead, so that he could get away to his own room. Another young boy lay curled fast asleep in the bed. When the candle flickered its friendly light down the stairs, I undressed and got in beside him. Billy, the boy, was nine years old, but small for his size. He was coiled in the middle, and his young flesh seemed baking hot. When he realized that someone else had got in beside him, he uncoiled and clung to me like a clammy oyster. He mumbled at first, calling me Ginger. In half-sleep he thought I was the other evacuee who had come to

71

Harald's farm, and had shared the bed until he ran away back to Belfast.

A further surprise was in store for me. Billy knew my mother. He had attended the school where she was caretaker. This vital connection with home meant that we would be sworn friends, and my rule of not associating with boys younger than my lordly twelve years would have to be waived. So as not to disturb the others, we talked in low voices of home, and about the gangs we knew and their renowned misdeeds. At last, excitements of the past twenty-four hours caught up with me, and sleep overwhelmed me, with Billy still holding on tightly. Then the loft shook with someone coming up the tiny staircase. I heard subdued hiccups, and a smell of drink suffused the roof space. Billy woke too, and whispered that it was Paddy the farm-labourer, who occupied a bed in the other corner of the loft.

An icy stab of dread went through me. No good Protestant would have a name like Paddy. Softly, Billy confirmed my fears —despite his drinking, Paddy would be first up in the morning to go off for Mass. He was not (and this was worse) an Ulsterman but actually came from the Free State. Surely he must be a spy for de Valera, whom we burned in effigy once a year. Paddy took off his clothes noiselessly, and heavy breathing replaced the hiccups. I did not relax until I was sure he had gone sound asleep. No one could tell what violence he might do us loyal Orange boys before morning.

And the next thing I knew was that day had come, and that Paddy was up. He was oiling his black hair in a bit of broken mirror as a preparation for going to Mass. Paddy sensed my critical stare. He turned, gave me a broad, matey wink, and was gone.

Through the loft window came the sound of clinking pails and Harald talking to the cows. Billy and I lay still and chatted. He said that Harald's wife would soon call us to get up. Meanwhile I had to retell, with suitable embellishment, the stories of the gang's activities along the sally-bush verges of the railway. Had we really held prisoners overnight in our disused chimney stack, and how had we stopped the Derry Express?

But, being Sunday, we had to occupy our minds with holier thoughts, and breakfast done, we were packed off to Sunday school. From the first, I was dubious about the old clergyman, who made us get right down on our knees to sing:

> *Children of the Heavenly King,*
> *As ye journey, sweetly sing;*
> *Sing your Saviour's worthy praise,*
> *Glorious in His works and ways.*

For me, bred to the lowest evangelical ways, this kneeling smacked of popery, as bad as turning towards the east for the Creed. I kept my eyes open for further signs. When Sunday school finished, we stayed on for morning service. Here again he behaved in a most unorthodox manner, for after giving out the number and first line of the hymn, he deserted his prayer-desk and went right round the church to perch on the organ seat. And there he stayed, playing through to the 'Amen'. He fluttered back and forth in his robes, pince-nez set precariously on the end of his long beak, like an agitated heron with two nests. Although he did not genuflect or cross himself or light candles, I marked him as one of whom, as a good Protestant, I had to be careful.

Before going to bed that night, however, my fear of Paddy changed to the greatest respect. Two huge horses lived on the farm, one of them young and having an internal complaint. The medicine for this consisted of a pill the size of a man's fist. A fist indeed had to be used in making the fiery beast swallow the thing. Paddy held its mouth open, and Harald put his arm down its throat. As I saw the veins on Paddy's arms and fore-head rise as though to burst, and the sweat stream down his

73

contorted face, admiration filled me. Harald's wife came nervously to watch, and pointed out that if Paddy relaxed his grip, her husband would lose his arm. What responsibility for the black-haired Paddy—and him a Fenian.

Monday presented its own problems. With a packet of thick slices of bread with butter and beef in our pockets, Billy led the way to a schoolhouse three miles away across country. We climbed hedges and jumped streams, and threaded our way through woods. Suppose I had run home—it would have been the streets again on the way to school, and dull brick buildings and hard asphalt playgrounds! I marvelled that in the nick of time I had been stopped from deserting Fermanagh's green acres.

The school proved to be modest, having only one room and one teacher, who taught every subject herself to everyone. There was no division according to age, except for the infants who were coaxed or coerced by senior girls. The teacher gave me work to do that I had learnt years before, so that the morning went by easily enough. Billy and I ate our lunch, and went outside.

During the morning session, many notes of enquiry and answer had passed as to where I came from in Belfast, my exact age, and above all, my fighting abilities. The twenty other evacuees there wanted to be quite sure about my prowess. With dismay I learnt that one of them had also belonged to a notorious railway gang, but not Gandhi's like myself. His was Tulip's crowd, our deadliest enemy. From now on there could be no co-existence between this boy and myself, no peace and no order, until one of us was vanquished.

Fighting was all right, but I had given it up. Too much damage could be done, and I had enough battle-scars already. I would be more than content to eat my pride. But when I got into the playground and heard everyone buzzing about the two Belfast evacuees, I knew a fight was inevitable. And so was the result, I reckoned, for Tulip's boy was two years older than me, and built more heavily. Coats came off, a ring formed and up went our fists.

No sooner had we started than I realized how things would go. The other had removed his thick glasses, and when I began to dart about him, he was quite lost. We hammered wildly, until quite by chance I struck his nose—really hard. The blood flowed and would not be staunched. His friends took him inside, and he was laid flat, with a penny on his forehead and a towel to catch the mess. Nothing it seemed, could be done. The teacher was so frightened (so was I, for I had a cousin who died in a playground fight) that she sent me off home straight away. By Billy's hand, she sent a note to Harald, saying that I was never to return to her school again.

I wondered if there would ever be an end to injustice in this world. I had not wanted to fight, let alone win at such a cost. What had the billeting-officer said, not unkindly, about 'behaving myself'? Once again the 'clean snout' that so concerned my mother was black. Life looked grim again. I had landed in a plight—debarred from the village school before the first day was out, and my nice new home in jeopardy.

This massacre brought the aged and peculiar rector to the house. I heard the rattle of his Ford car coming along the lane, where I lay enjoying my unexpected freedom. The cleric was feared by many, and so I bolted to the hayshed. A search for me began, and he sat in the house for an hour, and then becoming impatient, joined in the hunt himself. The others scattered themselves far and wide, but the old man pottered about near the house, and almost stumbled on my hiding place. I suppressed the laughter that threatened to betray me, when his finely polished shoe squelched into a fresh cow-clap. With guttural rumblings of irritation a veiny hand stretched out and, to clean the shoe, took a puck of hay from my warm burrow. I could hardly resist seizing his ankle and frightening the life out of him. But then the whole business would certainly reach clerical ears at home, and mean once and for all the end of the church orphan money. Farmyard games lost interest for the rector after that, and soon the car was bumping down the lane again.

The secret hermitage in the hay, came near to costing me my life. A delightful cleft in the great hayshed, it was alive with insects that explored every inch of the human form that invaded their world. Because Billy was away at school and there was no one to play with, I used to go there, lured by the smell and snugness of the hay. I would lie and daydream or count the strange hairs appearing on my body. Sometimes I would go so soundly asleep that hens would come and lay their eggs near me, each of us oblivious of the other's business.

Then one day, as the insect-races took place unnoticed across my chest, and even the satisfactory tan developing on my legs had ceased to fascinate me, my dreams changed to a nightmare which I woke to find a reality. Darkness had swamped my burrow, and the sweet scent had become suffocating dust and hayseeds. It seemed as though the whole shed had collapsed on top of me. To draw attention was impossible, for nobody would hear my shouts. I realized then what had happened. Because of bad weather Paddy had started to store away some rucks of hay brought in the day before. I had not been roused by the usual noise of the iron-shod cartwheels that went with the hay loading. Into my terrible entombment came a sudden idea, better than a ray of light. I remembered that my feet pointed towards the outside. Inch by inch I crept out, my throat and eyes burning from the choking dust.

My newly-won independence from school was not all spent in the hay or roaming over the ruins of a fantastic fairy-tale castle nearby. I was only too willing to help Harald and his wife with the steading chores. They accepted me as a proper milker, and collecting the pails I went out with the missus at milking time. The silly performance of stripping with a mug belonged to the past. The men worked in the stinking brown waters of the flax dams, and I had to take out their enormous teapot, and slices of bread still hot from the griddle, with butter running to oil through the holes. I could feed the calves by myself now, and rode the broad back of the Clydesdale mare to the blacksmith.

Such a delightful life could not last in a world bent on education. Before long, my case was packed again, farewells said, and the billeting-officer was driving me away. He took me to a part of the county as yet unsullied by my bad reputation, and where the village school had a headmaster equal to my pranks, a 'man severe he was, and stern to view'.

Chapter Six

The Master's Tenants

S tanding at the gate to welcome me in yet another home was Kate Lytte. Beside her, leaning on a hazel stick, was her old mother. The billeting-officer probably left me with misgivings, but he need not have, for I loved the house from the moment I arrived. By the way they had been awaiting me, I knew they regarded an evacuee as a human being to be welcomed, not a sort of monster thieving-magpie from the city slums.

Kate's small cottage could not compare in size with my other billets, but warmth and kindness had impregnated its walls. The cottage sheltered two other evacuees, brothers from Belfast. Kate showed me the bed I would share with Colin, the elder who was a shade older than myself. The brothers could not sleep together because the younger one was a bed-wetter, and had a rubber sheet. They were at school, Kate explained.

Old Mrs. Lytte sat at the table with a sock over her fist, cutting up young nettles to mix in the turkey food. She struck me as being the most aged person I had ever known, older even than my great-grandfather who reached a century. But the hardship of life had drawn the lines, and sunk the gentle eyes into frightening sockets. Already at fourteen she had married, and after bearing a large family, had been left a widow, with no means of life but her own hard manual work. She made me feel

I had always belonged to the little house, as she steadily chopped up the nettles, and told me stories of her early struggles. Her love for the children never dried up. To feed them, a twelve-mile walk into town and back to buy a sixpenny cow's head, was nothing unusual. In one day she had been able to pick up an incredible number of drills of potatoes for a few paltry pence.

Hardship was not followed by bitterness in old age, for the family, now thriving and multiplying, did not abandon her. Those near were always in and out with presents, an ounce of snuff, a rabbit or still-struggling eels.

The cottage differed not only from any of my billets, but from any house I had ever been in. Barney, the pet pig, ran around the living-room, and was treated as one of the family. A hen and a flock of chickens lived in one corner. And all around the big open fire, bundles of seeds and bulbs hung drying. The Lytte garden was the prize one among the tenants of the local estate. Though summer waned at last, there still remained sufficient fine days to take outside twenty or more pots and old saucepans of indoor plants. They decked the cottage window-sills, so that all passers-by admired the rioting crested-ladder and maidenhair ferns, the geraniums and fig-leaf palms.

'Give us a hand with the pots' was to be a familiar call in the house. Morning and night we would run back and forth with the make-do flower stands.

Nor were the flowers the only thing on which the cottage prided itself. There was the delph. Rows of hooks studded a white dresser, from which swung blue and white mugs and cups. Its shelves sagged with delph, and the door was left open so that people could admire it. Tourists were even reputed to have called especially to photograph the fine collection.

Only one of the old woman's sons remained at home un-married, Willie, and he was the bread-winner. Kate, his sister, ran the house and little holding. She was only a few months old when her father died, and she had been cradled in the bog heather, while her mother slaved at the turf-cutting with the men. Willie worked as a gardener on the estate. When he came home in the evening, he was always asked, 'How's the Master today?' meaning his employer, who was old and hobbled about on sticks. The Master had two children, who were never known as anything but Miss Alice and Captain John. Their mother, the Mistress, had been dead many years but was still remembered by the old tenants, and even by those born since her death. She had died suddenly and old Mrs. Lytte was one of those who had seen her spirit return to stand by the former bedroom window, brushing her long mane of hair.

When the other evacuees arrived home from school, they resented finding me there. But the aversions soon passed and Colin became sufficiently friendly to go and explore the village with me. His nose was flat, his shoulders square like a boxer's, and perfectly suited the nickname he gave himself—Collie Boy. But before we were free to go, the day's supply of water had to be brought from the well half a mile away. Even the rich farmers were obliged to use this communal well, for no other drinking water could be obtained for two miles. Having got the buckets home without wetting the sides of our trousers too much, Collie Boy took me to the old water-mill by the bridge. Some of its roofs were crumbling already, usurped by dense ivy. Owls flew round the deserted place, hunting for mice and beetles. Water moved in oily coils round the still-sturdy walls and tumbled over the remains of the wheel and weirs.

An old couple lived in a cottage near the mill, and in their field an enormous pear-tree flourished. Police warnings about raiding orchards were long forgotten, and in any case, this tree was not 'gentry' property so I had no misgivings when Collie Boy climbed it. Lodged precariously we shook the tree to make the last pears remaining of its crop fall to the ground. A few plopped on to the grass, but before we could get down, a sow ran to the tree and started gobbling them up. Colin stopped me from scrambling down. The sow had recently farrowed and eaten the unfortunate litter as soon as it was born. And now I saw wickedness in her eye, as she cocked up her head to look at us, hoping for more fruit or even a slice of leg. We dare not face the sow, and were most uncomfortable by the time someone rattled a bucket by the sty and drew her away.

Collie Boy was a talker, and while we were in the tree told me many things about the Lyttes and the district. He had once run away from the Lyttes' cottage, back to the city, but his father had given him such a thrashing, that he thought being away from home was not so bad after all, and so came back again to the friendly cottage. I was not to enjoy his companionship for long. News came that his mother was ill, and both brothers packed up immediately to hitch-hike to Belfast. They left in a legitimate manner with sandwiches and their bundles. We heard afterwards that they reached Belfast, over a hundred miles away, the next day after a night under a stack of corn.

No one came to take their place. The steady trickle of evacuees going back to the city every week was not lessening. People needed more than warnings about bombs to keep them from their homes. I was moved into Willie's room, in the younger brother's bed, as winter was coming on, and my little room was needed to house a lot of chickens. But I had no need of the bed's rubber sheet, and so it was converted into a very superior blackout blind.

At night, the Lyttes' generosity overflowed when the local farm boys and girls came in to dance on the stone-flagged floor. Kate roused the fire with a spray of sparks, and set the gramophone squeaking out a reel, while the hobnailed boots scraping on the floor sent out their own sparks to rival those in the fire. And unless your boots sparked it was not considered that you could dance at all. Ignoring the fact that I had never danced in company before, Kate insisted on the first night that I make up 'the sets', a form of lancers. The rhythm and body movements came easily to me and even the boot-sparks. More difficult was the swinging of my partner off her feet, an essential ingredient in the dance. When I eventually mastered this and lifted Kate right off the floor, this received great approval, for Kate made a weighty partner.

When brows could sweat no more, and hearts thump no harder, Kate called a halt, and she and I sang together, or put songs on the gramophone. Most popular was 'A Poor Little Orphan Boy' with 'A Mother's Farewell' coming a close second. But if anyone present had a death in the family, these songs were banned and we contented ourselves with 'The Ould Orange Flute'. How we loved this story of Bob Williamson, the weaver from Dungannon who played his flute in the Orange band. But he married a Catholic and had to flee the town. When he took the flute along to play at Mass, we laughed most for not a note would it give except 'The Protestant Boys', even though dipped in holy water. After that the priests decided to destroy the righteous flute:

> *At a council of priests that was held the next day,*
> *They prepared to administer auto-da-fay*
> *Sure they couldn't knock heresy out of its head,*
> *So they bought Bob another to play in its stead,*
> *So the ould flute was doomed and its fate was pathetic,*
> *'Twas branded and burned at the stake as heretic;*
> *While the flames roared around it they heard a strange noise*
> *'Twas the ould flute still playing 'The Protestant Boys'.*

Round about the district, many old country customs survived, and I learnt some superstitions to add to our strange Belfast ones. To turn the mattress of a bed on a Friday or Sunday was to court bad luck. Some still said the grace for light when the evening lamps were trimmed, and Catholics dug the sign of the cross into each new loaf. On passing a bereaved person on the road the greeting was 'Sorry for yer grief', or if a new coat or shoes were being worn, we all said 'Health to wear'.

Harry, one of the Master's horsemen, lost his brother while I lived at the Lyttes', and the old lady told me what to say if I met him. Leaving nothing to chance I waited for an hour under a dripping hedge on a miserable day for him, just to jump out and say 'Sorry for yer grief, Harry'. Alas, his life was full of sorrow. His new wife caused it all, people said, because she had a hen that crowed like a cock, and what soul could prosper with that? Custom ruled the Master's house too. When Kate went as kitchen-maid to the mansion during pheasant-shooting she had to sit in the servants' pew on Sunday, and must stand up and bob when the Master or Miss Alice entered or left the church.

Captain John came home from England for the pheasant-shooting. As the Master was too feeble on his sticks, his son conducted their posh friends through the woods. Strict instructions were given to me to keep away. Not even being allowed to go with the beaters, I took myself off for the day and went into an old cattle-shed used by the out-wintering herds. It was a scorching day. As I lay musing on nothing in particular in the shed, approaching footsteps cut the reverie short. They came from one of quality—a real tofty in knickerbocker trousers and cloth stalking cap, and beautiful strong shoes with overhanging tongues. He began to undress. Off with the knickerbockers and the long underpants, and on again with everything except the pants, which he rolled up and stowed in his game-bag. I, of course, concealed myself during this divesting ceremony, feeling rather like French courtiers who collected royal sheets.

At last the long day ended, and pheasants and shooters went to their respective homes. I went up to the great house to meet Kate and she allowed me to see the day's bag in the game-room. I waited for her in the big kitchen, and saw the Master's tea tray being prepared by the housekeeper and maids. What a parody of toast was his—so thin and warped that you could see through it, and with the best part of all, the crusts, precisely amputated. Like wafers of beaten gold this toast was laid on a silver plate with hot water underneath and covered by a domed silver lid. Among all the strange things I had seen in my life, never had there been such pomp and circumstance over so little. I went home with Kate deeply impressed by the toast performance. Such fragile rusks surrounded by so much silver and the work of so many hands!

On the slightest pretext I loved to go up the Master's drive to see the gardens or look around the steading of the home farm. Often I was entrusted with messages or food for Willie, and sometimes money to buy corn or a setting of eggs from the steward. The gardeners had changing-rooms in a wonderful rambling wing surrounding the walled garden. Willie's room was dim and resinous, full of telescoped flower-pots, and shelves of dormant bulbs. Windfall fruit lined the window-ledges and bundles of yellow raffia waited until next season's tomato plants drooped with their heavy green orbs. The leaf-mouldy room brought out the best in Willie, and he always gave me what I asked in the way of fruit.

My wonderful discovery was made when the threshing started, and all the Master's men were working very late. Many empty rooms threaded their way through this wing of the mansion's outbuildings, and I had long ago experienced the thrill of deserted houses. In one of them, I found a thick wad of paper, which someone had used to wedge the cobwebby window. I unfolded it and found a thousand mysteries. I imagined I had stumbled on vastly secret war-plans, and putting them in my pocket, ran off to the cattle-shed near the woods to see what it was all about.

Three papers made up the bundle, and they were all maps, about two feet square. I spread them out and pored over them. The first was a map of Petrograd Bay made from Russian surveys of the last century. Its importance and meaning lay cunningly concealed, perhaps by code, for all I could see besides the coastline was a pin-cushion of numbers spread all over it. Carefully folding it, I brought out the next. But it was similar except that it charted a part of the China Sea. Important documents though I recognized them to be, it was the third which was valuable. To begin with, it had been done by hand, whereas the others were printed. And then it showed the Mediterranean, but showed it badly. Even I could have produced a better map in school and decorated it with better printing. But this 'track chart' (whatever *that* meant) bore the date 1654, which I took to be the date of the piece of paper in my hand. Only a few, deliberate lines composed the map, and some curious numbers.

Yes, I knew only too well what it was—the map of a treasure island. All my family's troubles and poverty would soon be at an end. *Treasure Island* had been the only book which I had sat down to read for its own sake, as in our part of the world for a boy to read was regarded as cissy. But on the first occasion when a neighbour invited me to listen to the wireless (the devil's box as the most bigoted of the 'saved' school called it) I had heard a play—and the tapping of blind Pew's stick as he went to the 'Admiral Benbow' held me spellbound. Now I had my own secret map, and life suddenly had a marvellous goal.

I hid the maps in the hayshed. On the following day, I got some discarded oilcloth and made a treasure chest for the documents and buried it in the woods. I went often to that part of the woods to see that neither trappers nor badgers had scraped away the earth from the cache. My fourteenth birthday would have to come, of course, before I could start out on the great voyage. And if the war had not ended by then, years might pass before I saw the ancient chests of gold moidores and pieces-of-eight unearthed. Before then, there would be time to learn a little about treasure islands. I sorted out the brightest boys at school, and asked them about the islands of the Mediterranean. From my study of the secret map I thought it not improbable that the treasure lay buried on Formentara for it was such a small island and the vital data was scribbled round it.

My last thoughts at night were always of my hidden chest in the woods. And in the morning when Barney came to scratch himself on the apple-tree outside my window my mind would fly to the future. When rich I would hand out five-pound notes to every Free State soldier who would fight for our Protestant king, and such marvellous dresses they would be, that I gave to my favourite girls in the village.

Meanwhile, life had to be lived in the cottage. As I lay dreaming of the wealth in days to come, my eyes would wander from one to another of the many-coloured royal family pictures, which hung in the room shared with Willie. There was also a decorated verse of 'Jesu, Lover of My Soul'. Our beds were warm and comfortable, and every evening Mrs. Lytte tottered along to tuck us in. Patchwork quilts covered them, evidence of Kate's favourite pastime, and on the coldest nights, we put military topcoats from the First World War over us. Instead of a hot-water bottle, I had an iron pot-lid heated and wrapped in red flannel, and if all the lids were in use, a brick brought hot from the hearth. When the old woman's shaking hands had folded us in she would pronounce an individual blessing on each one, 'Good-night Robbie, God Almighty bless ya', and then 'Good-night Willie, the Lord love ya', and a similar benediction was given to anyone who came to stay. A general blessing was not considered sufficient. The callers who came to dance in the evenings went away with the same prayers. And anyone going on a journey had a solemn 'God speed ya and love ya', from the garden gate.

After the pheasants came the potatoes, and they, like the birds, had a special day to themselves. The Master allowed all his estate workers two drills of potatoes in a long hill, as well as their big gardens. The two drills produced more than a ton and there was only one day available for getting them dug and carried down to the cottages, to be put in pits against the coming winter. We made a very early start, and the hill soon became alive with movement and laughter from the numerous tenants, who turned out in force. Strong competition prevailed and the men who did the digging took second place to the women who picked up the potatoes. The one to finish first was Queen of the Field, a position held by Kate for several years. She strove to keep it. No matter how the rest of us might nudge each other in the rows, or throw potatoes at a neighbour's broad beam that showed good strong boots and red flannel petticoats, to say nothing of a length of naked thigh, Kate ignored us all and worked, reluctant to lose her title.

Enveloped in happiness at the cottage, I found school, irksome at first after my freedom, becoming more bearable. The previous dame-school affair paled beside it, for comparatively the new one was elaborate. Local people regarded it as a grand set-up, for it had been built over a well, and equipped with a pump which we were allowed to use at midday for drinking. A headmaster presided, a man renowned as a good wielder of the cane. Though he could still cane well, and I saw him do it, his prime was over long ago. I was now very big, and after one or two tussles with me, he used a different method.

I had a flair for mathematics, and when the seniors failed to solve a problem the headmaster would appeal to me, 'Can you tackle this, Robbie?' With pride at stake I willingly co-operated. My memory was retentive, especially for poetry. He put *As You Like It* in front of me, and playing on my pride again, asked me to study fat chunks of it. Shakespeare—who ever heard of him before, except when we crooked little fingers round a wishbone and said 'Bobbie Burns' while the other responded 'Will Shakespeare'.

Now, in these unusual phrases, I found a link with my own

experience. And having them photographed on my memory, I used to say them aloud on my wanderings in the woods:

> *Sweet are the uses of adversity;*
> *Which, like the toad, ugly and venomous,*
> *Wears yet a precious jewel in his head:*
> *And this our life, exempt from public haunt,*
> *Finds tongues in trees, books in the running brooks,*
> *Sermons in stones, and good in everything:*
> *I would not change it.*

Because we were a country school, surplus energies were not channelled into organized games, but into gardening. Afternoons passed on our patches where every kind of vegetable grew, and where a thorough practical and theoretical course on horticulture was given. Unbeknown to the silver-haired man with the blue eyes, my hatred of school and especially of teachers, was dissolving. I grew so to respect this unusual headmaster, that when someone deliberately punctured his bicycle, I devoted my whole dinner-time to mending it.

For all this, school was still school, and when an opportunity came of missing a day, I jumped at it. Winter was good for this. When any of the Master's tenants bought a standing tree, or one blown down in a gale, the Lyttes were often offered the minor branches free if they cleared the main trunk for sawing. We were always in need of fuel at the cottage. Ours was one of the biggest and best-dressed turf stacks on the estate. But it consisted of a light, mossy peat, mostly sphagnum, which burnt away too quickly.

Since Willie's work took him away all day, Kate and I usually foraged in the woods for sticks. We helped to build each other's load, and tried to make our own the bigger, just to prove who was the stronger. The fire devoured the wood so hungrily, that sometimes three trips were necessary in one day. But I never minded, and to sit over the open fire at night was more than enough reward. I loved to see the branches spitting and sizzling and breaking into crackling flames, and would try to recognize the ones I had picked up. Kate, proud of her strength, turned the excursions into a romp. When at last enough was collected, we turned for home. Looking exactly like the figures in a nostalgic nineteenth-century print, we bent under the sticks, following each other's footsteps in the snow against the sad silhouette of naked winter trees, while the sun fell low like a red hot cannon-ball searing the clouds with purple.

The village took an inordinate interest in its evacuees. A simultaneous rise in population and influx of outsiders had never been known before. Johnny-Longlegs provided an endless subject of gossip for the women. They maintained that he was much older than everybody said, sixteen or seventeen at least in their estimation. After all, everyone knew that he went to the local dances, smoked openly with the young men on the village bridge, and could do a man's work on the farm. The women accused his mother of wanting to save him from conscription, which was rumoured at that time, and of supporting him on government evacuation funds. I hated this tittle-tattle, for Johnny-Longlegs was a name given to me at school because of my height, and the village had soon caught on.

Nobody ever believed me about my age. At a sports day in a nearby parish, they debarred me from racing in my own age group, and even the one above me. I finally ran with those of fifteen to eighteen, and came in third. Suspicions were aggravated by my way of speaking which, for some unfathomable reason, had little trace of an Irish accent. One old hag even went so far as to put it about that I was a German spy. Only when I wrote home for my mother to get my birth certificate and send it, was the rising tide of gossip stemmed.

At school I had a circle of friends including the twins. These identical boys had four rows of beautiful teeth each, two at the bottom and two at the top of their mouths, and fiery spirits kindred to my own. Together we went to the deep river that clung motionless to its banks and fished for tiny silver perch, with perhaps a whole pounder on lucky days. With palpitating hearts we would sometimes glimpse vast pike, elusive in the slow-moving currents.

For a month the Master's men dammed the ford, so that they could get stones for the upkeep of the estate drives. Here the water spluttered and snarled between the glistening boulders, and the three of us came for the eels. In and out of the shallows we hunted the writhing fishy snakes. From the small streams that trickled through the dam, the twins sighted the biggest eel any of us had ever seen. A dozen times they brought it out wriggling with muscular protest, and a dozen times it went back, as they could not hold it long enough to kill it. And the last time it escaped altogether. A frantic search ensued, and I found it again, managed to hold on and killed it. Like a trophy the eel lay prone at my feet.

Then the trouble started. 'It's ours!' the twins shouted. I laughed at this and said it was not. They both set on me and we tumbled about on the bank and in the water, fighting for possession. I refused to yield my prize, but they began to cry, and one went off to report me for stealing *his* eel. The tears melted me. All right, they could keep their silly eel, I said, adding that it wasn't much of a one anyway. But it was, and I thought about it as I fished on after they had gone, and all the way back to the cottage. And there, on the table, served up for tea, was the eel. Kate, in all innocence, had bought it from the twins.

No such differences arose between Daisy and me. She went to the school also, and was my constant nymph. During the winter lunch break, she liked to organize dances, so that she could choose me as partner. She also provided the music by singing the chanting song:

The Master's Tenants

My mother she says I can marry, marry, marry,
My mother she says I can marry,
And she'll leave me her bed when she dies.

Shod in our rubber wellingtons Daisy and I clasped each other and moved like a pendulum to the monotonous rhythm. She was well informed on local matters and could name the father of every illegitimate child, and where the wicked deed had taken place.

But alas, Daisy could not provide the delights of adventure, and for these I turned to Betty, a handsome girl, also an evacuee. Betty was fourteen and liked attention from the boys, though she thought my overtures too bold, and simply tore up the dozens of notes I wrote her during classes without even reading them. Her resistance was a mistake for it inflamed my interest. Forsaking Daisy after school one day, I followed Betty, and we walked for a mile or so, and then she began to run. I ran too, caught up and tried to kiss her. But she fled screaming into her farmhouse billet.

Next day I accompanied her, and profusely apologized for uncourtly behaviour the previous afternoon, hoping to win an even greater advantage. In the middle of all this two sturdy sons from her farm sprang out. I was helpless and they subjected me to humiliating punishment and extracted a promise that I would never go near Betty again. Whether because of this affair or not, I never knew, but the old woman in the village who said I was a spy, began the rumour that I was soon to be a father.

For at least a part of Saturday I kept out of temptation's way —in the church. One of Kate's married brothers was the sexton, but more often than not, it was Kate herself who cleaned the church on Saturday, and I accompanied her. Once inside, while she busied herself with broom and bucket, I could give rein to my secret desire to open the wooden door to the high pews built like cubicles where the quality sat. The Master's pew being superior in its appointments, I sat in his seat, surrounded by a splendour of red velvet cushions and tassels, far richer than anything in the church at home. Not only was the Master a local squire, but he had once held endless offices and honours which Mrs. Lytte never tired of praising, and was an exalted figure in the hierarchy of the Orange Order. So great a man was he, in fact, that I expected by sitting in his seat, to catch a stray ray of his glory, and be transformed into a grand personage myself. But nothing happened, and the nearest I could get was to smell the specially bound and tooled hymn-books, for a whiff of highness.

It was a dark and beautiful church lit dimly with many heavy, stained-glass windows. Even in winter the sun struck their colours, igniting the saints to a new martyrdom of bruised-looking reds and purples. The building had the smell of sanctity, of damp hassocks, and mildewed hymn-books. Even the rector's cupboard in the vestry smelt dingily of cassock. The first time I discovered them I could not rest until I had donned the flowing robes, and mounted the pulpit. But it was not entirely a theatrical gesture for I sank to my knees on the carved stool, and prayed quite earnestly, expecting a marvellous revelation because I was arrayed in such holy garments. Then the hanging lamps had to be filled with paraffin. And when everything else was ready for the Sunday I would sit at the organ, and try to find soulful chords to fit my mood.

Time went by, I was very happy, and the idea of leaving the Lyttes' cottage never entered my head. I enjoyed winter nights especially. After supper Willie and I would go visiting, his brother the postman's house about five miles away being the favourite. His wife read tea leaves and I lived between each visit waiting to see what my fortune would be. Her subtle art largely foretold the mail which I would receive. A brown piece of stem on the side of the cup indicated a parcel, and if it was near the rim it meant I would receive it soon. Since I heard from home quite often the forecasts proved remarkably faithful.

Spring came very early, and with a prolific rush. Cats appeared, smiling blandly on the doorstep with families of sportive kittens, and hens led flocks of fluffy chicks through miniature forests under the rhubarb leaves. The old turkey, who had been spared her children's Christmas fate, showed signs of wanting to rear another family, and on seeing any of us in the garden, ran up and meekly lay down at our feet. Then Kate knew it was time to get on her bicycle, and take it up to Tom, Mrs. Billay's turkey-cock. Indeed, on the road, it was not unusual to meet good country wives with turkeys under arm, intent on a similar mission to Mrs. Billay's.

Although women were usually banned when cows were being serviced, it was their province to attend turkeys in season. We loved to hang about round Mrs. Billay's cottage to watch the callers come, with the turkeys safely under arm. But poor old Mrs. Billay got so annoyed at the lateness of some calls made on her, or rather on Tom. Before she went up to an early bed a notice would appear on the door, 'Tom won't see anyone till morning'. The housewives were not put off so easily, however. They feared their turkeys' desire for courtship might not last till morning. So they shouted through the letter-box for they knew that Tom was roosting inside with his mistress. And always—for she had a heart of gold—the old soul got up, for she understood only too well how the cottagers depended on the sale of their Christmas turkeys for clothes and pin-money. With a reminder that it must be 'a quick one', the door was opened. Tom's passion would already have sent his feathers into a shivering halo while his comb dropped like a frond of love-lies-bleeding.

I could have spent all my life with the Lyttes, people I loved, and amongst the country sights and sounds. But it was not to be, for the Master died and the whole of our little world collapsed.

Old Barney, the pig, was already gone. He had outgrown his box in the kitchen and lived in a little hut in the orchard. Under the trees he had been free to run about, and to keep an eye on the kitchen door so that he could sneak in and look for left-overs in the saucepans or up on the table. Coming home from school one day I saw a big mallet by the dresser and a strange assortment of knives.

Outside I found poor Barney tied head downwards from the clothes-line to stiffen. Kate watched to see that cats and dogs did not interfere with him, and when night came he was brought in, placed on the kitchen table, washed and shaved. The following morning we put him in a fine bed of fresh yellow straw and took him by horse and cart to market. And cruel bets were made as to how much he would weigh. The very same evening, amid a heap of onions, Barney's liver was served up for supper.

When the billeting-officer came for me once again, he could say nothing, as I had broken my previous record of six weeks by staying five months with the Lyttes.

The parting was sad. Kate took me to her generous bosom, the old woman waved her hazel stick and gave endless blessing, and even Willie shed a few tears as I climbed into the car.

Chapter Seven

Herdsmen of the Scillies

The parlour floor decided it all. Until returning from school on the Tuesday evening, I had been in two minds about my new billet.

Through Sunday dusk, the billeting-officer took me into Enniskillen over one bridge, and out of it by the other. I had already been over the county's main roads in search of a home. But at last he succeeded in getting the car up a narrow lane, and I shamefully forgot about the Lyttes in wonder at the farm-house standing at the end. The walls were low and hugged the ground. A warm thatch covered them and moss-balls grew on the roof like green hedgehogs. Candlelight glowed through the tiny windows.

Sitting on two long benches in front of the kitchen fire was the family of grown-up sons and daughters. They made me immediately belong to them when Mrs. Garreton, their mother, brought me in. No pretence of being 'gentry' hung about her, for although it was Sunday she still wore an enormous sack-apron wrapped round her small body. Her voice was soft and gentle as she invited me to a place at the hearth. At the time it did not occur to me that I had not seen the farmer himself.

Bert, the sturdy eldest son, commented on my linen shirt, and said what a fine thing it was—all his life he had wanted one like it. Like his mother he looked as if Sunday clothes meant nothing to him. Shavings from his carpenter's bench still needed to be brushed from his thick bush of golden curls. When he stood up, stretched himself, and said he was going to bed, he came over and rubbed my shirt between his fingers and said again how much he admired it. I felt so flattered, and wanted to give it to him at once.

Before we all went to bed I had still not seen Farmer Garreton. But I heard him come home late, after I had been shown into the smallest imaginable room off the parlour. Two of these box-rooms opened from the parlour, and in a large room adjoining the kitchen, Mrs. Garreton slept with her whole brood of sons and daughters. After I was in bed and asleep, Farmer Garreton blundered into the box-room next to mine. His bed-spring clanked as he threw himself down. Then he broke wind with such enthusiasm, that I thought he had invented a joke for my amusement, and was deflating a rubber balloon.

In the morning I did not see him either. Mrs. Garreton gave me a huge breakfast, as the walk to school was a long one, and packed sandwiches while I ate. Just as I was ready to scamper down the lane to try and follow her instructions cross-country to the schoolhouse, she called me back. We went into the big field in front of the house. Small, wild daffodils leaned and nudged each other in the wind, and tinted the field with a wash of pale yellow. Mrs. Garreton picked a bunch and gave them to me as a present for my new teacher. Once upon a time, such a thing would have horrified me—flowers for the teacher! But now I knew the country schools well, and how a little tact and diplomacy could remove the stigma of being an evacuee. Days off were more easily wrung out of friendly rather than hostile teachers. Considering that less than twenty-four hours before, Kate Lytte and I had walked over the hills to church in tearful anticipation of parting, I went to school on that Monday morning with surprising cheerfulness.

I found the school, and Mrs. Stokar who received the daffo-dils with unfeigned delight. I liked her immediately. This was fine because apart from a farmer's wife who taught the small children, Mrs. Stokar was alone. The grand school I had just come from was a thing of the past. There were no luxuries like built-in pumps. A thing which pleased Mrs. Stokar more than flowers, was for one of the children to bring a bucket of water to school, or a midday walk to the well.

On Monday evening I saw Mr. Garreton. He was in the dimly lit byre feeling the bones of a cow about to calve. He was very large and frightening in the way he shouted at the sicken-ing cow. I was glad that he did not speak to me. But things were different on Tuesday. I came home from school and made a dash for my little room to change into an old pair of dunga-rees which Willie Lytte had given me. An enormous bellow from Farmer Garreton followed me as I ran across the parlour. 'I'll cut the bloody balls off ya,' he roared, and came after me as though to put this threat into force. Too late I remembered the morning's warning about the parlour floor. During the day, it's rotten floorboards had been taken up, and a thick bed of cement installed. And now across the middle lay a clear spoor of my footprints.

I fled to the farm's most romantic retreat—the privy. It was an old stone hut lichened with bright yellow scabs, and quite hidden from the world by thick shrubbery. I thought it un-likely that the irate Garreton would pursue me to this lonely dovecote. A generous supply of nurserymen's catalogues pro-vided stimulating reading matter. What bliss it was for me to imagine '50 sturdy 1 yr. lavender bushes for 25/-' or a whole '100 giant gladioli for 6/6', and the most exquisite shrubs, spiraea, tamarix, deutzia, cotoneaster, japonica, and philadel-phus for less than the price of a bar of chocolate each. I loved these catalogues, many of them years old and out of date, and spent hours over their tempting offers, making up imaginary orders. What a garden I planned for my island home on Lough Erne when I went back there from my treasure island. Another joy of the stone privy was its own music. A stream gushed at the side of the pit, and after getting used to the idea that the seat was not going to collapse and cast me out on to the green mossy stones of the stream, I could relax and listen to the peaceful gurglings.

I could not exactly live in the lavatory, and so kept my distance from Farmer Garreton. He made no attempt to conceal his dislike of evacuees, and had not the wit in him to consider that all might not be alike. His experience of them previous to me was of shortcuts to school being taken through his crops. But he was of such a cross disposition that I had the consolation of thinking that if his anger had not been over one thing, it would certainly have been over another. I trembled at night when I heard him go to bed, for fear that he would burst in and thrash me with the wide leather belt that kept his adipose tissues from sagging. His sons often came in for a dose of bad temper and their grievances were later to be aired in a spectacular family lawsuit. The farmer's uncouth behaviour probably derived from his ailing stomach, whose borborygms sang all night like a faulty ballcock.

The tension under which I lived must have told more in my face than I imagined for Mrs. Stokar frequently enquired if I were happy at the farm, and listened sympathetically to the grosser episodes. She often asked me to stay on after school, until her son Stephen returned from Enniskillen. Stephen was seventeen and went to Portora, the public school in the town. We became great friends and this meant that I only returned to the farm late at night to sleep. Farmer Garreton found cause for irritation in this and insisted I must go straight back after school and pull my weight with the farm work.

Mrs. Stokar thought otherwise. Perhaps she regarded my contact with her son as the most vital aspect of my current education. One day after school she got out her car and drove me home. On the way she explained that she was going to collect my things and take me to another farm. In an hour I was installed in my seventh billet.

The little house had lost its thatch and had corrugated iron instead. It lay nearer the school and was the Saggarts' home. They herded cattle for an absentee landlord, and from the start treated me as if I had always lived with them. An old uncle headed the family, and enjoyed the title of 'His-self'. The only woman was Emily, whose husband helped uncle with the animals. Her two brothers worked in the town, one as a storeman and the other as a lorry-driver. Both cycled out to the house at night, to eat and sleep with the others in the room opening from the kitchen. His-self's bed was up in the loft where, until I arrived, he had been alone. Now a bed was placed close alongside his, and even then we were squeezed for space, and my bed touched the sloping roof.

His-self took to me at once. I became his favourite, confidant, and fellow-conspirator. He told me of his many years as a trapper in the lonely desolation of northern Canada, but added, significantly, that he was now unfortunately reduced to poaching and fishing. This was a leading statement. The cottage stood in a small close surrounded by a wood, and beyond it, two large forestry plantations stretched a long way. All the cattle were out-wintering, and grazed in rough pastures that were gradually being re-afforested. This prolific tree-cover helped to conserve tremendous colonies of game. And almost without asking me, His-self had a willing recruit for his poaching.

Not uttering so much as a whisper, we made our way through the pine darkness of the plantation in search of pheasant and woodcock, and snipe in the bottoms. The chirruping and croaking, the hiccuping and bleating, could be heard everywhere. The pheasants were so abundant that Emily's domestic fowl shared the same nests in the woods. The hens

99

would never lay their eggs in the boxes provided for them at home. I always had to look for eggs somewhere out in the woods, and often found a female pheasant brooding on a mixed setting.

On the other side of the old wood, the river Scillies flowed, and His-self and I spent many hours there. The Saggarts were poor, and a large proportion of the food supply depended on uncle's skill with gun and rod. His fishing rods were very elementary affairs cut straight from the forest, but in his hands, what power and fight they could muster! Big pike and rudd ran under banks already bending with spring's fretwork of green. Most in demand, however, were the average bream about three or four pounds. We never thought of this coarse fish as tasteless and unpleasant, because Emily had such an art in making sauces to go with them.

The lines were set up at our favourite place, a bend in the wide river. Here the water passed languidly, its gentle surface movements suggestive of a rich catch below. His-self settled contentedly to a pipe, and maybe a doze if the weather was hot. I stayed awake, and alert for anything that looked like a bite. At the least suspicion I roused the old herdsman, and he changed instantly to a Red Indian on the warpath. Several of the lines might go at once, and I would have to deal with some. If I could barely land them, His-self would grow apoplectic in fear that I would let the fish go, and run up and down screaming and shouting unintelligible instructions. Should the water start heaving and rocking with pike tactics, and I could not find the gaff, his whole body quivered, and vast oaths sent the moorhens into guttural flight to safer distance. But by the time the lines were reset, and the catch had gasped its last breath on the bank, he would be his amicable self again, and fall asleep.

Whatever the result of the day's hunt, we always went home for the evening milking of the two house cows, and afterwards I fed the ferrets, my special task. When the boys came home from the town, Emily would lift the great iron pot of locally-ground oats off the fire, and set it on a stool. Armed with a spoon and mug of milk we gathered round the pot, and dug into the hot porridge, and cooled it in the milk. No matter what quantity Emily cooked it always disappeared, and was followed by an anxious scraping of the iron bottom for the tasty burnt bits. This communal way of feeding was quite a novelty to me, and I thought myself such a man to be given a spoon and told to battle for myself.

Uncle and I went to bed early, for we often set out in the pre-dawn for the river. In our favourite bend was a large hole, and we fed it with boiled corn, so that the biggest bag could be taken before sunrise. At night, in the bedroom under the roof, His-self performed a fascinating, unvarying ritual. It consisted of undressing, except for his dark grey Oxford shirt which served as a nightdress, looking out of the skylight to judge the next day's weather, listening for any unusual sound coming from the herds, scratching himself slowly and methodically, winding his large pocket-watch, and finally getting into bed under a pile of clothes with his trapper's fur coat on top. Sleep claimed him at once, a slumber marked by heavy contented breathing and snatches of impolite conversation.

I did not settle so readily. Although I was tired also, the loft had too many distractions to allow immediate rest. Under the beds lay a number of wooden boxes, and I soon discovered that they held hoards of rationed and scarce food. Full cartons of jelly had been hidden there, and as soon as His-self began to snore, it was time to put out a furtive hand and divide the con-centrated cubes. Then I would lie back alone under the roof sucking the sweet fruit flavours, listening to the wind soughing in the woods, or to bullets of rain exploding on the galvanized iron. On still nights the deep-toned, bubbling notes of the sedge-warbler pierced the silence, plaintive and sensuous like the song of nightingales, without beginning or end.

But the best hour of the day for bird-song, was when Himself pulled on his old breeches and I sleepily tucked dungarees into my wellingtons. It was barely four o'clock, but the cock-pheasants were crowing, and the cuckoo let fall his sultry flute-notes. Moving through the woods, we would hear the garden-warbler gushing with the sweetest song imaginable in his low trilling warble. Hurrying out of the black forest, we crossed pastures where the cattle still lay, their shaggy coats glazed with dew. Peewits whistled to us, and by the time we had robbed the river hole of our catch, the sun was up. In its flood of liquid gold, all the birds on earth, warblers and songsters, joined the pulsating crescendo of a perfect spring morning.

With full day responsibilities came also. By the time I ran down the lane to join my friends on the way to school, I was already tired. The early rise, however, did not dull my concern for inspecting the numerous nests that clustered along the road in thick hedges. In the beginning, evacuees were blamed for stealing birds' eggs as fighting weapons, easy to throw and making satisfactory splashes. The accusations were justified. But the importance of conserving birds and their part in country life was carefully explained. This patience saw ample reward, for the evacuees became staunch guardians of the frail mossy balls and the intricate constructions of rootlets and mud.

School under Mrs. Stokar became an absorbing business. The small building had little to commend it from a practical point of view. In its one room, the wooden benches ranged in rows facing the teacher's desk. An iron stove provided the heat, and its crazy chimney-pipe rose up to disappear through the ceiling. Yet with everything against her, Mrs. Stokar managed to keep six different classes all going at once, and in such a way that all were interested in the work. Her genius was in stirring enthusiasm in even the dullest of her flock, with botany and zoology as specialities.

For the dangerous buffer period between classes when idle

hands could have invented devilment, she also had a plan. When our work was finished, we could take down a volume of the *Encyclopaedia Britannica* and delve into it. What a storehouse of fantastic things we thought those giant tomes. There was absolutely no restriction on what we could look up—and therein lay Mrs. Stokar's secret. At first we gloated over nudes in the art section, licking our chops at the unashamed hussies in a Rubens, or a stripped-off female in a Boucher, or any typical writhing heap of torso from the salacious classical centuries. And with a Michaelangelo reproduction, we reckoned to be pretty wicked, by catching the girls' eyes and making them look at what was what. But we quickly found that sort of game grew stale, and when the *Encyclopaedia's* resources were exhausted on that score, and art had yielded up its all, we turned the pages to more serious matters. Unconsciously we absorbed a dozen topics, and lost ourselves in Eastern customs, or became mesmerized looking at tape worms in a sheep's head. During break intervals, we could get permission to go beetle hunting in bogholes, or make clay models outside.

Some change in me must have resulted from this stumbling on the unsuspected pleasure of learning, for Mrs. Stokar decided I must sit for a scholarship at Portora. On fine days I sat in her private garden to study, with a local boy who was also to sit for the examination. I had to adjust myself to a new idea, that of staying at school until my eighteenth year. The notion was not quite so loathsome as I would have previously imagined. My shipyard apprenticeship would have to be abandoned, and the treasure island expedition postponed—perhaps for ever.

The greatest revolution in my life was that the bad old days of school in Belfast were over and done. I found that learning was not a war waged by heavily-armed teachers trying to find the slightest flaw in a child's make-up as an excuse to cane. Nor was it the biggest osbtacle in parents' way—parents who were forever wanting to get the school-leaving age lowered, so that the few shillings of a message-boy's packet might be added to the family wage. I wrote now to my mother that it was thought likely I would get the scholarship. But the reply contained no reference to it.

Spring could contain itself no longer, the weight of leaves, the bursting songs foretold the imminent summer. The more Mrs. Stokar tried to bring my weak subjects up-to-date, and plied me with homework, the more distracted I became by life with the herdsmen. The two possibilities tore me asunder. I was filled with the excitement of wearing the public school clothes and becoming a real tofty, complete with top hat. But the next moment I would catch sight of His-self setting out for the Scillies, his war-wounded leg causing him to limp a little. Such a pang would assail me then that schoolbooks were ashes in my mouth.

In the end, my homework remained uncompleted, and when some major event on the farm occurred, I often stayed away from school altogether. I hated to hurt Mrs. Stokar, but what could I do, it was impossible to live two lives. The farm had the stronger pull, especially when the vet came to dress the calves, or when I went out on a big rabbit drive with 'my' ferrets. Then Emily fell ill, and became so distressed at being helpless, that I volunteered to do all her jobs. I cooked the food and tried my hand at baking bread. The men were amazed that a city boy could go out and pick a plump hen, wring its neck, pluck it and have a good meal served up in as quick as or shorter time than Emily would have done. Poor Mrs. Stokar, she took all this hardly, but it was spring, and I could not miss the bream waiting for my line down by the river, and the secret excursions to the woods with uncle's knowing companionship.

An intimation that this idyll could not last came from Belfast. We evacuees felt the hair on our necks rise, with the news that German bombers had swept over the city, killing nearly a thousand people. We wondered how many of our friends who had run away, to go back to the close, dangerous streets, had survived. But greater concern than for Dizzy Murray or Collie Boy, was for my own home. With a hot feeling in my stomach I wrote home.

Two awful days dragged by. No answer. It could mean only one thing. I became frantic with worry, and decided to go into the city and see for myself. But the evacuation authorities said it was not necessary to go, they would make enquiries if I did not hear in a few days. Things, they said, were bound to be a little delayed. Mrs. Stokar agreed with this decision, and also refused permission. Then a good excuse occurred to me. Papers regarding my scholarship had to be signed by my mother, and so I suggested taking them home. A great deal of personal persuasion would be needed to get my mother's signature, to send them by post would be futile. Still Mrs. Stokar forbade me, concerned only with my safety.

Anxiety built itself up inside me all that day, and when I got home to the woodland cottage, burst out. His-self was very human, and understood my feelings. He was also easy to persuade, and having no official position to keep up, gave his blessing on my scheme. My luck had turned, for Sandy, the elder nephew, was taking his lorry into Belfast the next morning.

At almost our pre-dawn call for river trips, Sandy crept up the stairs to my bed, and whispering so as not to wake His-self, told me to dress. Downstairs we moved in the dark getting his bicycle out. I sat on the crossbar, and he rode me six miles into Enniskillen. A large truck was waiting which Sandy and another man were driving into Belfast to collect a load of farm meal. The journey lasted over five hours, the most exciting of my life.

Sandy and his mate seemed to stand about for ages before we climbed in and the headlights swung on to the main road. Once under way, I really felt as if something was happening and relaxed a little. Sandy's mate was about thirty, dark and unshaven. He had so much experience in driving, that he looked careless, leaning only one hand on the big wheel, and constantly glancing away from the road. One after the other he told spicy stories, and did not spare my ears as I was being treated like a man, and felt entitled to this regard as it was my thirteenth birthday. Pin-up girls, all leg and bosom, covered the driving cabin, and as the truck roared on, we all three smoked, filling the cabin with blue haze. We shouted at girls on bicycles, honked the horn at drivers with cattle, made fun of each other when we stopped for nature calls, and divided the hours by calling at transport cafés for tea and buns. In the thrill of the journey I forgot its purpose. The other two wanted this to happen, for they were older and knew what I might find at the end.

Half an hour away from my home, anxiety gripped me, and when the lorry pulled up at the end of our street, I could not believe my eyes, for it stood brick for brick just as I had left it. Hardly stopping to listen to their arrangements for picking me up at the end of the day, I ran down to our house and burst open the door on a strangely quiet house. Our tomcat sat humped up on the window-sill like a teacosy, waiting for someone to throw out the bacon-rinds that lay glued to the breakfast plates. The place seemed much smaller than I remembered it, but unchanged, except for large cracks in the ceiling and windows from the bombing. I went upstairs and found my mother in the familiar brass bed where we had all been born. She was sound asleep. I guessed she had just come off night-shift from the munition factory. Her dungarees lay over the bedrail and I fingered the fine steel dust that coated her clogs. The distinct family odour filled the room, a smell of old sweat that I recognized as home.

When I called, she opened her eyes, and looked in astonishment. When she recovered from surprise she got up and set about preparing a huge meal, as much in honour of the visit as my birthday. But she was no more surprised with my lorry-trip than if I had arrived by Rolls Royce or ass and cart.

The scholarship papers were put in the fire—such nonsense, I did not belong to those kind of people. When I was fourteen, I would come home and be apprenticed in the shipyard. A man was lost if he did not 'serve his trade' when young. The more I pointed out how much I would eventually earn if I went to Portora, the more my mother carried on about my father and his unskilled companions 'on the corner', who had always been out of work. The far west and Mrs. Stokar seemed momentarily so remote, so removed now that I was back among the people and places of my origins, that the documents' crackling flames ceased to matter to me. To find my mother alive instead of dead, and our house intact and not a desolate heap of bricks, was all I demanded of life then. My mother looked so much older, and unwell, no longer the young woman of my first remembered days, though still she was only forty. All the struggle of bringing us up without a father's support, had grown into a weary mask, and filmed the clear amber eyes. She needed me in the shipyard at fourteen, and I must come.

Neighbours called in to see me, amazed at my physique, and declaring that I must be 'courtin' strong up the country'. My elder sister was fifteen, working in the laundry, and displaying her first engagement ring. There was a better birthday party than ever I had. Although the house had not changed much during my year away, for me there was a difference. I had grown used to the open country with woods and rivers, and a sky never dull even when overcast with rain. But here the streets were like shut boxes, the air smelt dirty, and out of the windows were not apple trees but lamp-posts without children swinging on them as before the war.

I saw clearly what I would have lost by running back to the city. Even during the unhappiest times in the country, escape was possible to the beauty of Fermanagh's meadows and hills. But from here there could be no escape. Even the first novelty of war held no more magic. I knew that had I returned to be cooped up, I would no longer have found interest in the silver barrage-balloons swaying in the weak sunlight or waiting for nightfall to study the geometric pattern of searchlights combing the sky. I was happy to have been home to find my mother and sisters safe. But I did not want to stay. I had a full year more in the west, before my destiny in the shipyard would tear me from the countryside I loved. As the clock ticked round to five I waited anxiously for Sandy and the driver to knock at the door.

Our journey out to Fermanagh again was slow and grinding, for the load of meal weighed many tons. Soon the headlamps were switched on, and the chromium-plated cigarette case went to and fro again while the driver laughed, showing perfect teeth that looked so white against the black, two-day beard. Once we stopped and let the engine cool off. When the lights were switched on again, they caught the startled gaze of a sheep, lighting up the red depths of its eyes. The two points like a twin Mars burning on the road, stayed in my mind for many years. We shooed it away, started up the engine and crawled over the hills, heading west. The cabin became hot and I yawned. It had been a full day, charged with emotion, and the swigs of beer I had taken from the driver's bottle, made me heady. I began to nod and soon found a pillow of greasy dungarees on Sandy's lap.

Owls and stars possessed the whole countryside when Sandy and I trod quietly up to the little iron-roofed house in the early hours. But though tired out, we went over to the spa-well, and lying flat, drank of the cold, blue water. I knew that my excursion would not please Mrs. Stokar and went next morning prepared for the worst.

For the first time I saw her angry. She stormed at my flouting her advice and at the disobedience of the evacuation authority's rule. Anger changed to distress when I told her that my mother, far from signing the scholarship papers, had burnt them. But I did not hear her reproaches, having the songs we sang round our kitchen fire and our laughter at the lorry-driver's jokes still ringing in my ears.

Mrs. Stokar, being made of sterner stuff than most, was not discouraged by this interruption, and took up coaching me for the examination, where it had been dropped.

A few more blissful weeks passed, His-self and I going as before to the river and woods. Then one of the local school-girls took me to peer through the window of Mrs. Stokars's house. And there, by the piano, a new divan bed was stood on end. It had arrived the previous day during my absence by the Scillies, and all the children had concluded it was for me. Yes, I was going to be moved to yet another billet—Mrs. Stokar's own house, where there could be no dodging what she considered my proper work.

Going home that afternoon I saw the grocer who travelled round the farms, and also traded in evacuees, coming down the lane with my suitcase in his hand. There was no opportunity of saying good-bye to His-self, or the brothers, or even to soak a few slices of bread in milk for the ferrets.

It did not take long for me to learn of the herdsmen's rage at my being uprooted so callously and transplanted down the road to the school residence.

Chapter Eight

Lost Horizon

My interest in bicycles began in our street at home. The insurance clerk left his machine outside the house, when he called one day for the weekly shilling. I was only eight, but could not remember him coming on such a thing before. When he marched through our little hall and into the kitchen to see if it had been a good week for us, and whether my mother had the precious shilling, I noticed the cycle clips and darted out to touch the beautiful contraption.

Possessively I drove off the children ringing the bell, and accepted a bribe from a friend to let him ride it to the nearest lamp-post. He was far too small to mount properly or even get his leg over the crossbar. He made the allotted run in a curious fashion, but straight and fast. Envy filled me at this mastery, and waiving another bribe, I tried it myself. With pounding heart I clung to the handle-bars and pedals in exact imitation of my friend, but fell off in a heap. I was astonished that the cycle, in my hands, was no more than an inert tangle of metal. The insurance man came out, and found the helpless bundle on the pavement, with his bicycle on top. His angry words about inter-fering with his machine were not nearly such punishment as the way my reputation would suffer for not being able to keep the thing upright.

For the rest of the Belfast years, my skill remained unproven.

But now Mrs. Stokar was asking me to take a bicycle and go to the well for water. The early experience rose up to mock me, and I felt too ashamed to say that I could not ride. It was humiliating to see Stephen, her son, go swinging off on his, with a bucket, and only one hand on the handle-bars. So I waited until later in the afternoon when Mrs. Stokar went into town to collect her son and daughter from school, and then went into the shed. I could choose from four cycles kept there. After consideration I selected an old-fashioned lady's one, as it had no embarrassing crossbar.

Making sure that nobody was watching, I made a few tentative movements, and gradually got the knack of balance. After half an hour, I found myself going at what seemed fabulous speeds, with the bicycle completely in my control. Within a week I could cycle all the way across the rough farm track to the well, and spill little water on the return journey, when only one hand held the machine and me together. Graduating to a man's bicycle came naturally after that, and soon I was riding everywhere. Style followed mastery, and I could mount with a flourish, ride up hills standing on the pedals, ahead of everyone else because of my long legs, and when fleeing free-wheel down the other side, I could lower my head and shoulders over the handle-bars, to increase the speed, so that the wind bellied inside my shirt like a filled sail.

At first I had sadly missed my early morning sallies to the river with His-self, but cycling filled the empty place. My world became bigger, and instead of local streams and woods, the whole country waited exploration. Stephen and his sister took me everywhere in search of cairns, giants' graves, cave writings, prehistoric sea shells. The islands of Upper and Lower Lough Erne became familiar. And so did the caves. Our side of Fermanagh was riddled with caves through the subterranean chalk. The dark chambers echoed our voices as though we walked in a cathedral nave. The electric torch would suddenly reveal mysterious pools, or flash on the deadly swirl of an underground river, or stop our feet just in time from going into bottle-neck potholes. To mark our way, we laid a trail of thread behind us, unwound from a reel, for in the damp gloom, retracing steps or taking the right turning without some guide were impossible. As the torch beams swept a roof, showing the multitude of Daubenton's bats spotted like crockets on a Gothic tower, I was swept by the dread of being lost and doomed to die in the labyrinth, sealed for ever in a clammy tomb.

However dangerous our trips may have been, no objection could be raised for they were basically educational, and my weak English underwent improvement simply by being in Stephen's and Wendy's company, for they spoke 'nicely'. Fishing was allowed too, at the proper time, though the old dawn excitements were no more. The rods which His-self cut from the forest were replaced by elegant bamboo ones, and the old man's snores by endless public-school chatter and clichés—'Prang-ho' and 'the mater' being the most frequently used. And the catch was different too. Our supper did not depend on any 'wee taste of bream' we might catch—more often than not the houseful of cats got away with the catch. The dream of faraway places and the idling rivers and lakes, drew us, not the threat of going hungry to bed, and we fished for the beautiful gillaroo by fly, and trolled for ferox and char.

Sometimes Mrs. Stokar got the car out and took us to interesting sites, but the best days came from roamings by bicycle. And I often crossed the border into the Free State, and felt few qualms in my friends' company. At one time it would have been to me like knocking at hell's gate itself. We never had trouble with customs either side of the dividing line, even though Stephen had a great eighteenth-century rapier fitted on to his bicycle which looked suspiciously murderous. The first time we went over, I was surprised to find it no different from our own Protestant side. Grass and trees were just as green, the river just as cool. Even the people looked like people, and no dirtier than our own. None of them tried to kidnap us, not even when we went apprehensively into Catholic churches to blow out votive lamps in our excess of Protestant missionary zeal.

Along the mountain road just by the border, we found an old churchyard, fallen to disuse years before. Nothing more than a lichenous shell remained of the church, and the intriguing vaults were easily entered. The room-like tombs, half sunk in the ground, or leaning with age, had floors punctured with holes, and shank-bones and skulls littered them. Through the years, rats had done their work well. On a dreadful day, some-one shut me in a vault where the bodies were not altogether disintegrated, and where rats had dragged limbs and shrouds through the rotten coffins. In the dimness, I read a woman's nameplate—Rebecca West. I never forgot it. The joke of shutting me in could not have lasted more than a few minutes but for months afterwards, in terrible nightmares, I was always dragging my legs hopelessly, trying to run from the fearful Beccy who pursued with outstretched strangler's hands.

In search of a less gruesome, and long-since rifled, burial place, we climbed Mount Belmore, to a vast megalithic chamber and cairn, where all sorts of interesting things had been found. But my first climb up the slopes of that beautiful mountain, piled like a green wave about to break over Fermanagh, was won-drous for another reason. In the bog-heather I saw a ewe bear a lamb. The miracle was enacted against the background of a radiant sky fleeced with white clouds, herded along by the sensuous wind of early summer, and the rugged flanks of the mountain, warm in a fondling sun. The lovely pink of the umbilical cord like a slender stick of seaside rock, the tightly curled coat of the new lamb determined to stand up at once on its own feet, a lone kestrel winnowing the pregnant air above the russet sculpture of the mountain, filled me with a new sensation, a kind of fullness, a rhapsodic passion which I could not express. I felt I wanted to stand on top of the mountain or roll in the heather, or lie and gaze for hours at the implacable cerulean enamel over my head, and then die in the rapture of the day, before the sun's rich yolk dipped behind Belmore.

The early weeks with the Stokars passed amiably enough. I did not go into the schoolroom for roll call, but worked in the house. This preferential treatment rather went to my head and I cultivated a snobbishness to other evacuees which they must have found quite unbearable. I refused to go out jumping streams with the other boys at midday which I had once so loved. At every opportunity when the house was empty, I would slip into the bedroom and dress myself up in Stephen's Portora clothes, with the bright yellow-striped blazer. Not being able to resist showing myself in public, I took the bicycle and cycled in the smart outfit down to the main road. By lucky chance I met a friend of the Lyttes—a daughter of the Master's steward. She was reckoned as respectable because she 'did the books' for a seed merchant in town. Impressed by the uniform, she made me very much the godling.

Sheila, who lived three miles away and came by bicycle, provided my only point of contact with the school. She was a large girl and sat at a table in the corner, learning shorthand. On arrival at the school I had possessed no slippers. This was a serious state of affairs for the children were obliged to leave boots and wellingtons in a little porch, and wear slippers in the classroom. Several other evacuees had been in the same predicament, and this was remedied by the girls, who offered to make some in their handwork class, to save us running around in stockinged feet. Old felt hats were cut up for the soles, while the sides were knitted. The results were pronounced satisfactory after critical inspection and testing by the slipperless. Sheila had volunteered to do mine, though she was very resentful of my even talking to her. In a genuine rash of enthusiasm over the slippers, I gave her a tin of butter scotch. But she only took one and returned the tin. Not to be put off, I bought marshmallows, and then liquorice all-sorts, and put them in the drawer of her table, but they always came back.

And all the time, the inexorable date of the scholarship examination drew nearer. Still nothing concerning me was definite. Letters to my mother produced no answer, she refused to be drawn by means of the post. I knew she was annoyed because I had been moved so briskly from the herdsmen's house, for she had some personal experience of them. In Sandy with the lorry, the remote west, and the postal addresses she got my sister to write on my letters had become reality. 'I like that fella,' she said of Sandy on the day they brought me into Belfast, and felt specially attached to him, as he had promised to look after me. In country terms, their life was equivalent to hers, and she understood them. But for the grand people who took me away from Sandy, and talked posh about things far above her head, she had no sympathies. And as for the scholarship, she had already heard more than enough about it.

One thing which helped to antagonize my mother against the well-meaning Mrs. Stokar, was a letter sent concerning my clothes. The good lady had assumed when I appeared from the cottage in the woods looking like a ragamuffin, that it was the fault of those in charge of me. But when she saw the pathetic contents of my suitcase, and realized that my possessions amounted to what I stood up in, she sent a long list of things needed to my mother. Again my sympathies were torn, half for my mother who had fought poverty for us in the lean years, and half for Mrs. Stokar who burned with determination over my future. Of course, nothing happened over the list. Instead I was given an old pair of Stephen's trousers, for I went about almost indecently in a pair of shorts bought when I was eleven, for Willie Lytte's ex-dungarees were far beyond the patching stage. And I had only boots, the plimsolls having long ago expired from overwork. I wanted very much to wear shoes, but knew well enough that my mother would not hear of it, in her view what could I be after shoes for with a good pair of boots to my feet? Keeping up with Stephen's grand public school friends became increasingly difficult. To explain the boots I lied that my ankles were weak and needed support, and bluffed my way through many ungentlemanly questions aimed at my odd wardrobe.

But now pressure was applied, and letters must have fairly rained on the little house in Belfast. Confused and worried, my mother could not follow what was going on at all, and so decided to come west herself and sort it all out. She had a boy-friend who worked on the railway and they would brave the perils of far Fermanagh together. In the nature of things, her visit was foredoomed to failure. She created a stir on arrival by refusing to use the children's earth closets. Having eased the discomfort of a long journey, she settled down to business. An added difficulty was that the Stokars could hardly under-stand her heavy Belfast accent. My mother proudly declared that she had been sent to work in the mill at twelve years old, and had never stopped since. What she had, what I had, was the result of her own sweat. Distrust of high-falutin' ways of carrying on burned in her eyes as she spoke. She suspected her life and mine were being undermined in some way or other. Mrs. Stokar temporarily retired, but brought reinforcements in the form of an important ecclesiastic, who served on Portora's board of governors. The sight of the 'cloth', especially with its well-turned baluster legs in gaiters, put my mother on edge. Fortunately there was just time to bundle the boy-friend discreetly off to the pub. The whole business was so much more serious for her, now that the great black beetle peered into her guilty eyes. (She could not relax for fear the boy-friend would burst in, perhaps rolling drunk, from the pub and offer the cleric a bottle, or try to see if he was wearing trews under the 'black kilt'.) But still, my mother stood her ground, and in her own weird dockland patois, pointed out her straitened domestic circumstances. Poor cleric, he pleaded, wheedled and reasoned. But my mother's mind was made up—I would go straight to the shipyard at fourteen, and no monkey business.

After the visit, eddies of coldness blew into my life. I think Mrs. Stokar lost heart and gave up caring, and perhaps understandably so. She had been battling against great odds solely to get me the advantages of a public school education. With her aim almost within grasp, it had been snatched away, and any future progress blocked. I could make no further pretences with Stephen and his smart friends, and though I continued to share the same bedroom with Stephen, a gulf separated us, that grew wider and wider. I took to going off on my own and waylaying His-self in the woods or along the banks of the Scillies.

Intense examination coaching stopped, and I moved back into the schoolroom for lessons. There, the last battle was fought. The farmer's wife who taught the infants had always disliked me, and now that she could treat me like an ordinary evacuee without giving offence to the Stokars, her hour of triumph had come. On this particular day, I found her chuckling over a letter from my mother, written out by my sister. Could I possibly, asked the farm woman dangling it like a dirty thing between finger and thumb, could I *possibly* count the number of mistakes in it? Of all its enormities, the greatest, apparently, was the fact that my mother had signed herself 'Mrs. Harbinson'. What an ignorant person she must be. I burned with shame and anger and at the word 'ignorant', lost my temper and went berserk. Rushing to the iron stove I picked up the poker and threatened to knock her brains out. She ran screaming to the residence.

Before the bell for afternoon school had rung, the evacuation authorities were once again seeking a new billet for me.

Chapter Nine

The Promised Land

Maggie lived only four miles from the Stokars' school. Like everyone else, she knew all about the turbulent evacuee. News in the country travelled fast. But when the billeting-officer called and asked if Maggie would take me in, she said 'Yes' without hesitation.

And for twenty years after that day, I was never to hear her say anything but that the most ordinary girl was good looking, that the ugliest would 'make the grand wife for some man', or that the biggest rogue or tramp that ever walked was 'terrible respectable', even though he might have been 'in and out of jail all his life'! With unerring instinct Maggie singled out the good in everyone and stoutly refused to see the bad.

She ran down the lane to meet the wayward child of the city, who had already rampaged his way in and out of eight other homes. Her hands, marked by years of work about the farm and house, were folded comfortably over her apron. Bright eyes and a smile as wide as the Scillies, regarded my height. I knew what she would say, about not believing I was only thirteen. 'It's the great cub ya are,' she commented appreciatively before going on to praise everything about me. This small woman, rather late in middle-age, with the lively face that held darting expressions of happiness like a river full of fish, looked up at me with love. Her name for me became the general one, and I was always known as 'the Cub', or 'Our Cub' to outsiders.

Mrs. Stokar had discharged her duty to me at the top of the lane, and had gone back, perhaps in sadness. Now Maggie, chattering away, walked with me towards the house. I could not even see it, for Maggie's was the longest farm lane I had known. First it passed a stretch with fields on either side, and then turning slightly its ruts ran, like furrows, between the peat bogs, where the curious brown architecture of stacked turves had been excavated. Then we walked in the shade of overhanging trees, passed meadows and a cherry orchard, then gardens. And on a low rise in the ground was the house, white in the sun, its front door open.

Maggie talked all the time, and laughed at nothing in particular except for joy. Her astonishment over my size was replaced by amazement that I could do the milking. In earnest of my skill, I promised to do the Sunday milking so that she could go off to Bundoran on a big spree.

As the old Chinese believed to the extent of it altering market values, a house has a spirit. When Maggie took me into her big farm kitchen, I immediately loved it. In terms of walls and roof it was as benign and approving as Maggie herself. The house, in short, liked me. No pretence hung about that room, which was very much the everyday, working kitchen. Half was paved with heavy stone flags taken from an ancient castle nearby. The other half, for some reason or another, had never been completed, and was a miniature mountain range of holes and broken cement. But nobody minded—it was great for falling over when dancing, and that was always good for a laugh.

Maggie was convinced I must be starving and fainting away for 'a drop of scald'. She sat me down and busied herself at the fire. I started to count how many different kinds of wallpaper were in the room, and reached twelve. Maggie's approach to the problem of interior decoration was an extemporary one. If she saw a nice bright pattern while in town, and it took her fancy, she would go in and buy one roll, irrespective of whether she intended to use it immediately. When a patch of the kitchen wall was reckoned to be dirty, a square of the paper was cut off, and stuck on with flour and water. The total effect from a few years of this treatment had produced a most alarming patch-work-quilt effect. Bulges in the walls helped to create the idea of quilting. Years later, I showed her interior schemes in a glossy English magazine. The walls of the same room were treated differently, in true contemporary spirit. But Maggie was not over-impressed, all she said was 'Ya see my style's all the rage over there now.'

But in spite of the gaudy designs much of the walls were covered by tradesmen's calendars. Age had blackened some of them, but Maggie could not bear to destroy them, for perhaps they illustrated a touching scene of kittens, an old blacksmith's forge, or a homely cottage with roses round the door. Besides the calendars, a dozen newspaper and magazine photographs were nailed up, depicting at least two generations of the royal family. More for necessity than art, onions and bacon hung richly from the ceiling, a year-round reminder of Fermanagh's abundance.

An old bell also hung there, its silent tongue lolling out. No one used it now, but it was highly prized none the less. Maggie's mother once had a cottage in the grounds of Lisgoole Abbey, and the bell had been fixed in her room. A long wire connected it with the big house, to be pulled if the owner was ill or wanted comfort in the night. Both Maggie's parents had died before I was even born. Her father could remember the cruel days of the Famine. From the stories Maggie told me, I felt I had known them, and rather thought of them as grandparents. Perhaps Maggie's house-spirit was connected with this. I could picture Maggie's mother going through the dark winter woods up to

the ghostly abbey, where in the massacre of 1641 it was burnt
full of women and children, to see her grand lady. The invalid
and her doleful bell jangling in the night, must have been a
presence in the life of Maggie's family. I was shown the doctor's prescriptions, still preserved, written in a spidery hand.
The ink had faded a little, and the dryness of the paper made
them like old documents. Maggie gave me one which I kept
ever afterwards. There were other heirlooms of her mother's
old mistress—the discoloured dentures and woollen knee-caps
that long ago succumbed to the moths.

It was difficult to know of which place Maggie talked the
most, the abbey or the castle. The lordly silver stones of the
castle went to making of humbler buildings when their days of
splendour passed. Some of the stones in Maggie's house bore
the marks of a careful mason's tool in serrated lines of dressing.
And the front step, which bowed out in a half-circle, had come
from a battlement turret of long ago. Musk-bells grew by the
step, and here Maggie paused in her tour of the house. The
smile in her wide brown eyes vanished, like the colour draining
from Mount Belmore when clouds obscured the sun.

She indicated the musk. 'They all lost their scent, Robbie,
every single one of them. They say it was from fumes of poison
gas tainting the air in the last war.' The solemn eyes looked
from me to the bright yellow bells. 'The end of the world is
coming, surely,' she reasoned, 'the preachers all say it—no
difference between summer or winter. It's all in the Book of
Revelation, so the preachers all say."

Staunch Protestant though she was, Maggie certainly was no
gloom and glory type. And after a passing moment of sad
reverie, the sun of her smile shone out again, and we went to
look at what was to be my bedroom. In a way that I had grown
to accept as usual, a tiny room opened directly from the
kitchen. A twirly iron bed painted white occupied one corner,
surrounded by lots of deep red chintz. Her father had died in it,

Maggie told me proudly, when nearly a hundred years old. She picked up some clothes-brushes I could use, and said the old man had made them, using hair from his horses. The bristle part of them was patterned in roundels and squares, formed by using both black and white hair. Towards the end of his life, he was totally blind, and confined to bed in the little room. As though it had all happened only last week, Maggie said how his door was kept open, so that he could hear her clopping over the flagstones in her clog-shoes, or playing on her fiddle.

Maggie was a vast fiddler still much in demand at dances. Every tune that anyone ever knew, from 'The Sprigs of Kilrea' to the 'Air on the G String', itched at her fingers' ends. Despite her hands being more like the clawed feet of an antique table, gloved in flesh, they flew nimbly enough over the strings. Her father had been the last for many miles around who could remember the Great Hunger. By all accounts he was a character.

All my life, from five years old, I had never revealed to anyone the secret about my own father. I would have died rather than let the smart Stephen sneer at him, or the 'gentry' I had stayed with, or even the kind Mrs. Morsett who was posh and might not understand. But Maggie looked straight into my soul, and I told her he had been a 'windy-cleaner', and had a fatal fall when he was twenty-seven years old, and how my mother had wrestled with poverty, and how my sisters and I had been parish orphans. This set the seal on Maggie's affection for me. Emotion sprang into every crevice of her brown face. 'Sure he was but a poor boy,' she said in a wavering voice. And she could not trust herself to speak again, until we got into the sitting-room.

'What a powerful woman yer mother must be. We must have her up for a long visit when we get the corn cut.' Would there be no end to Maggie's kindness I wondered? City evacuees being laid at farm doors was bad enough so far as most country people were concerned, but parents visiting their brats was the limit. And here was this woman who had not known me an hour, *wanting* my mother to come for a holiday. It was no idle thought, for a letter was shortly sent to arrange it.

I remembered my reception in other farm billets—in none of them had the work stopped specially in order that the evacuee might be welcomed. But Maggie, who ran the large house, did the milking and churning, tended the calves and poultry, baked fresh bread every day, had left it all to show me round the house, stopping in every room to give its history. Scattered about the farmhouse were fascinating old clocks, remnants of needlework, examples of craftsmanship, and pieces of fine glass. The dining-room, never used now, was still called the 'Wee Lodge Room', because local men of the Orange Order had used it before their new meeting hall was built. Maggie showed me rows and rows of drinking glasses; the swirl of bubbles in the varying thickness of the glass, and the slight deviation of the rims, showed them all to be hand-made and very old. They had come from Lisgoole Abbey and were consequently revered.

One glass, a small goblet elaborately engraved, fascinated me more than the others. Maggie said that when her father left the stewardship of Colamber Manor in Longford, Colonel Coffee had given it to him, and the glass had been his great pride and delight for it had been used after several famous Protestant battles. Because I so admired the beautiful glass, and because she so wanted to express her love and give me security in her house, Maggie took the precious heirloom from its place of honour, and gave it to me. It was my turn to be incapable of speech. The goblet was hundreds of years old, and in my eyes, the oldest piece of glass in the world. For me, the Queen Victoria Jubilee mug that belonged to my grandmother had been the touchstone of antiquity. The glasses and cups in our own house seldom survived a year. Comparatively I was a stranger, and yet had been given one of her dearest possessions.

Maggie hung the blackened kettle on its hook, to boil water for the third brewing of tea since my arrival—using me partly as an excuse to have another cup herself. While this was in progress I played the gramophone. Only one record remained as all the others had been borrowed and never returned. So we had Gracie Fields singing 'The Little Pudden Basin that belonged to Auntie Flo', not less than ten times. Each repeat sounded worse than its predecessor on account of the thorn needle broken off from the hedge outside, which was getting very broad and frayed indeed.

Apart from putting the needle back at the beginning of the groove each time, I paid little attention to the antiquated gramophone. The masses of books stacked in odd corners of the kitchen had caught my notice. Books, in fact, littered the whole house, and many of them were beautifully bound and tooled, and in remarkable condition for veterans of two famous libraries. A large proportion dated from the eighteenth century, and even the most up-to-date rows of the *Irish Farmer's and Gardener's Magazine*, were well over a century old. Subjects ponderously treated in the books ranged from *The Conduct of the Allies and of the Late Ministry in Beginning and Carrying on the Present War 1712* to the hardly more likely *Gout—its history, its causes and cure*. There were *Selections of Psalms and Hymns, used at the Chapel of the Molyneux Asylum for Blind Females*, 1854, and also a first edition of *The Seasons* by James Thomson.

Age and venerability did not give the books any financial worth, however, their interest was entirely intrinsic. Even this had declined since Maggie's father died, for he had seen the great castles thriving, from which they came. A shed outside the house was also crammed with books, mostly on botany and medicine, but damp had worked at them and glued their mottle-edged pages inseparably together with mildew. Many of the books indoors were useless too, for farm labourers sitting by the kitchen hearth at night had torn pages out to make spills for lighting pipes or candles.

As Maggie unfolded her epic of days gone by, I realized that their farm, along with abbeys and castles, had fallen from its former state. Hired labour could not be afforded now, except for odd weeks when the potatoes were set, or the threshing machine came. Land and cattle were tended by Christy himself—Maggie's brother. And until I came only those two lived in the house.

Christy was a small man, and looked nervous when he came into the kitchen on that June day, and saw me standing on a stool looking at the books. It would have been hard at that moment to foresee that more than anyone else in my whole life, he was to fill the place of my real father whom I could scarcely remember. Christy spoke shyly to me in a quiet faraway voice. I felt reassured, for it had seemed improbable that Maggie's brother could be as kind as she. But he was, and through the months ahead his gentle voice and strong hand was to teach me the running of the farm, crop rotation, and the methods of marking a good beast at the fair. When the haycart was emptied, he would take me over to examine the dizzy insects, scrapping amongst the seeds at the bottom, and instruct me as to their names.

However busy Christy might be in the fields he always found time to stop and point out a bird winging low over the corn, or the name of a flower hiding under the hedge. When trails of rain drifted across so that Mount Belmore disappeared, he taught me indoor work, how to cobble or repair harness, and the uses of a carpenter's bench. Christy was reluctant to offer criticism of my work, but I soon got to know by his look, whether he was pleased by my stitching of the ass's breechings or if I had waxed the thread properly. I soon learnt to know a well-dressed stack of corn, and how to set the teeth of a crosscut. I could graft fruit trees, skin a fox, put bar-frames on the bee hives, and vet a cow sick of the red water. All the time I sensed that Christy cared about me, and was not merely training me to be useful about the place for his own benefit. Because of his shy love, which I had unconsciously sought through the years, I willingly became pliable in his hands. For Christy, I would have done anything.

With different skills Maggie applied herself to the house. A 'great barn', she called it, because of the difficulty in doing the cleaning single-handed. But she loved the place, and the thought of leaving it for somewhere else never entered her head. Although she would have died rather than move, Maggie nevertheless had firm opinions as to what constituted the ideal house. Such a one existed down in the bog, a tiny two-roomed cabin with mud walls and thatched roof, where a family of twenty-two lived in company with their animals.

Maggie thought her own house was in need of only one more piece of furniture, and this was a 'press' by which she meant a wardrobe for the clothes. Possession of a wardrobe was the only thing that I ever knew Maggie to desire. Except for this, she demanded and expected nothing from life, never suffered from ambition or a wish to be one-up on the neighbours. I never heard her speak in jealousy. But she *did* want a press. Although this was by no means a frivolous wish, poor Maggie felt almost ashamed in wanting one. She would not speak to Christy directly about it, but got at him through me. When Christy and I went to a sale together, I was to use all my persuasive powers, if a press went up for auction. But her brother was content without such modern innovations. The backs of the doors held nails enough for ordinary clothes, and every room had its beautiful sea-chest with brown paper and pepper to fold the Sunday suits in. The thick walls had rough holes cut in them to hold the linen—huckaback towels, and old sheets like sail-cloth. Sprigs of bog-myrtle were put in these recesses to keep moths away from the best personal linen that must only be used in a fatal emergency, or the final dressing for the grave.

Of course, Maggie and Christy had no radio. What, indeed, would they want a thing like that for, to be like Harry Maguire who was forever running into town getting batteries charged instead of being in his meadows. In this respect they were like we had been at home in Belfast, though they did not have passing trains at the farm, by which to put clocks right, as we had done. Instead they listened for the Angelus bell, blowing its doleful, sublime sound across the hills from the Catholic chapel. Maggie would pause from mixing the hens' food, or from testing potatoes cooking in the round iron pot, and on hearing the bell, reach up and correct the hands of a tardy cuckoo-clock.

The weather forecasting so essential to farming was equally as unscientific as clock synchronizing. For long-term forecasting we had to rely on *Old Moore's Almanac* bought the previous December at the fair. More immediate needs were dealt with by a barometer which Christy said had never once misled him—a long strip of seaweed—*sugar laminaria*. Some chance wave had washed it ashore at Bundoran years before, when Maggie was on her last excursion. Unfailingly the seaweed dampened when rain threatened, but went hard and crackly for fine days, that Christy knew would be good for haymaking. Limp or crackly, rain or sun, they made great efforts to get their potatoes 'planted with Paddy and dug with Billy'. The enigma of this saying was solved by Maggie who explained that if the seed potatoes went in by St. Patrick's Day in March, there would be some ready for eating at the twelfth of July celebration of King Billy's greatest victory.

Maintenance of the house and farm buildings rested on Christy's shoulders. If a new sty or floor was needed, he went to one of the plantations, loaded some seasoned timber into the cart, and I drove it away off to the sawmill, and within days the new structure appeared. The old tomes on the kitchen shelf suddenly became as dry as dust on that first day when Christy asked if I would like to go with him. Out in the golden afternoon walking along with Christy, who was older than Maggie, I thought it the most wonderful day of my life.

We went down to a fir plantation at the back of the farm. The ground was springy with old needles. I was rather shaken when Christy said he had planted the wood. The soaring pine pillars, their sighing in the wind barely audible, and the shady underworld stabbed here and there by burning spots of sunlight—had these really sprung from the little grey-haired man beside me? To me it was a marvel, difficult to comprehend. I had always loved trees, even the strangled ones that struggled against Belfast smoke, and the trees in the city cemetery, but I had never seen one planted.

Pleased that I found the wood so wonderful, Christy pointed to a large spreading chestnut still flaring with a thousand white candles. He said he had planted it too, as a conker when he was my own age. I could imagine him as an eager boy prising the shiny kernel from its spiky shell, and putting it in his pocket. I knew what clothes boys had worn in those days by looking at old photographs in my previous farm billets, so Christy would have had knickerbockers. Then one day he would have fished in the pocket, found the conker and have buried it in the earth. Perhaps he forgot it, until the day when he found it sprouting. Now it stood out on the summer landscape like a giant statue of the Enlightened One, a memorial to the little boy who loved trees. I understood how he had felt, for in Belfast I had refused every year to pierce the fine kernels polished like mahogany marbles, in order to string them and do battle with my friends. I thought the conkers much too beautiful and precious to be destroyed in this way, and kept mine along the window-ledge. But why, oh why, I asked myself now, had I never thought to plant them?

Christy's plantation impressed me even more than the engraved goblet. I wanted the autumn to come quickly so that I too could plant a chestnut in order to measure its growth against my own. Christy's concern with trees led him to plant them still, though he was old now and certainly would not live to see their full-grown splendour. In cutting wood, Christy left the trees that he liked. Perhaps in cutting the hedge, a particular ash sapling would appeal to him, so he would slash all round it sparing the slender young tree. In this way, seen from the hill, the whole farm looked heavily wooded.

We did not go down into the wood on that first afternoon just for daydreams. I was given one end of the cross-cut and we made eight lengths of fir trunks. Then we laboured with them down to a small stream and built a bridge. Before milking time, it was completed, and I was so excited I insisted on dragging Maggie away from her jobs to see the wonder of the structure. What an entry in my diary it would make, and what a boast for my letter home—'I have built a super bridge with Christy that can carry the binder.'

When we got back to the house, Maggie was standing by the back door, her face flushed as she finished making the butter. She had no complicated methods of churning, but simply used a primitive dash. Christy had made this also, from a short pole with two pieces of wood crossed at the bottom, held by nails. Maggie stood at the churn pumping the dash up and down like a piston. She tried to make the butter form with the same demoniac energy as I had used in the rectory bath. But churning was often left until late in the day and the cows lowing for the second milking. Then Maggie would be naughty and run to the kitchen for a drop of hot water to force it on. At last the heaping, golden pile of butter was taken up in a wooden bowl, washed, salted and maybe brightened with carrot juice, and finally pressed into a shamrock mould or one of King Billy crossing Boyne Water.

Maggie also produced her own starch potatoes for the

laundry. My meteoric rise in height and weight went on un-
checked, and a year's country food, reaching a climax in the
enormous meals set out by Maggie, had smoothed out all the
hollows in my face, and thickened up the thin covering of flesh
on my limbs. Filled with content, and conscious of the rising
sap of adolescence, I was assailed by vanity. I fancied myself
still in certain clothes and that was why I always found time to
grate potatoes for Maggie, so that she could starch me a
beautiful white collar to go with my Sunday suit.

I regarded Maggie as the cleverest woman with her hands
that I had ever met. She could make her own candles, and her
jam always amused me. Half an hour or so before tea, she would
go down the garden, pull a handful of soft fruit, and have
enough jam ready by the mealtime. Many of the local people
preferred her bour-tree wine to her dandelion or quicken-berry
vintages. Whatever Maggie did was accompanied with squeals
of laughter, and there was a stock of jokes for each occasion
which never failed to amuse us as though for the first time.
Flour came by the hundredweight and was stored under the
stairs along with the flutes and drums of the Orange band. The
empty sacks were boiled to remove the blue lettering and trade
marks, and then Maggie's needle turned them into sheets. To
unpick a flour sack quickly demanded no little skill. Anyone
with a prominent or sharp nose became the butt for one of our
jokes—'Och, hasn't he the fine beak for rippin' flour sacks!'

Throughout that unbelievable first day so many memorable
things had happened to me, that by milking time I determined
to show Maggie just how capable I was. Hot jets jumped and
sang into the bucket, and I went so rapidly that a heavy froth
formed on top. I had learnt that in milking skill was judged by
the amount of froth, the best always produced a high head, so I
worked away furiously to impress Maggie. When the first
bucket threatened to brim over, Maggie showed utter surprise
and said that not since arthritis had forced her mother to give

up, had she seen anyone milk like it. But I had not finished the cow, and the tiny Kerry-blue when her teats had been eased with the froth, gave another full pail.

Christy was summoned to the byre and he brought a friend who had called at the house on his way to an early *ceili*. Both farmers watched my performance approvingly and at last Christy admitted that milking was a thing he could not do himself. I had imagined that Christy could do anything and found this odd. He promised to take me whenever he went in to the fairs, and I could test the udders for him. This would save the embarrassment of always having to find a neighbour to go with him. To be asked by the experienced Christy was honour indeed and I wanted to know how soon the next fair would be.

After milk, came water. When Maggie and I had finished with the cows and had carried the thick creamy pails into the dairy, we set off to collect fresh water for the stone trough, to keep the milk cool until it was collected in the morning. We walked over several fields in the mellow airs of early evening and came to a brook, an inferior one, with water like pale tea. When the trough was filled, we started out again for another well—the far spring. To have a bucket of clear spring water in the house as the last job of the day was a deep satisfaction to Maggie. Knowing that the farm needed no more attention till morning, and that she could settle down to enjoy the neighbours' *ceili* with kettles full of spring water, was worth more to her than a win in the Irish sweepstake.

The far spring was quite a sacred thing, divined by Maggie's father. It lay far from the house, and every evening for the next thirteen months, and many times during the years that stretched then into the future, I enjoyed that leisurely journey to the spring-well with Maggie. She thought nothing of taking the short cut through the haunted orchard and jumping down the steep bank on the other side. Even in high summer parts of the rushy steppes beyond were a quagmire and sucked noisily at our feet as we went through. No light glimmered from round about, for the nearest house lay hidden by a shoulder of hill, and the nearest down the valley was a mile or more away. Picking her way carefully, Maggie brought me to the well. And as we clanked our buckets to lower them in the mysterious crystal depths, the noise disturbed a heron fishing in the nearby brook. It rose majestically, and flew overhead with lazy wing-beats, measuring its span against the first appearing stars.

Down went our buckets into the perfectly round hole that lay in a small depression against a hedge. The stones that lined the sides of the deep hole had also come from the castle, brought and laid by the water-diviner himself. Unlike so many wells in Fermanagh, it had never been known to dry up in summer. Its cool water was clear like glass, and tasted pleasantly of minerals.

Maggie and I never hurried over this nightly pilgrimage, and lingered by the well once our water was drawn. Some-times one of the herdsmen would come over for a chat, for in summer they used our well to get water for their outlying stock. A sycamore spread its branches in a magnificent canopy over the well, rising out of the ground close by, in four thick columns. In spite of the dusk we could read the initials carved into the trunks. Generations of herdsmen had made them, who passed that summer way. Down the hill they had come in all the years since Maggie's father had stopped as his rod of halse started to spin at the hidden presence of water.

Having drunk deep at the beauty of the place, we reached down and tightened our grip on the handles, and set off back to the house. Often the plaintive heart-stirring *wee-wee* of cur-lews would follow us, or the drumming of snipe. Maggie's knowledge of birds was not so wide as her brother's, but she could recognize the snipe, and laying her free hand on my arm would say, 'That's the wee weather-blade, Robbie'.

Time was ours. When we tired, or threatened to spill too

much water by laughing, we set our buckets down for a rest. A bad patch of ragwort was a good excuse to stop again while we pulled it up by the roots. A ruined cottage, tumbled to pieces at the bottom of a slope, held peculiar fascination for Maggie. She always rested the big bucket by its scattered stones. There followed the slightest silent pause, in which the scent of honeysuckle and sweet-briar we could not see, seemed to make the air more luscious than before. Maggie recalled visiting the cottage once when she was a very young child. And though no believer in ghosts, she regarded the house as still occupied, for her the ruin was still the home of Mrs. Hassard with the red cow and white turkeys. Now perhaps she would sit down on the moss-covered hearthstone, and tell of long-dead loves haunting the crumbling masonry.

And then the last lap back to the house to see how many people had come in to *ceili*. We lit the paraffin lamp and slipped one of Maggie's hairpins on the glass to save it from cracking.

Chapter Ten

Meadowsweet Summer

An alarming noise from the yard, just outside my window, woke me next morning. I looked out and saw the old wooden tub put there, hopefully, to catch rainwater. Maggie's twelve beloved Aylesbury ducks squabbled for room to turn somersaults in the few inches of slimy water at the bottom. Out of the flurrying white bundle, yellow beaks and webbed feet would appear for a moment and then vanish beneath feathers again. The quacking and squawks of protest deafened the birds in the nearest trees, in a dissonance at variance with the morning calm.

Maggie's step sounded hurriedly on the stairs, and I saw her pass the window, driving the ducks back into their crawl. She knew that not all would have laid eggs in the night, and have buried them under the soaking black mess, that had been fresh rushes only the day before. When she came back I went into the kitchen to put on my socks and boots with her. First she probed under a pale silver heap of ashes and unearthed some embers still glowing from yesterday's fire. Since the house was built, the fire had never been allowed to go out. Summer and winter, a welcome to the hearth was there for any caller, and, except at night, some pot or kettle always let out a gentle curl of steam. We took our socks from hooks in the deep fireplace, where they had been warmed and aired since we went to bed.

They had kept good company in the dark hours with rows of rabbit skins being cured. To pull on her socks Maggie sat on a stool to the left of the fire, the traditional place for the woman of the house. The big iron crane that carried the cooking pots and ovens was hinged on this side, and swung in that way to conform with an old superstition that the crook must follow the sun.

Then Maggie put on her shoes. One half of the pair consisted of a worn wellington boot, and the other, a plimsoll. This was a white one originally, but now reduced to a nondescript canvas colour, and with its frayed edges and torn eyelets, looking rather sorry for itself. But it was a great comfort in Maggie's life, for the large hole on one side allowed the escape of her bunion, which she referred to affectionately as 'my wee buddy'. With the first brew-up of tea well on the go, Maggie was ready to face her long day.

I was beginning to expand, like a young dragonfly drying its wings and feeling the sun's warmth. No more school during six glorious weeks of summer holiday. Simultaneous equations and the volume of cones, parsing and syntax, and all the frantic scrambles of homework belonged to the dead past. Cows were waiting at the gate, anxious to get into the byre where fresh bedding was strewn on the stalls. Patient eyes pleaded for the great burdens of milk, made heavy by summer lushness, to be eased in the quiet coolness. And beyond the milking stretched the whole day free, and then tomorrow also, and the day after, vanishing in an infinitive perspective towards autumn. For the second time, I did the milking, happily and in record time.

Afterwards, Christy wheeled the two big cans down the crooked lane, on a flat, home-made barrow that ran on a solid wheel of wood. If the milk lorry that collected it was late, the milk would be sour before it reached Enniskillen, and so be returned to us. Such a thing was a great loss to the farm, which depended solely on the creamery's monthly milk cheque.

Keeping the precious fluid cool was a worry for Maggie and
Christy. The hours spent during the day in carrying up fresh
water from the bog-holes scarcely repaid our efforts to save the
milk. On the hottest days, hiding the milk churns in hollows
of the hedge was the last resort, even then not always effective
if the lorry was very late. The cans stood in the shade like
diminutive knights in armour waiting in ambush. The dry
drains by the hedge were a complete lattice-work of mare's
tails, the biggest I was to see anywhere in the world. They grew
high above the milk churns for miles along the road, as though
long rows of green poodles queued up *en masse* for a dog show.
But down in the bogs even these were dwarfs compared with
the hemlock, which soared on sturdy jointed stems higher than
a man. Eight or nine feet in the air the frail green umbrellas
opened, holding the delicate white lace as a screen against the
sun.

As we returned up the lane, leaving the milk by the roadside,
Christy cast a critical eye on the hayfields. The dew still lay
heavily over the meadows, and he decided to put off work
there until later. Meanwhile there was the bog. I followed
Christy to the tiny brown cliffs cut sheer with terraces out of
low-lying fields. Here the air had a special tang, a sharp purity
which the sweet mown fields or the honeysuckle delirium of the
lanes did not possess. At the bottom lay the brown, unmoving
pools, and beneath them, no one knew what antiquity of forests
fallen and decayed centuries and centuries before.

For Christy the bog meant work and fuel for Maggie's undying fire. He showed me how to clamp turf. The peats, if only
partly dried of the bog water, were built on the ground into
little pyramids. If quite dry, big stacks were piled up. And as
with every job on the farm, the building demanded no little
skill. Spaces must be left between the separate, brick-shaped
lumps of turf. And through these holes the winds blew from
one season to the next, drying the peats, hardening the soft,

wet bricks, and lightening their colour. The sun, which would soon suck up the dew, had only a minor role in the drying and making of good burning fuel.

Christy's turf was quite unlike the Lyttes' spongy lumps of ancient moss, but was black and hard. Small twigs of sally were used for levelling the pyramids, but the most perfect constructions were not proof against the weasels. Sensing something, I would turn suddenly and look back at my neatly-made row, just in time to see a section plundered by the animals, who dived through the wind holes, knocking it all down.

The mowing machine could not get into some of the small closes, and these fell to Christy's scythe. He stood amid the high grasses, and with the slightest sigh of steel against stem, laid the green harvest at his feet. I envied those full swinging sweeps of his, and the way the blade, flashing now and again, seemed to be part of him. In unvarying rhythm, rocking smoothly from side to side he passed up the close, and down again. And always the grass fell in precise ranks, like soldiers drilling to a word of command. Christy never paused, except to wipe the sweat from his brow, or to clap a hand on a cleg that had succeeded in piercing the dark mahogany rind of his neck.

The little fields tilted and curved gently to follow the hill's gentle rise and fall. Here the meadowsweet was really queen-of-the-meadow. Its sickly creamy foam was a siren to clouds of pale copper butterflies, lured like careless navigators from their course. But these flowers were a great hardship to me, for I had to pick them, and black heads also, out of Christy's swathes. Unaccustomed to the constant bending, my long back would begin to ache in all sorts of unexpected places, and muscles never used before would make their presence felt. I looked to see if Christy too was growing tired, but nothing stopped the pendulum slicing into the phalanx of grass. Occasionally a corn-crake would be disturbed, then Christy might pause, and look at me to see if I was watching its ungainly darting in the last island of standing hay. And sometimes he would draw the hone from his hip-pocket and sharpen the blade with skilfully gauged pressure, making a ringing music in the quiet field.

Mastery of the scythe was not all that captured me about the little reaper. In every province, patient, enduring, I soon found he ruled supreme. His was the rough hand in the ploughlands broadcasting corn from a seed-apron just as his fathers from immemorial time had done—his the hand. that made such straight, tidy windrows of the harvest, and later in the year the hand that fed the sheaves firmly and evenly to the frantic pulse of the threshing-drum—a hand that could, if needs be, wield a flailing stick and dress the finest royal stack. Christy's was the hand that for me became the symbol of manhood. I no longer regarded hairy-chested roadmenders, or sweat- and sinew-covered blacksmiths as monuments of strength. This little man, grey and a little sad-looking, became my pattern. As thatcher or mason, ploughman or carpenter, hedger or woodman, Christy was consummate. I followed him closely, awed in silent worship.

At midday, a whistle was blown from the house, Maggie having first banged it on the step to shake out the earwigs that crept into it every night. Across the countryside we could hear the piping of whistles from other farms, as though answering ours in imitation of dawn cocks. We could always tell which farm was ready first for its delicious meal of bacon and cabbage boiled together in the same pot. And, of course, Maggie knew which unfortunate housewife was behind with her morning's work by the time of her whistle-blast. Sometimes our meal was over and we had been back in the fields an hour when the Angelus would ring, reminding the faithful of their noon prayers. And then we realized that in her concern over time and missing the milk lorry, Maggie had wildly adjusted the kitchen clock earlier in the morning, quite regardless of the real time. This state of affairs would be aggravated if the chapel bell had tolled during the morning for a funeral which Maggie had mistaken for the Angelus.

Work in the fields gave us roaring appetites and we sank down gratefully to dinner, glad of the kitchen's shelter from the burnished sun. Refreshed and filled with new vigour we went out once again, this time armed with cans of sour buttermilk, to work until quite late. We were too busy to return to the house for tea, and Maggie brought it out in a basket. I knew that inside would be something made specially for me—an apple tart. Maggie had soon discovered my love of these and would bake it on the oven bottom, without a plate, so that it came out more like a dumpling covered with sugar over the sides in a burnt, delicious candy.

The day marched on and my piles of unwanted meadowsweet and black heads grew into nice heaps for burning. Shadows fell now from the opposite direction, and trees that had shimmered in the sun's direct rays now darkened into silhouettes as light fell behind them. Maggie took a pitchfork and worked with us, for an hour or two. Every field had its history, like every room in the house. She did not stop the work, but went on talking as I led the donkey with the gatherer. 'Up in that corner, Robbie, the wee penny-schoolmaster had his hut. Ya should have seen the wee shanty, so fallin' down, it needed a great stake to prop it up. Then all the cubs, who hated goin' to school, went one night and pulled the stake away, and down came the whole place. Weren't they great?' Christy said nothing, but by his chuckle, full of remembered joy, I knew he had been one of the mischievous cubs.

While working at the hay, Maggie kept a weather-eye on the lane, in case one of the maids from the local mansion-house came up for a cup of tea on her day off. And in spite of chatting, and convulsing with laughter so much that she had to cling to the pitchfork handle for support, she listened for the dog barking. He never failed to warn of intruders. The house was locked and the key put under a special stone in the garden, but nevertheless, Maggie was anxious about the rambling tinkers who frequented the lanes and slept in the haysheds. Unlike most of the neighbours, Maggie always welcomed the tinkers and gypsies into the house if she were there, but even so would not trust them. I think she invited them in for fear of being cursed. She would tell with dread of a local woman who went into town and met a gypsy she had turned away from her door without a cup of tea. The gypsy had spat at the woman and cursed her by fire and water. Little cause to wonder that the woman's hayshed went afire, and a stirk drowned in the lint-hole, all in the same month as the curse.

Giving a shriek, Maggie would sometimes drop her rake or fork, and bolt madly down the field, careless of the swathes she trod on. This was a signal for Christy to go and deal with a wild bees' nest. We marked the place with a stick, and at night returned to gas the nest. As many as twelve might be found in one meadow, much to Maggie's distress. Other bees than the bad-tempered, swift-to-sting, wild ones of the hayfield hummed about the house and garden, for in front stood the domestic hives.

Fifty years before, when Christy and his brothers were young and all living at home the big gardens had been a show place. But half a century did not pass without leaving changes even in the garden which seemed to me like an eternal paradise. Could the robust group in the red velvet photograph album really be Christy and his brothers as playful, devil-may-care boys hating the Boers as I hated the Germans? They were gone except for one, and for Christy, who alone of all of them was left to look after the overgrown gardens. Flower-beds had disappeared, and only the fierce, bloody bullets of peonies broke through the rank weeds. Out of loyalty, of course, the bed of orange lilies was kept in good order, so that we would have decorations for the twelfth of July.

Thickly flourishing shrubs recalled the garden's lost glory more than anything. Japonica survived the striving seedlings and tangly masses of *azalea pontica*, that lifted its tiny golden candelabra on a million twigs and scented the air too luxuriously, too prolifically with its sweet smell, as if the subtler honey-suckle had been distilled. It lured me to take deep breaths with my nose close to the flowers, as the copper butterflies were lured to the meadowsweet. Golden bells, these were indeed, as Maggie called them, ringing with the silent magic of their heady incense. At night, the scent lay in dense layers on the air, so that walking up the lane, the new-mown hay would mingle with the azalea smell, then be lost, only to be caught again when the yellow shrubs were far behind. I thought that all the plants listed with such exotic names in the Garretons' privy catalogues had taken root here, purposely to bind my heart to this wild garden, this farm, this home.

From all the blossom, besides the limitless bog heather and myrtle, the bees had more than they needed. Often I found them quivering on the window-sills, too heavy with pollen to move. From the day of Maggie's birth, the hives had not been shifted, but she had never in all the long years lost her fear of bees. When they swarmed she did not like the new hive to escape, and ran to call us to deal with it. If we were far away from the house, perhaps working in one of the farthest fields, and could not easily be found, Maggie resorted to an old method of stopping the swarm's flight away from the farm. Putting some pebbles in the bottom of a bucket, she rolled them round and round, shook them up and down trying to drown the noise of the queen bee by the din.

Although the bees might be controlled Maggie's fear re-mained. Using her dread to tease her, I would make stray bees angry and come buzzing after us. She was terrified they would get in her long hair, and although she half-ran at all times as her life was a busy one, she would fairly spring into the house and

lock herself in. When the air was clear and she could safely un-
bolt the windows again, she would scold me, always ending
with the story of the church sexton. He had been down digging
a grave when a swarm passed over. It dropped suddenly and
landed inside his shirt, making him dangerously ill.

Maggie's instinctive watch on the lane for visitors, kept her
alert not only for maids and tinkers, but for the Old Fusilier
and the Darkie. Blazoned with medals from an impossibly
large number of campaigns, the Old Fusilier came to peddle
pins and bootlaces. So did the Darkie, but he was a Sikh. A
man who wore bangles was bound to be intriguing, and I
longed to see Darkie unwind his uncut hair from beneath his
pink-icing turban. He never left our farm without a present of a
plump fowl, cackling and struggling under his arm.

Christy did not deem these callers to be any particular concern of his, and carried on with his work. But he always left the
meadow for the deaf and dumb man who came collecting for
the institute. He was accorded great honour and treated to one
of Maggie's outsize meals. While the guest ate, Christy went
upstairs to his room and unlocked the wooden chest where his
money and family papers were kept, and Maggie and I looked
through the man's book to see how much the quality had sub-
scribed. He passed his jotter back and forth, he scribbled and
we scribbled, and so carried on a lively conversation. Because
he could express so much in this way everybody voted him as a
most 'powerful sport'. More important to us, however, was the
fact that he always brought news from distant cousins and
friends of whom we would never have heard otherwise. We
followed the point of his pencil as if it were a ticker-tape
machine, wondering what on earth would come from it next.
The cousin up in Killeshandra, we would learn, had got a new
bull and had three acres of potatoes in, while poor James away
in the Blue Stack Mountains had married a lass the width of two
creels, but he had got £650 with her, so he couldn't complain.

And our old rector, who was across in the Free State now, still wore his rainproof with the green paint all over it, and his wife had been thrown from a horse and killed.

As the youngest and nimblest on the farm I had to build the ricks of hay—or rucks as we called them. The trampling of a ruck required a good sense of balance and no fear of heights. When the structure trembled and I stood a great distance from the ground, it was a temptation to place the forkfuls of hay under my feet and finish the ruck quickly. But Christy's expert eye knew how the stack must be shaped. With his fork he patted and prodded it evenly, and then piled up more for me to distribute, until I thought myself miles in the air, on a cloud that shook and shivered at every step I took.

Not many days of practice at this art were necessary before I became moderately efficient. But no success could match old Archer Rosshill, a local cottager. His cow ran dry, and in return for a free can of milk from Maggie, he came to help us with the rucking. He was over eighty, and tried to dance jigs on the very top of the rucks, and sing one of his rude songs. I liked Archer in other ways, but hated to work with him in a hayfield. He went out of his way to show the world that at eighty he was still an undisputed champion. No matter how vast the loads of hay I pitched up to him, to the point of rupturing myself or breaking the fork, he was equal to them. He flicked the hay miraculously into place and bellowed to me in a Scottish accent, 'Come now lad, don't think I was born hopping round inkwells'. His wife was not without distinction, for she had been operated on for gall-stones, 132 of them, which afterwards were proudly displayed in a soup tureen on the dresser at their cottage for all the world to count.

Work in the meadows not infrequently went on until after ten at night, especially if bad weather was predicted for the next day. Then, if the hay was unfit for rucking, we resorted to lapping. To do this back-breaking job, the hay lying on the ground had to be lightly shaken and deftly scooped up into loose balls. The rain caught us during my first summer at Maggie's. And that was on the Fort hill. Just to be sure we lapped, for it was St. Swithin's Eve. Before we had got to bed the rain came, caressing at first then pounding down, plopping musically into the tub by my window. Such a violent thunderstorm boomed over us later, that Maggie came downstairs to put a tablecloth over the mirror in my room. It rained for days, and much of the mown hay rotted in the fields, whereas the laps up on Fort Hill, dried out afterwards, and were perfectly safe.

A complete circle, twenty paces wide, crowned the top of the Fort hill. Round it ran a low wall. Christy associated the place with ancient invasions of the Danes. But neighbours were in no doubt that it was a home for the 'little people'. Two white-thorns guarded it, sloped in one direction from the wind, and twisted into grotesque shapes, like scraggy cattle with wild horns and tails flying in the wind. Landscapes of unsurpassable beauty surrounded the high Fort on all points of the compass, melting in soft tones of forest, field and mountain into vast skies.

A chain of lakes extended on the other side of the house, and from there Belmore presided over the lesser hills, gradually building itself up to the cloud-drawn climax of summer evenings. To the south lay Benaughlin where the sun played snakes and ladders with cloud-shapes first in fluorescent greens and blues, and then in inky veins and russet patches. There was Knockninny southwards too, where we went on the Methodist spree and were obliged to sing a doxology in the heather before eating our rain-sodden sandwiches and drinking our sarsa-parilla.

The Fort fascinated me more than any other part of Maggie's farm, and not only because of the views. I was told that its two trees were 'lonely bushes', because, reaching back into time, they belonged to the days of eviction when the poor gathered under them for protection. I perfectly understood what these people had suffered. In our small Belfast house we had lived for years in dread of the rentman evicting us because of our mounting arrears. The trees' kindness in sheltering the destitute had been magically rewarded for their timber was immune against the woodman's axe. One man who disbelieved in this power, and tried to cut them down broke his arm on them.

And these were not old wives' tales. My information came from a highly reliable source. He was the oldest person around and enjoyed much respect as churchwarden. He told me that he was a friend of the 'little people', and not only had he seen them, but a rarer privilege, heard their concerts up in the Fort. But I remained unsure about the reality of the Fort's powers until Freddie, quite unsolicited, confirmed them. He was Maggie's and Christy's married brother who farmed nearby. One night recently he had been in a party on Home Guard patrol, and had fainted when he heard the banshee circling the Fort with its wail of death. They were all stout Protestant men and heavily armed, but their hearts quailed, even though the banshee was only wailing for a Catholic who died before morning.

When we finally got round to rucking the hay on the Fort hill, I stayed on at the mound until after the stroke of midnight. But nothing happened and I was disappointed, for I was not a sceptic and had not mocked the churchwarden's 'gift of the little people', or doubted the banshee's visitation. Only a cock pheasant and a score of rabbits found shelter under the 'lonely bushes'.

The heavenly music of the little greencaps up in the Fort was apparently not to be one of my delights at Maggie's. But I scored success in other fields—as a Don Juan. Not only had my bad name, and the trouble of my previous billets, preceded me to the farm, but also the fact that I was a 'great one with the cutties'. How this came about was not clear, for apart from molesting Betty on the way home from school, and bombarding Sheila with sweetmeats, I had exerted myself hardly at all over girls. Still, as usually happens in such cases, the reputation, having been earned justly or otherwise, must be lived up to.

We were out clamping in the bog one day when Maggie called. She wanted to introduce me to a niece of Flynn Carroll —a neighbour singular among us because he could speak and roundly curse in Gaelic and wore five waistcoats at the same time. Niece, however, could not lay claim to any special quality. Not only was she afflicted with acne and myopic too, but weighed not an ounce under fourteen stone. On her side she had comparative youth, was a renowned baker and had the attraction of a good farm of land, to which she was heiress. Anxious to do her best by me, Maggie whispered at an opportune moment, that I should accompany Ethel home, and, on the way, give her a 'wee squeeze'. Accordingly, when we were out of sight from the house, I tripped the astonished woman up and rolled her in the meadow lush with the best timothy. In return I got such a box on the ear that I thought the eardrum must be broken. Though profitless, the episode lived long. The trampled patch in the tall grass was pointed out by Maggie to all and sundry, as the place where 'Our Cub gave big Ethel a grand squeeze'.

Chapter Eleven

Sunday Posh

A Sunday morning would have to be very still before we could hear the bell, as we lived a long way from the church. But as soon as we crested the far hill on our bicycle, its summons reached us. There could be no mistaking it for the chapel one, which had been rung all morning for successive Masses. Like the architecture which housed them the two bells were quite distinct. Ours was a hard, clear, decidedly Protestant note, while the chapel's made a sad plaint, and belonged vaguely, in my mind at least, to the night flight of curlews.

Up at the cross-roads, when we came bowling along, a dozen youths and farm-labourers would have met, and we all trundled along to church together. In the delectable air, still fresh from lingering dew, we pushed on the pedals under the shade of leaning ash and overloaded chestnuts, tall choirs of beech, and miles of hedges bursting with birdsong and devil's garters. The red faces and working-day hands emerged awkwardly from Sunday suits, and many a neck was to feel the rasping edge of a starched collar long before sermon time. Under the ancient yews, we waited, watching those who arrived by foot or pony and trap. Couples who perhaps had been dancing on a farm kitchen's stone floor the previous night, did not now mix. The occasion being a solemn one, the girls stood on

one side, and boys on the other. But all the same, much courting was done by the going to and fro of the eyes.

At last, the number of arrivals began to dwindle, and the bell
set about its summing up, a steady toll eminently suited to the
vigorous arm beneath it that pulled the rope. I sat in the choir
because the body of the church was so crammed and few men
would brave the gaze of the whole congregation to walk down
to the chancel seats. The people filled the church up from the
back, working towards the front, until latecomers must instal
themselves under the rector's very eyes. They probably
thought that the rector had clairvoyant powers, and could gaze
into the soul of those who sat near him in the front rows. The
back, somehow, was safer. Eyes could peer between fingers
during prayers and look for new hats and hair styles without
turning round.

Division of the church into choir and nave was purely an
arbitrary one, for nobody could distinguish between the choir's
efforts and the lusty singing of the more martial hymns by the
congregation. In consequence I could make as joyful a noise as
many of the old crones in the choir proper. Our churchman-
ship, of course, was of such a lowness and evangelical disposition, that exceeded even the most reasonable demands that
loyalty to our Protestant king could demand. Psalms and
responses were not sung, but divided into alternate verses,
recited by rector and people. Two old men, deaf as posts,
bawled out in revivalist fashion, their voices far louder than
anybody's. The effect of this was very disturbing as every Sunday, without variation, they were a verse behind the rest of us.

There were other stars who appeared on the bill in a similar
manner during prayers said by the congregation. 'Our Father'
was a favourite for late entry, and it usually got off to a start
like a fugue. The general law governing these performances
seemed to be that the later you started, the louder you prayed.
Unlike a Bach fugue, however, the prayers never came to a

grand finish, but trailed away, the voices finishing in the reverse order from which they began, in a series of 'Amens'.

'Amens' were old Jane Dockson's special province. Hers was the most discordant voice during the whole hymn-singing. Nobody ever mentiond the subject, but it was fairly plain that she could not read the words in her hymn-book, and so she relied on a very resounding 'amen' to make her presence felt. 'All things bright and beautiful' provided the only exception, for she knew it by heart and shouted it at the top of her voice.

All of this was the more remarkable in view of the fact that old Jane was really a Roman Catholic. In the body, she came to our church from the farm where she worked as housekeeper, dressed in the Victorian clothes bequeathed by the old farmer's mother. In spirit, she came to the Church of Ireland clothed in humility, and full of grief that her inward allegiance had received no outward recognition. She was forever imploring the rector to turn her round three times on the chancel steps in front of the whole congregation. She found consolation at the Methodist preaching-houses and gospel tent-meetings. Here she could respond to the evangelist's appeal for on-the-spot converts. When he pleaded for those who wanted to be saved, to put up their hands, old Jane's shot up like a distress signal. With Jane there was no question of being saved once and for all. If a special mission lasted six nights, up went her hand six times. If an embarrassed evangelist tried to avoid the hand, she would shout wildly 'Jane over here!' One English divine, not forewarned about her, on seeing her hand go up on the second night running remonstrated with her. She admitted to being 'saved' the night before, but had taken the name of the Holy Boy in vain when the sow would not be driven home, and needed to be 'saved' again.

Acceptance into the fold of her choice was not all that grieved Jane. In her ancient bosom another desire consumed her—she wanted to sing in the choir at the parish church. Being turned three times round before the 'Lord's Table' did not compare with this wish. But being prevented from this during divine service did not mean she could not do so when the place was empty. With the big music book opened anywhere, and propped upside-down on the choir stalls, she would give a good bellow of 'All things bright and beautiful'.

Fame of a sort, she did eventually have, but not in a religious sphere. The red lamp was responsible. One of the farm hands told her that war regulations prohibited people from walking out in the blackout unless carrying a rear light. Since the poor old soul was heavily in love with the boy, she believed his every word. No amount of laughter and derision could make her remove the red lamp pinned on the back of her once-grand velvet cape.

And as though to compensate for an age without a name, fate gave Jane one glorious hour. She was called as witness in an important law case. On entering the crowded courthouse and seeing the barristers in their wigs, she apologized to the judge, 'Ya'll forgive me now, for I never thought 'twould be so stylish, or I would have worn Ma's wee brown wig myself.'

To have had Jane Dockson in the choir, would certainly have been a remarkable thing. It might even have meant that my cherished dream of sitting in the gallery, would lose its attraction. But things had changed up there, although all sorts of devilry was still practised. The most exciting gallery days came to an abrupt end when one of the largest landowners in those parts had taken himself off to the Methodists after feeling insulted. His head was large and bald, and once, as he snored through the rector's boring polemics, someone successfully aimed a water-pistol at the polished pate below. He woke with a start, made the rector lose his way in a sheaf of papers, and jumped and shouted 'Spitting in the house of God', and stumped out never to return.

I took my mind off the sermons by watching the wasps that

built in the rafters. Droning monotone or rousing harmony seemed to leave them quite unmoved. The fact that they were physically unmoved was due to the sexton's avoiding them like the plague, for he was the man stung while down in the grave. But at last the rector pushed his papers together, and amid a stirring and stretching and cracking of stiff bones and smoothing out of crumpled clothes began his 'Now to God the Father. . . .'

Now to our relief, we could squeeze into the tiny porch and out into the sunshine. We youths and boys crowded to the wall where our bicycles leant, and without stopping for a fresh liaison with the girls, crashed rusty chains over dry cogs in a race toward the lake. Flinging off the imprisoning Sunday clothes we flung ourselves into the cool, grateful water. Within minutes its placid surface had vanished as twenty lusty bodies thrashed with arms and legs, in an ecstasy of nakedness and vigour. By the time the girls went by, the first energy had dissipated and we floated on our backs, or drifted lazily with only the slightest paddling movements. We knew the girls would come, though it was by no means their shortest way home, and waited for them.

None of us possessed a bathing-costume, or really cared who saw us. But mainly because we had just been in church, and because it was Sunday, the girls shrieked and shouted to ask if we weren't ashamed. Of course not, neither were they. The most brazen of the would-be-shocked girls was serving-maid at the next farm to us, and she was always wallowing in the muddy bog-holes which were far from private. And I knew from personal investigation, that she certainly never wore a bathing suit.

On Sunday, the only day when no work was done, we ate more than at any other time of the week, and Maggie's midday dinner left everyone incapable of thought or action for hours after. When we were all satisfied, she took up her station to see if her brother Freddy was coming. As soon as he came into the kitchen, Maggie asked him for the 'wee paper'—a Scottish weekly. She refused to budge then until she had read the latest instalment of a serial about a dog called Trusty Rover. Maggie loved animals, and had so spoiled our own dog Carlo that he was useless with cattle and an obstinate ewe would send him flying. But her sentimental attachment to Carlo had not dulled his wits as a house-dog.

Carlo was an essential defence for a house in a lonely position like ours. His ears were very sharp and he set up warning whenever he heard footsteps. If he barked in the daytime, Maggie rushed to the hall window to see whether tinkers or visitors were coming. Should it be someone grand, like the music teacher from town, then Maggie fled upstairs, to put her dentures in by the time they arrived.

Should Carlo bark during sleeping hours, we all woke, as it might be something serious, for the border ran near the farm, and the I.R.A. troubled the district. The dog was useful for betraying the presence of predatory creatures other than humans—foxes. We had almost a hundred hens who refused to roost in the henhouse, however expertly Christy may have built it, and preferred a laurel and box thicket by Maggie's window. Early in the morning at least once a week, foxes came to prowl round the trees. When Carlo woke me by his savage, staccato yapping, I wondered if the fox was running round the laurel as people said, and making the hens drop from their perch with dizziness. Poor Maggie, who seldom got more than six hours' sleep in an ordinary night, would be up shouting out of her window and throwing everything within reach at the fox.

Although I was alone downstairs in my little room off the kitchen, I felt quite safe to hear Carlo padding with a soft click of claws up and down the wooden staircase, or the gentle thud as he sat by my door scratching behind his ears. He never left the farm except for three or four days in the year when a couple of dozen dogs went off together and held a canine carnival in the fir woods. After it was all over he would limp home, bleeding, exhausted and hungry, his black wavy coat full of brambles and burrs, his paws swollen and aching with thorns. He looked at us with such soulful eyes that Maggie had not the heart to scold him. Then he slept for two days haunted by terrible nightmares, and thereafter was a perfect gentleman until next spring.

Carlo belonged as one of the family. We hardly thought of him as being a dog at all, and Maggie spent her affection for animals as animals on the cats. The seven fawn ones lived, more or less, round the house. But there were others semi-wild, and living like savage tribes in the jungle which only Maggie ever saw. They were born and bred in rabbit burrows and because of unfettered freedom and a diet entirely of their own choosing, grew to dimensions quite dwarfing their fawn cousins. Sometimes I caught just a glimpse of these great and elegant brutes, slinking stealthily through the grass like miniature tigers. Suddenly a mass of claw and fur would spring from the camouflage, and there would be one less rabbit. Hunting was not beneath the dignity of the domestic cats. Indeed, they regarded it as an essential parental duty, and having produced a brood of kittens would go out and bring home a couple of carcasses for the family every day. The wild cats were much more sophisticated than they pretended to be. At night they crept around the steading on low bellies like the foxes. But the cats were after courtship with their refined cousins, the fawn ladies. But as soon as their serenade screeching began, Carlo made such a row that the savages fled back again to their burrows and bushes.

The rights which the tame cats could enjoy were strictly defined, and even those who were given milk in the byre were not allowed into the kitchen. They were thieves—as bad as the hens who, on seeing the door ajar, were into the pots, up on the dresser, and trying to escape through the window or up the open chimney when Carlo approached. One poor hen had its feet burnt off this way, and for years after Maggie carried it night and morning to a quiet part of the garden, away from the other hens who pecked it badly. After the unfortunate burning the hen changed its black and white feathers once a year into pure albino. The only other curiosity among the hens was a favourite of mine called Mother Reilly. She had always been bandy and walked about in a most ungainly way. One day a tinker called and gave Maggie a present of a goose egg, no doubt appropriated on his way out from the previous farm. Maggie set it under Mother Reilly who was always broody. Sure enough a very fine gosling was hatched. Within months he had far outgrown the bandy hen. She, proud mother, still refused to roost, but slept on the ground so that her gawky foster-son could stick part of his neck under her wing.

When Maggie settled to her study of Trusty Rover's latest adventures, and had temporarily withdrawn from reality, Christy took his brother and me on an extended tour of the farm. We visited every field, and regarding them solemnly, pronounced judgements as to the prospects for the crops, the state of the hedges, or which trees should be felled. Such appraisal of the general situation, and the summing up of the future hopes, was not considered to be a sinful deed for a Sunday. Actually to work or lay a hand on a tool would have been, and all that was manually allowed was the feeding of calves, milking and drawing of water. A certain social taboo rested on such activities but an even stronger one was the dread of divine retribution. This respect for the unsleeping eye of God was ineradicable, unchanged no doubt since pagan times. The way of transgressors was covertly watched for signs of evil reward, which would come as certainly as bad luck came from the gypsy's curse. Those who made crooked cattle deals, or maltreated serving-hands or beasts, besides Sabbath-breakers were fit subjects of punishments—and by strange coincidence wrath often fell on them. We appreciated this more forcibly than ever when a farmer who turned out after church to win a field of barley, had to destroy his whole herd the winter following because of foot and mouth disease.

A similar fate was meted out on the cattle of another man who broke an unwritten law about birds. We all enjoyed mallard which could be got in plenty from the numerous lakes. But wild geese were forbidden prey, especially the Greenland white-fronted that lived in a colony nearby. Not only did this farmer break the taboo but had the affrontery to serve up the birds for the threshers' dinner. I had the news second-hand for I did not help at this threshing, but I did once go down to bring back the ass collar which he had borrowed. It was supper-time when I arrived and the farmer invited me to stay, and they gave me what they called turkey's egg. When I got home with the collar I told Maggie of their hospitality. She was very sceptical about it being a turkey's egg. I could not forget and worried about it until at last the pains set in, which lasted for twenty-four hours. Thinking of it years afterwards I was sure the strong yolk of the egg was not responsible so much as the auto-suggestion that I *ought* to be ill.

The ban on Sunday labour was irksome to me, and I was not convinced of the divine wrath in spite of Maggie's calamitous tales about the ungodly. A gorgeously sun-drowned Sunday often followed a week of constant rain. The day would have been just long enough to clear up a meadow already ten days cut, so that it could be turned, tedded and rucked before night-fall. To stand idly by, merely looking at it, became even more aggravating when Catholic neighbours turned out after their Mass with forks and shouts of pleasure. Of course, they worked under protection of the devil, and their byres were blessed with ivy and quickbeam and maybe an old Queen Victoria threepenny bit.

Passing methodically from field to field on hot, still Sunday afternoons, the week's labour seemed to fall into place. Christy's Sunday boots creaked a little and a film of dust and grass pollen settled on the polished toecaps. Nobody could mistake the Sunday walk for work. Yet it was not forbidden for ears of corn to be plucked, and rolled in the palms of our hands to tell us when to order the binder. And fearing nothing we could stick our hands into a ruck of hay to see if it was heating. Age-old wisdom and experience half-learnt, half-inherited, shone in Christy's and Freddy's eyes as they looked over the land. This done, and the barley husks thrown to the wind, we went into the barn.

What a romantic place this was for me, where all the machinery and harnesses were stored. On Sundays it formed a kind of men-only club where deals and finances could be freely discussed. When we first got in, nothing could be distinguished, then slowly the dark interior grew visible. First the tiny slit windows would emerge, holes so small that on the brightest day only a glimmer of light could filter in, and on grey winter afternoons, none at all. Then, way above our heads, the immense beams of the roof appeared, quite white in places from generations of swallows who built nests all along them. And behind them the darker spaces never penetrated by human eye where bats hung in somnolent silence. And then I would see the slope of the sturdy walls, and could make out their roughness. A lichenous patina of varying colours spread over them like a map of some hitherto-uncharted continent. Here and there in the walls, an iron spike or a hook projected. One of Christy's forefathers had knocked them in for a purpose not remembered any more.

As we sat talking in subdued tones a wedge of sun would lie on the floor like the gleaming blade of a sword. Out of the dark surroundings the cats' eyes glowed or flashed like emeralds. They prowled about restlessly, or came unexpectedly to rub against my legs. From nests made amongst old plough-chains and blinkers, kittens squeaked pitifully, unheeded. I gave my-self up to the barn's smell, which was always delicious. The walls had an old smell, as though granite and lichen had once been compounded by pestle and mortar and allowed to go richly mouldy. These stones had a different smell from the weathered and desolate blocks of a disused house or a ruin. It was a smell redolent with the days of summer sunshine on the breeze-rippled cornfields—a scent distilled from the oily heat of machinery, and from the musty tang of skins and wool clippings hung up to dry—an incense offered up as though in a church, from barrels of tar and bags of lime, swallows' droppings, and saws kept set and shiny in oil. And there were the sacks too, mealy and pungent, which stored the corn in winter, and which in summer were hung on lines like the battle flags in Ennis-killen cathedral.

I used to imagine myself returning one day as a blind man, and being left without a guide to stumble about the uneven ground of the steading. I pictured my senses starting and tingling as a whiff of the well-loved smell reached me. And I heard my voice grown older and deeper, saying with the certainty of sight, 'Ah, this is the barn where they kept the best spring-cart'. And the spring-cart it was, that made the place holy to Christy and his brother. Under a huge tarpaulin rested the cart, the last masterpiece by their father. In all the tender, sad love with which a jilted lover might look at her trousseau, the brothers carefully adjusted the cover on a Sunday, just in case the cats had moved it. The two raised arms of the shafts pointed up in the gloom to the rafters and the swallows' nests. And here the cats crept like acrobats, malicious eyes following the darting wings for a chance morsel. Of course, the spring-cart was much too good and sacred ever to see the light of day, even if we had grand visitors to drive into town.

Maggie would have out her best china for the tea when we got back. Boiling away with knockings and bubblings in the big teapot were two eggs. These were for me. In every snack and meal eggs were included, for in Maggie's opinion I was not broad enough to match my six feet of height. She waged a continuous campaign of feeding me up, and slowly but noticeably I was continuing to fill out. The tea-time eggs received a slight staining from the strong brew in the pot, which was left stewing a long time to draw out the tea's fullest, blackest strength. As we ate, Maggie regaled us with the most exciting bits from Trusty Rover's weekly adventures.

When the table was cleared again and the eggs scooped empty, it was time for me to display what Maggie called my 'posh'. She had herself been responsible for wakening my love of glass and china and making a collector out of me, by giving me Colonel Coffee's engraved goblet. Every week since then, some object had been added until a sizeable collection resulted. Maggie often went to cottages and farms and, telling them about my 'posh', would come away with a prized breadplate or an old china gravy ladle. From different sources she procured four moustache cups. I thought the lip strainer pieces at the side very novel. After a year the collection had exceeded all hopes and although of outrageous proportions, I could not part with a single plate. Many of the best pieces were given to me, but others came from auctions. The most revered of all my plates and cups and jugs, and a motley crew of glass and paper-thin china was undoubtedly my blue vase, which came from a sale at a cousin of Maggie's.

Cousin Edith had not been on speaking terms with Maggie, and never acknowledged the fact that she was the niece of Maggie's old father. Maggie was upset about this. The old lady's grand airs, her precious manner and the way she minced daintily about the town exactly like a tiny Dresden figurine, did not worry Maggie, nor the fact that Edith deliberately turned away if we passed her in the street. The cousin lived in state near Enniskillen and we often passed her out walking on our way into town. In summer Cousin Edith was conspicuous by her faded Edwardian parasol.

Edith's parade of class and wealth had no effect on Maggie whatsoever. But what she could not bear, was that another human being, and a relative into the bargain, should dislike her. Maggie never had enemies in her whole life. Cousin Edith's pride distressed Maggie. As we rode our bicycles along the six miles into Enniskillen, everyone, herders and public schoolboys alike, had a greeting for Maggie. Edith's snobbery wounded her. She felt in no way inferior to her cousin, and was equally proud of her family. Maggie often spoke in awe of her father who recalled the family's dire poverty during the Great Hunger when they lived in the south of Ireland. But as Maggie found satisfaction in boasting that her grandparents had been as poor as Soupers, Cousin Edith liked to remember her big house full of treasures brought home from her travels. She had lived for a time in Greece, and then in Italy. It was even rumoured that she could mutter a few heathenish languages, and it was known for a certainty that Cousin Edith could talk with the Frenchies.

But Edith, in common with the grass of the field, fell to scything time. After she was decently buried with obsequies of death matching the style of her life, Maggie had a bright idea. She insisted that Christy and I should go to the sale of the cousin's possessions. Christy thought this a good suggestion and when his mind was thoroughly made up, Maggie added that we might just see if a 'wee cheap press' was to fall under the hammer. Having thus brought her main motive in sending us out into the open, she grinned, hoping that Christy's objection to modern innovations was at last vanquished.

Full of excitement, I set off with Christy. I had never been to the auction of a complete home before, and found it hard indeed that fellow humans could manhandle and joke about treasured possessions in such a crude way. When bundles of doilies and tablecloths were thrown about for a shilling, I could only imagine the little, grand woman sitting under her garden tree, spending years on the elaborate lace borders. And oh, what misery that proud breast would have suffered, had Cousin Edith seen the next desecration. Her very chamber pot, that for years had been most zealously hidden behind valances, was now lifted on high, exposed to the gaze and laughter of rough farmers and out-of-work labourers. Involuntarily I glanced round expecting to hear small footsteps coming down the stairs, as the indignant woman struck her frilly parasol over the jeering heads.

I wanted to make a bid for everything that came up—each bundle of linen and every blade of cutlery. Christy remained unmoved, his calm unruffled by the seething unquiet all around. In a lifetime he had been to many sales. Not even a wardrobe with four big doors, as fine a 'press' as ever there was, could make him part with ten shillings. Not that he was mean or begrudged Maggie her wish, but his natural shyness and fear of being noticed in a crowd froze his eye and kept him from winking at the hard-mouthed auctioneer.

Then the vase came up, and I could contain myself no longer. The vase was undoubtedly the finest thing of the whole day's business, yet nobody other than me, made a bid. Pretending to be exasperated at the dwindling appreciation of his customers, the auctioneer let his hammer fall and the beautiful thing was mine for next to nothing. On the way home I unwrapped it a dozen times from its straw bedding in the ass cart, in order to gaze at its base of blue ceramic, glazed with a sapphire's depth and brilliance. Round its bowl, in an idyllic world, white figures lived a pastoral existence amongst white trees, and a white stream that ran on endlessly, joined to itself. Deep calm infused the scene as though a sun which never set bathed the figures and the running water in its golden shafts. The figures with their perfectly moulded bodies reminded me of the police cadets swimming, and of our Sunday bathing in the lake on the way home from church. One relief in particular seemed to be a photograph of myself and the many hours I spent in Fenhill's mossy wood, getting ready to plunge into the lake.

Was this Greece, or was it the summer dome of nattier blue over the waters of Erne?

> *Where the dark cypresses smile in the water*
> *Out of deep sky unflecked, deep into heights.*
> *Where the cool lapping stream runs,*
> *Twixt old and mystic cypresses*
> *And scattered stones of the hillside,*
> *Comes running a boy*
> *To dip and bathe in the upturned heaven*
> *Mirrored in the stream.*
> *Through cool depths, like a little silver fish*
> *He darts, and dives from the dappled pools*
> *Into the burnished amber air*
> *Laden with the heavy scent of olives.*
> *His dark eye gleams, and follows swiftly*
> *Where myriad fish swim, and others slide under the bank.*
> *A flash, and his smooth arm cuts the water*
> *And the flow of fishes from hand to hand*
> *Runs back to its brown house of weeds.*
>
> *The boy laughs, white teeth smiling at the sun,*
> *And climbs to dive again.*

I had a series of Japanese boxes too. These were gilded with scenes of emperors travelling with their courts in a vast retinue. Here the lakes and rivers they passed were inlaid with mother-of-pearl. The boxes were cunningly made in diminishing sizes so that they fitted one inside the other, the largest containing all the rest. On this box, like a lacquered biscuit tin, I set my

blue vase every Sunday amid my pieces of Coalport and Belleek.
A personal victory was involved in this display—if Cousin
Edith had been too proud to put her dainty foot over our
humble threshold, I had at least secured a trophy, and brought
it back to stand on the kitchen table. There could be no denying
the vase's beauty, though some people seemed to find the
nudity of its figures too strong for Protestant taste.

· The first of our Sunday visitors to come and admire the 'posh'
was Joe Montgomery, who called on his way home from the
Methodist preaching-house. Joe was considered a special friend
of mine, and because of this his eighty-odd years seemed of no
matter. Our common ground was Belfast, as many years before
Joe had worked in the Botanic Gardens there. This lent him the
prestige of a man-about-town, for neither Maggie nor Christy
had ever been on such a vast journey as that to Belfast from
Enniskillen. Such a thing hardly entered their mind. Yet they
loved to hear Joe and me talking about the jungle city of linen
spindles and gantry forests.

Besides the reputation he enjoyed on account of having
lived in Belfast, Joe basked in the approval given to the devout.
However, he had not always been so religious, and at one time
his name had been a byword for everything to the contrary.
For Sunday preaching he dressed in fine knickerbocker
trousers and tweed jacket, cut as though to clothe the quality—
which indeed they once had. As gardener at the local mansion-
house, Joe waited for important visitors to come, and then
paraded round the walled gardens with his shirt-tails hanging
from the holes between the patches of his trousers. This adroit
piece of chicanery never failed. The owner would spot Joe
working in a place where the approaching guests would be sure
to see him, and all he could do was to ransack his wardrobe and
find a pair of trousers. A terrible *paralysis agitans* afflicted Joe,
but in spite of this, he felt obliged to give the full history of
every pair of trousers, and to illustrate his talk by fumbling

hopelessly under the waistcoat to expose the name of the smart London tailor.

In younger years Joe had worked hard and efficiently, saving his money for an annual holiday in Glasgow, the occasion of a great drinking spree. His father had been a celebrated toper, and 'drank three farms of land down in Tyrone' as Maggie often reminded us. One of Joe's jaunts proved to be the last and the means of his conversion. Across the channel in the grey Scottish city he had been put to bed rolling drunk. Next morning he woke up to find a fat negress lying beside him. His head cleared at once. He leapt out of the bed thinking it was the devil himself. Joe caught the very next boat to Ireland, and still in a condition of terror gave himself up to the preaching-house redemption. According to local accounts his public confession provided one of the most rousing testimonies heard for many a year.

But the day came when poor Joe could no longer make the length of our lane nor stand with shaking head to look at my 'posh' spread out. The last I saw of him was when Christy took me to visit him in the dread workhouse where he lay near the bed I had occupied.

We never attended the preaching-house on a Sunday afternoon, except when a wonderful harvest-thanksgiving broke down all barriers of conformity. But Maggie tried to go at least once a month to evening service in the parish church. In winter, we had to take our old bicycle lamps with us filled with carbon and water. The lackadaisical ways of pre-war were now over, and lamps were compulsory. Often our faulty lamps failed to light after the service, as the water had seeped into the carbon. Or perhaps the wind blew in a gust and extinguished the tiny flame because the glass was so broken. But we did not mind overmuch, the moon and stars gave a better light and except on rainy or cloudy nights, were more reliable. I was only caught once for riding without lights and then by a dear old constable who had been many years in the force without even a single arrest to his credit. 'Don't ya know there's a war on?' he asked me, pretending to be stern. When I explained about the carbon he said, 'Well, I should be gettin' away home to yer bed quick, before ya meet a policeman.'

Though all too small for the morning congregation, at night the parish church was almost deserted. Maggie was once the only person in the congregation apart from the sexton, while I alone looked into the nave from the choir. But the rector went through the entire service, quite undisturbed by the sound of his echoing voice. On the way home Maggie was anxious to avoid the main road, as the crossroads were supposed to be frequented by a sex maniac, who was said to spring out and attack unsuspecting females.

Instead, we wheeled our bicycles over a bog lane, past the farm where old Jane Dockson worked. It was a very ramshackle house, though people said a lucky one, because it was shadowed by a vast rookery, and had a spring-well in the parlour. Rex, the dog, would give warning of our approach and out the dame would come. Jane talked to the dog as an equal, and when she recognized us said to it, 'Visitors tonight, Rex, what a treat!' She insisted on being told the text of the rector's sermon, and if we had her favourite hymn to sing. But whether we had or not, she did not allow us to leave without a cup of tea, a slice of her delicious buxty, and at least three verses of 'All things bright and beautiful'.

Chapter Twelve

Those Endearing Old Charms

My brave new world did not lack connections with the past. The most annoying was undoubtedly school. It tore me away from the barn and fields, and all to no purpose now that the scholarship was no longer an aim. I had to forgo the wisdom of mists and seasons, the watching of badgers and the building of rucks. I hated September's coming and the hours I must sacrifice to the dry philosophy of books.

Until the very last minute on the morning that school started, I delayed going. I had got up early to help with the milking, and then took the cattle out to pasture. Along the muddy cow-path I ambled with the beasts, a fringe of birch saplings rising on one side with delicate vertical strokes like a Japanese print, and on the other side an orchard now almost bare of its summer-johns and peach apples. And at the foot of the thick hedges, bound in cocoons of gossamer, lay the jacks-in-the-box with flaming jackets of varnished red. Past the remains of the ruined cottage we went, the blue-roan yearling stopping to scratch her back on the gate leading to the rushy steppes. There was no hurrying the animals. Even if I wanted it, they refused to be closely herded. They always went in a loose file, spaced apart by fear of each other's horns. Some of them were set high like deer antlers in a baronial hall, and others swooped downwards like a sport-cycle's handle-bars, while the poor, hornless polls went in special dread of the heavily-armed Kerry-blues.

Away to the right, before reaching the good meadowland, stretched a wild thicket of bour-tree and ash, hazel and guelder rose. Much of it bowed under shaggy coats of ivy, and a network of fern and mosses threaded through the jungle. Purple loosestrife kept to the wet side, its sumptuous, vivid spires still spearing the shroud of late summer. Trees that could no longer bear the weight of smothering creepers, lay rotting amongst the briars and nightshade. The gloom of this wood was primeval and dank with decay, odorous with the rich black earth.

Sitting on a fallen tree, I dreamed one of my sad, long dreams of being isolated from the too-clamorous world that threatened me again in the form of school. Carlo sat patiently at my feet, his sides heaving like bellows, a pink strip of his tongue lolling out, dripping from the exertions of rabbit hunting. I thought wistfully of the vanishing summer, not realizing that Maggie would be worried over my delay. Risking her one plimsoll in the hoof-holes of the pass, she came to find me. With a very poor grace and a wry smile at her concerned look, I went off to school.

But the outlook brightened on meeting the school van. It came rumbling along the road, a perfect cowboy wagon from a Western, for it was horse-drawn and covered by a round canvas top. I would not have been surprised to see bearded men inside with wide-brimmed hats and rifles at the ready. Instead of whooping Red Indians, the shouts were from a swarm of boys who helped me into the dim interior, where for the rest of the journey we indulged in every kind of devilry. When we came to a hill, we all had to get out, as the driver also owned the horse that pulled the van, and he had no wish to see it expire on our behalf.

In this way we covered the miles to school, picking up more passengers, and finally creaking to a stop outside my new school. I already knew of its reputation—a high one on account of its having three teachers, one a master known as a real 'Trinity gent'. An undergraduate air clung to him still, but his chief interest for me was that in spite of being small he was more than a match for me, a fact I discovered during the very first break. While waiting to take us all home again the school wagon lived in a sinister structure, shaped to accommodate the van's round top. Its architect had planned no windows, and the resulting darkness and warmth were recommended by other boys as an excellent place to eat lunch in company with the girl of one's choice. I was very busy playing Don Juan in a pleasantly wanton manner, when the headmaster himself surprised us. For all my superior size, I knew I had met my Waterloo as he marched me off to the classroom for a good caning.

In spite of intolerance towards the delights of love, he became my friend, almost overcame my objection to returning to school, and managed to teach me a few things. My earlier flair for mathematics now gave way to new interests. Discovering my passion for birds and farming, the master gave me an outlet in essay writing. Pages and pages were soon covered and I could not write quickly enough to put down everything that had ever happened to me in the country. No such fluency came during the day's first lesson, however, the wretched minutes devoted to our catechism *How we differ from Rome*.

With the sun climbing higher outside, the birds circling over the hayfields, could the little booklet matter? In any case I had been through the stuff before, and would never be able to remember whether this or that was said by Henry II or Henry VIII, or which pope was which in 1221, Pope Honorius or Pope Adrian. With my thoughts following Christy through the fields and the sound of his saw in my ears it was extremely unlikely that I would care much about the horrid book and its pedantic dates of everything from the day of Pentecost to A.D. 432, or its miserable comments on writings in Trinity

College to Augustine's boring papal mission of 597, and Henry II's conquest of Ireland in 1172 and its subjection to the popes until the glorious year of Reformation in 1536.

I didn't care. And though question ten in the book cast decided doubts on the existence of Purgatory, I was completely convinced of it as a reality, for during this lesson the cane came into play more than any other. As we mumbled and wept over the unwilling responses, frozen in our mouths more often than not by the cane that was supposed to release them, I longed for four o'clock to come. And whatever pleasures the rest of the day might bring, I was always relieved when the van stood waiting outside, and the old brown mare in harness.

The thrill of riding a cowboy wagon could not last for ever. It was a tedious journey with too many hills to get out for and walk up, and detours into every farm lane, and the wasting of time that could be spent with Maggie and Christy. I could have been working in the fields nearly an hour by the time the wagon went by our lane, and so after the first weeks I walked to and from school. Another Belfast evacuee came with me, a younger boy, who always joined me in old Matt Sheridan's field for a feast of raw turnip. But my friend lived with his great-uncle, a crabbed ex-prison warder, who almost broke his stick on my bottom, the day he discovered us at work. I had the distinct impression that he did not approve of his nephew having me as a friend. I could no longer now be passed as a boy of thirteen, for I showed every sign of needing a shave, and my bad name was still whispered in horror, despite Maggie's good words on my behalf.

Taking Matt Sheridan's turnips proved to be the end of my light-fingered practices. Unexpectedly, Maggie changed me in that way as she was doing in others. She had to go into town to collect medicine for a sick animal. At the vet's dispensary she was asked for the fee. But the medicine was already paid for, a bewildered Maggie explained, when Christy left the prescrip-

tion in the morning. An argument followed, and though reluctant to do so, Maggie came away with the bottle or else the
beast might die. I met her coming up the lane, her eyes red
with tears, and her soul burdened with anxiety. Worse by far
than Cousin Edith's rebuffs, was that anyone should suspect
Maggie of cheating, even if it was only a bottle of medicine. So
ill was Maggie that she was up all night. In the morning I had
to cycle into town and pay a second time for the medicine. But
when I arrived the mistake had been discovered and I returned
with the money and a note of apology which helped Maggie's
recovery. But I was never to forget her distress, and her high
regard for honesty and a good name. Had she learnt of the
dozens of eggs I had stolen and sucked at Fenhills' farm, I
would have died from shame. The only way to make sure of
never being found out was never to steal again.

Seedtime and harvest dictated the timing of school work.
The headmaster was a wise man, and understood country ways
and the lives of his children who all came from farms. Even the
youngest did jobs at home in the byres and went out to help
win the harvest. And so our holidays were movable feasts
ruled by the crops and work in the bogs. How wonderful it
was, therefore, to hear that after only a month at school we
would be given a big holiday for the potato digging.

Compulsory war-time ploughing of certain percentages of
arable land was a great burden in the neighbourhood. Most
farmers worked single-handed, assisted only by their women-
folk and a horse or donkey, to win enough hay to last through
the winter. We had to have a tractor to come and break our
own lea. But Christy turned our two acres of potatoes and
turnips himself, with his long slender Fermanagh spade. He
had to dig them up too, and I gathered up the harvest, carrying
the pink and blue pebble-like tubers to the pits.

That year, the potato ground lay down in the direction of
the bog, enclosed on all sides by thick, waving sallies. And the

only drawback to this was Joey Calaum. He slaved enormously on the land and no amount of effort seemed to tire him. But he was simple. I would be bent over a potato rill happily picking away, then I might feel a presence behind me. Sometimes a shadow would fall over the turned earth. Joey would be standing quite motionless behind me. The first encounter terrified me. The apparition stood so close I could hear its breathing. A stout barrel body was clothed in sacks. One was tied round the waist as a skirt in lieu of trousers. Above it, the remnants of an old fur coat appeared, mangy and bald in places. And on top of this fur shirt, another sack was tied, like a cape. A face, quite covered by hair that merged with the fur, glowered at me. A grease-sodden cap crowned it all, scarcely able to hold in the mass of coarse wild hair that escaped in a fuzz from under it.

The eyes that peered from the thicket of hair betrayed the vacancy of his mind. In his hand, a huge knife hung nakedly. It was supposedly for cutting turnip tops, but on that first day, I was not to know but that the ape-man was after my blood. I did not stop to make his acquaintance. Christy assured me that this caricature of Neanderthal man was in fact as harmless as a sleeping baby. But a long time ensued before he ceased to startle me, or I could be near him without fear. On occasion his brother Martin would work alongside him. At the ringing of the Angelus he would give Joey a dig in the ribs and swear at him to say his prayers. Off came the horrible cap, and the jungle of hair started out as though it never would be crammed in again.

Even Maggie had a shock the day she went to the front door and found Joey standing there. He held a new-born calf in his arms, having carried it half a mile, a feat of strength alone that would have taken two men. He had found the cow calving, and picking up her offspring had brought it to Maggie, the horns of the Kerry-blue butting him behind, and his sacks and fur shirt were covered with slime and blood. But this was nothing compared with his gory state on finding the carcass of a dead bull. The beast had been killed in a road accident while being taken into town, and was buried nearby. Several cottagers hurried out after nightfall and sawed off juicy joints of meat. But not Joey, he waited until morning and half climbed into the carcass, tearing and devouring the raw flesh like a wolf.

In the mornings I usually took a bucket and ran down to the bog-holes, and drew up its beautiful yellow water to wash amongst the heather. For toothpaste I used the solid type because it was cheap and the bright pink tablet lasted a long time. One morning I forgot my toothbrush and went back to the house for it. When I got back to my alfresco bathroom Joey Calaum was there eating the toothpaste. I made no attempt to salvage it. Joey I knew would eat anything, and had no idea of quantity or quality. A fine joke amongst grown-ups was to ask, 'Well Joey, and what did you have for breakfast this morning?' A glint of intelligence would flash in his eye. 'Ten cakes of fadge and two churns of butter, by the Holy Boy.' A cake of fadge was a round of home-made bread weighing three pounds.

For all the strength of a massive body undistracted by a mind, Joey's efforts in the field were overshadowed by his brother's. Martin, after all, was the owner of thirty-five acres and four heavy milkers. Conversation with Martin always opened about the same thing—'Isn't the tillage a holy terror, how will a man keep his bullocks at all, at all.' He was a champion worker, ploughing all his own fields, sowing them, and still finding time to hire himself out for a substantial part of the year to other farmers. He was proud of his prodigious strength. He wrote to a Sunday newspaper offering them his life story for a hundred pounds. The editor replied that he would be interested to see the story. And here Martin revealed his mastery over canny city dwellers. Sure the editor wanted to publish it without paying him. This went on for years, Martin bombarding the editor with letters. But he would never part with the story because of his conviction that the editor, being an Englishman, intended to steal it from him. The money first or no story. Of course, *we* all knew the story backwards. It was a tale of his arms' great strength and how he had pulled horses from drains, and removed fallen trees from roads when six men or more, united, had failed to do so.

The world of Martin's mind did not always coincide with the real world, and when conflict between the two became unbearable he removed for a time to the asylum. Before going he would come round the farms saying good-bye. After one of his treatments, I went over the hill to visit him, taking presents from Maggie. His cottage was among houses what Joey was among men. The thatched roof had all caved in, its ruins and rubbish lying where it had fallen. All the rooms were derelict and cluttered with pathetic rafters that stuck up like the ribs of a long-wrecked boat. Grass and nettles sprouted from the decayed straw, and the windows gaped without glass or frames. Only the kitchen was still used. To alleviate the inconvenience of having no roof over their heads, the brothers had put up a few sheets of corrugated iron round the chimney-piece, and lived under them. I could see slashes of sky between the sheets, and a fascinating starry effect was obtained from the nail-holes punctured in the sheets. Only a guess could be made as to their efficiency in a rainstorm. Yet smoke ascended peacefully from their hearth, spiralling from the empty shell as though the roof and windows were whole, and life going on in the grass-grown rooms.

I left Maggie's gift on the wall, for the brothers were not at home, nor anywhere near. I wondered if they were watching me from behind a hedge, for their dining-table was only just left, the remains of recently-cooked food scattered over it. This table was in fact a cart standing near the house, and a dozen hens perched on it, swarming into the milk and pecking for tit-bits into the stewpot. Thinking the brothers might be hiding in the byre, ashamed that I should see the condition they lived in, I peered into the dark cobbled shed. A cow stood in the dimness, and sitting under it with a great teat in her mouth, was a little girl from one of the nearby cottages. The cow champed its jaws, completely at ease. The child, preoccupied with her feed, did not notice me, but kept her moist red lips busily sucking. I crept away, resolved to try this idea for myself at our next milking.

Maggie and the people who had grown up with the Calaum brothers accepted them as part of the local scenery. I never could think of them as anything but extremely odd, to say the least. But I realized they were good neighbours nevertheless, to be relied on for turning up at threshing time, or for helping to corner an unusually strong calf that needed dressing. Good neighbours were essential in our isolated community, for emergencies requiring outside help often occurred. Next to this, Maggie rated her bicycle in importance. The bus stop was remote and the nearest telephone lay three miles away. If Christy was away from the house, Maggie never loaned her cycle, in case some urgent thing cropped up, and she should have to get on it and away off for help.

Fair days were the exception to this rule, when I borrowed it. The headmaster understood about fairs also, and allowed me to go once a month to fairs at Derrygonnelly and Enniskillen, besides more local ones. At the very first fair to which Christy and I went together, we went in search of a donkey. Beaming from under a smart pork-pie hat and waving a cattle-dealer's dandy yellow cane was little Tom Kirlan from the workhouse. He came over, listened carefully as we described just the sort of donkey we wanted, and then conducted us through the long passages between the animals. We walked along the ranks of rumps, and when a hind leg flew out in temper, or a golden pile fell on Tom's good clothes, he gave the luckless beast a generous feel of his yellow cane. And before I realized it Tom was forcing Christy's hand and a young lad's with a lot of spittle between them, over the purchase of a tall, white ass, said to be only five years old. While the 'luck penny' was being drunk I led Jenny away home. But in spite of her supposed youth, Jenny proved to be a most promiscuous lady. For years afterwards she kept producing foals, though she was never taken to stud. The nearest jackass lived four miles away. On still, starry nights the lovers must have crossed fields and hills to meet. But by morning Jenny was always back in the proper place. She was a good worker, once started, but when approached with bridle, Jenny sensed an end to her freedom in the pasture and turned both hind legs in sprightly defence.

Life never went on long without some event among the beasts. About the time of Jenny's arrival, one of the heifers was ready for calving. I grew more and more excited as the evening wore on. In spite of the beast's dropped condition, Christy went off to bed declaring that no calf would appear before morning. But Maggie was not so sure and said she would sit up all night, just in case. She was worried about Tim, the red heifer, because it had always been a delicate calf. When it was born prematurely in winter, Maggie had it brought into the kitchen, and had reared it herself, patiently feeding it from a bottle. I begged her to let me stay up also, and in the end she gave in. No doubt Maggie half-suspected my real motive, that of missing school the following day. A note to the headmaster, delivered by hand to the horse-van driver, saying that a cow had calved, would secure permission for absence. Christy climbed the stairs after our evening visitors had gone and the gramophone was put away. Maggie made up the fire, brewed a last cup of tea, and then sat gazing into the flames. The world outside, and the house itself, subsided into silence. Now and again Carlo scratched, or the stairs would give a sudden loud crack.

Maggie's head nodded. Her hands, never still or idle from

dawn to dusk, relaxed and fell open in her lap, looking strangely awkward now that they had nothing to do. Down her back hung the hair that had not been cut once in her life, although she often complained how unruly it was. When her supply of hairpins ran out, and the peddling Sikh had not appeared for months, she kept her bun in position by long nails. Listening all the time for the heifer's cries while Maggie dozed, I began quietly to put up the hair, tying it in knots with waxed string, as there were few clips or even nails at hand. My handiwork cost Maggie days of painful untying accompanied by gales of laughter that followed her pretence at annoyance. But she agreed the time had come to do something decisive. I persuaded her to go into town and have it done properly at the hairdresser's.

I had visualized a modest cutting, but there were to be no half measures for Maggie. The egg money had swollen since the pullets started laying, so she was going to have 'a real do'. Off the great tresses were to come, and the remains to be permanently waved. Christy said nothing but thought much over this proposal. I tried to turn Maggie away from such a drastic course. But her mind was set on it, and off she went on her bicycle. Delighted with the shiny, scented glamour of the saloon, Maggie sat down under the bulbous hood of the waving machine, and flicked over the pages of magazines. She felt fine. But the afternoon wore on, and the fascination began to ebb, as she realized that lighting-up time was not far off and she had come with no bicycle lamp. She also thought of the calves crying to be fed, and the cows streaming their milk with impatience.

Conscience-stricken at the damage caused by her silly vanity, Maggie called for the assistant, but no one answered. She wriggled and squirmed, trying to release herself from the grasp of the machine's tentacles. In her struggle with this electrical Apollyon, her inexpert fingers found some of the operating knobs, and on turning one, nearly roasted her head. Eventually freeing herself, she rushed from the scene of her temptation, though not without leaving a good deal of hair in the machine to complete its curling. Poor Maggie, never would she forget the night she sat sleeping by the fire and the abortive vigil over Tim's calving, which did not happen that night after all.

When the calf did come the second night, I was still wide-eyed with the thrill of it. The restless stamping started before the last visitors had gone. Then the heart-stirring cries of labour sounded above the soughing of wind-racked trees. Lighting the hurricane lamp Christy and I hurried to the byre. Maggie stood outside with a bucket of hot gruel. Convention ruled that she might not be present at the actual birth. As soon as Tim's difficult delivery in the lamplit bed of bracken was over, I put my head round the door and announced the offspring's sex to Maggie. It was a bull calf which pleased us, for at that time, the government paid a good subsidy on bullocks. While Christy wiped the young calf dry with hay, Maggie comforted the cow with tender words and the gruel.

A mask had to be made for the young spindly creature. This gasmask-like affair was made from a tin with holes punched in the bottom to prevent the calf from eating solids until a month passed. The calves objected to being muzzled, and after each milk feed fought furiously. The old-fashioned practice was quite effective though unnecessary, the tin being tied by string round the budding horns, that were soon to be burnt off. The burning of the horns was cruel. But it fitted unnoticed in the pattern of farm life, and it never occurred to anybody as a fit subject for sentiment. Cattle-dealers did not like bullocks with horns, as they ripped each others' flanks when travelling long distances in train-wagons or lorries.

Many superstitions attended the calving, and Maggie would never use the beastings. As the calf could take only a little of the strong yellow milk, the rest was given to the pigs. On the other hand Maggie never allowed me to put silver in the bottom of the bucket for the first milking. Only Catholics indulged in this practice. But though the beastings never splashed on silver, our cattle were often cured by charms in preference to the vet's methods, or when he had given up hope. Many of these charms were inherited by Catholics. We never hesitated to ask them over to give a cure for milk fever or to deal with an attack of the red water. And anyone who had charms for the cure of human ailments was sure of Maggie's enthusiastic support, irrespective of whether they were Catholics or Protestants.

Charms were passed on solely to relatives, and only on deathbeds. Many took the form of weird medieval herbal concoctions mixed with snails, bladders, rabbit tongues, mice eyes, nettle seeds with acorn flour in pig's blood for good measure. Others consisted simply of amulets. The treatments varied in elaborateness. For broken bones or sprains, the patients' eyes were blindfolded, all other people in the house were sent outside, while the charmer muttered his secret words over the injury. Tom, a lad from the Free State who came twice to work for us, could lead people to water in order to cure mumps, shingles or eczema.

I was very anti-charms when they failed to cure my warts. A local farmhand had given me his charm, and rubbed the growths with milk of devil's churnstaff, but with no success. My hands were really disfigured with the wretched lumps, and so I persisted nightly, scalding my hands as I placed them under the steaming sap of burning ash, exclaiming above my agony:

> *Hot ash spittle, hot ash spittle,*
> *Make my ugly warts grow little,*
> *Curse the bunions of Monea*
> *File away my worts by day.*

Even Maggie had to admit that Christy's caustic stick used for the bullocks' horns was more effective than anything. Love potions were, however, not to be disputed, and obviously more efficient than charms. They provided all the pleasures desired by ancient satyrs, and even a Methodist lay preacher was said to have recourse to the naughty roots when all else failed to produce a son and heir.

Maggie's accident turned me finally against verbal charms. On the hard January frost her wellington slipped, and she fell, hurting her arm. Unable to milk, or use a broom, or feed the pigs, she felt useless and looked very sorry for herself. Any suggestion of calling the doctor was brushed aside as though we were making a fuss over nothing. Next day she decided to visit the charmer who lived up by the Hanging Rock. The roads were too rough and dangerous to risk going up by bicycle, and we persuaded a neighbour with a car to run Maggie there. More than content, Maggie came home with a little bracelet of wool tied on the bad arm's wrist, like a Hindu farewell memento.

Days passed, the arm grew more painful, while swelling and inflammation appeared. We felt convinced it was broken. After two weeks, Maggie's suffering was terrible. The woollen thread had done nothing, but even then Maggie would not hear of proper attention. A friend of a more rational turn, took the matter out of her hands and asked the doctor to call. He had been the one who attended Maggie's mother, though since her death Maggie had not had cause to call him, for in her whole life Maggie had never been ill or in hospital. He took one look at the arm and said with no uncertainty that unless Maggie went to hospital, she would lose the limb. There could be no denying the authority in his voice.

X-rays revealed breaks in two places, and for days we were worried that the reset bones would never knit. But a strong constitution pulled her through. When she was well enough to go again with her buckets to the spring-well, she still treasured the charmer's rag of wool. The charm-lure did not leave her despite such weighty evidence of its failure. Superstitions hedged her about as before, and I would sit by the fire brazenly washing the devil's vessels. This swinging of the chains and hooks of the great crook across the fire, was traditionally a most unlucky practice. But I did it deliberately to show her my disbelief in all the devil's tools—vessels, back-rods, moon-sickness, glass eyes and withered hearts.

Christy expressed no opinion on the question of charms other than a quiet affirmation of his trust in them. His attitude was slightly more critical than Maggie's however, and over the broken arm, he was in favour of calling the doctor. Christy could exist with no difficulty in the ancient inherited world of a half-magical Ireland as well as in the modern one. He relied much on instinct and tradition in running the farm, but readily accepted new aids and methods where they really helped. It did not occur to Maggie and him, that to believe in charms but not in ghosts was illogical. But that was the case. Neither of them gave credit to the tales about the ghosts said to haunt the neighbourhood.

Our own old orchard had a particular reputation for the supernatural, and, of course, the 'little people' lived under the 'lonely bushes' up in the Fort. They did not deny their own brother's experience of hearing the banshee while on the Home Guard patrol, and explained their own lack of this experience by saying that they had not the 'ear' for her cry. I never saw anything either, though Christy and I went to every field and hill at night during the trapping season. But what we did see, Maggie included, from time to time, were shadowy forms of tinkers going to coil up in our hayshed, and the weird balls of burning gas rolling over the bog at twilight, the mysterious will-o'-the-wisp, or the bog-sprite who could not cross water.

People who came to *ceili* at night often turned to talk of experiences with ghosts, or adventures with rebels during the 'Bad Times'. When they had gone and I undressed alone by the candle the stories came vividly to life. Snuffing the friendly flame, I would lie down in the darkness, gazing apprehensively at the window's pale square of light. Until I heard Christy load his rifle before getting into bed, I could not rest. But even after falling asleep, the ghost stories pursued me, to the point of terror when I would wake again in a cold sweat. By the window a voluminous maple tree responded in movement to every shift of air on windy nights. As I lay asleep, its sound would penetrate my fantasies, in the dread tones of a tragic symphony, its heavy boughs sawing up and down like bows playing the tautened strings of the wind.

When gale force was reached the wind wailed down the parlour chimney like a fiend, and I would lie motionless, wide-eyed in bed, convinced the banshee was circling the house. When storms swept over us laying the land bare with stabs of stark light, Christy got up and called me to dress. As the thunder rolled and boomed in the caverns of heaven we pulled coats about our shoulders and went out to the byre to see if branches had fallen on the roof, or if the animals had panicked, and were choking on the stakes. In cold reality I recognized the roar of the wind buffeting the house for what it was, and found no fear in the threshing maple as it swayed to the wind's will. The fear of rebels and spirits was exorcized, and once in bed again with the byre made secure, I slept so soundly, that when Maggie came to call me next morning, she thought I was in a mood for evading school.

Chapter Thirteen

Winter Prelude

The bright orange arils of the spindle-trees, set in their satin-pink ruffs, lit up the November hedges with a surprising brilliance. Up on the hill, the stinking dogwood had changed unexpectedly into a thing of beauty, wearing a fairy-tale robe of burgundy. Around the little wooden privy that Christy and I had built, the concealing bour-trees drooped their black, shiny drupes, the red stems too slender to carry the bursting abundance. In the warm nutty groves of furze, where the wild cats held council, enough smears of fiercest custard blooms remained to attract the yellowhammers. The snowberry, the most persistent of all the encroaching bushes, hung thick with its spongy white blobs, and Maggie foresaw a hard winter with so much fruit waiting for the game birds. But only a few yellowish roses lingered in the gardens, and in the morning, dew was cupped in their petals like oil in a chalice. Down by the vegetable garden the rabbits had already broken into the winter greens.

And still there was no sign of the thresher.

We grew tired of waiting for the big day. A false alarm alerted us in the first week of the month, when news of the great machine's coming had sent Maggie off to kill her Rhode Island Red cocks. But we had nobody to share them with, for the helpers were not called in. When the thresher did come

Maggie would now have to serve up duck. The hens had gone off laying for want of corn, though Christy had spent several mornings with his flailing-stick.

Then one morning, when we had almost forgotten about it, the unmistakable sound came across the fields from the lane, the chugging and rumbling of heavy machinery. No time was left now to feel vexed over the long delay. Some neighbours had already seen the thresher on the road, and before even it reached our royal stacks, were on their bicycles, coming up to work. I had to run off, over the big hill, past the dogwood and heady furze, in order to call the Calaum brothers and other out-lying helpers, the cry on my lips being almost a call to arms, 'The thresher's come, the thresher's come!'

By the time I got back, breathless and sweating from running, Maggie was covered in flour, making the rich, dark brown bread, thickened with molasses from a neighbour's silo. The poor Aylesbury ducks had put up a great fight, but the odds were too great, and at last they were caught, plucked, and now simmered away in the oven, with a gentle fire of turf shovelled on top of the lid.

Out in the field, the cold winter morning soon became a tropical noon. The engines heated up, and chaff flew like a pestilence, clogging our nostrils, while sack after sack of golden grain was carried into the barn. We threw off jackets and jerseys, and even Flynn Carroll peeled away two of his numerous waistcoats. The only one who worked on oblivious of the heat was Joey Calaum, to whom all things were equal. None of us had ever seen him without his sacks and fur coat. Had he removed them, we would have thought his skin was coming off. He worked fiendishly, and we had not long to wait until he amused us. Several farmers had brought dogs with them. As the thresher devoured more and more, the stacks of corn shrank and rats shot out in all directions, streaking for cover in the hedges. But the dogs were too quick for them and their grey corpses lay strewn over the field. The prize ratter was a sharp little terrier, and during the battle took a dive for Joey's fur coat after a rat. He knocked Joey down and together they rolled in the deep chaff, while the other dogs came to start on the fur as well with snaps and barks. Joey collected himself together, declaring the terrier had bitten him, and stood up. His cap had come off, and the great fuzz of hair, the sacks and fur coat were covered with corn dust and empty ears.

My job was to lace and tie the full sacks of corn with an enormous bodkin curved like a scimitar. But I broke off early before dinner, as Maggie had no one in the house and needed me to help with the serving up. We dragged the large refectory table to the middle of the kitchen and loaded it with plates of duck, vegetables, and a whole churn of fresh butter. There were stuffed rabbits too, and a gigantic ham for those who did not want a half-carcass of duck. As the last place was laid and a delicious smell hung about the room, the men trooped in to do justice to the meal, hungry and thirsty after heroic efforts at threshing.

Christy sat at one end of the table, presiding unobtrusively as head of the house. I expected his brother, Freddy, to occupy the place of honour in the deep windsor armchair at the other end, but Maggie insisted on my sitting there when he refused, saying 'That's Rob's place'. Maggie was far too busy, filling glasses and dissecting birds for second helpings, to take a seat herself. I never felt so important or so pleased in my life as I did at that dinner, seeing the rows of red country faces beaming over heaped plates, while dogs lined up outside the window hardly able to wait till their masters carried out the bones. I was proud indeed of my country home.

To my right sat a neighbour known as 'The Little Thank You Man'. He scattered thanks as liberally as a sower broadcasting seed. If you met him on the road and remarked how fine a day it was, he would answer, 'Thank you, a topper!' An enquiry about his invalid wife elicited a 'Thank you, she's had a bad night, thank you'. Seldom ruffled by anything, Maggie was irritated by him. He loved tea, and when she had filled his huge mug five times, and made as though to replenish it again, he placed his hand over the top and said, 'Thank you no, I never take more than one cup, thank you.'

When no more could be eaten, and tight buttons were released, the old men lit their pipes. A good all-round scratch began, for the chaff dust filtered through the thickest clothes, setting up unbearable itching. The younger ones and I went out to the orchard. Here the bottom hedge was riddled with rabbit burrows, and Jason Nesbutt loosed his ferrets. When the evil pink eyes flashed in the dark tunnels, out rushed a score of rabbits to the watery jaws of the dogs. The bedlam of yapping dogs, screaming rabbits and swearing men, all mixed in wild confusion, would have given Hogarth himself fit subject for comment.

Jason Nesbutt was mostly responsible for the uproar, being the wildest character for miles round. When I misbehaved or reports of my past seeped through from old billets, people declared that sure, but wasn't I just another Jason Nesbutt. I accepted this as a compliment for Jason was very much my hero. He lived alone with his father in a tiny cabin on the mountainside. Their relationship was a simple one of hatred. Much of the wildness centred round this uncomplicated emotion. A story had it that his father had thrown him from a boat into the deepest part of the lake when Jason was a tiny boy. It was meant to teach him to swim. Whether true or not, Jason certainly swam powerfully when I knew him. On our Sunday mornings, coming home from church, he flung his strong body into the water and went across the lake and back almost before the rest of us had undressed. Jason's diving was expert too, and he would cleave the water as gracefully as the great-crested grebe. None of us could remain under water as long as Jason, who swam in vast depths down to the lake bed in search of a sunken boat loaded with loot from an old castle. When he was seventeen I saw him riding his bicycle up the church hill, a steep incline which other cyclists walked. That was not all, however, for a buxom woman balanced uncertainly on the crossbar. Jason would rather have died from heart failure than give up half-way.

Jason set me a fine example at a church social where dancing was not allowed on account of its being too 'worldly'. We were reduced to playing party games, children, adults and aged alike, joining in 'The farmer wants a wife'. Since the girls were too timid to choose Jason as the dog or even as the bone, he contented himself by collecting mementoes of them. Scented handkerchiefs were his particular fetishism, and by grabbing them boldly we collected half a dozen each by the end of the evening. This introduction to erotic stimulants roused a dormant appetite. After the handkerchiefs, I had no need to learn from Jason.

In the church choir-stall in front of me, two sisters sang. In spite of approaching the late teens, they still wore their hair in long pigtails, braided with bows of blue ribbon. The cable strands glinted like gold and seemed to have absorbed the whole summer's sun and the glory of the cornfields. It was difficult to decide which of the two I liked the more. Interest changed to fascination and then to obsession. When I first joined the choir I rested my hands on the hymn-book rack, so that when the girls sat back during the lessons or sermon, the soft blonde braids touched my fingers, sending an electrical thrill along my arms, down into my stomach. But such passive contact was not enough, and I took to surreptitious stroking, one hand covered by the other.

One Sunday morning I applied too much pressure, and the game was up. They looked daggers at me, and carefully draped the plaits over their chests. The aggressive male was not so easily rebuffed. Jason's methods had to be adopted. After church, I waited behind a tombstone and then followed them, determined to untie a ribbon as a souvenir. I crept close, jumped out and seized a rope of hair. But outraged innocence swung round and would not let me go until her sister beat me on the head with a bicycle pump. It was well worth it, three strands of hair came away which I kept in a captive handkerchief for years. Pious souls hearing of this rape, pronounced it most ungodly. I could not at that time reply that I only followed a precedent set by a one-time dean of St. Paul's, who wrote:

> *Who ever comes to shroud me, do not harme*
> *Nor question much*
> *That subtile wreathe of haire, which crowns my arme;*
> *The mystery, the signe you must not touch,*
> *For 'tis my outward Soule,*
> *Viceroy to that, which then to heaven being gone,*
> *Will leave this to controule,*
> *And keep these limbs, her Provinces, from dissolution.'*

I was highly delighted when Jason changed his job and came to work at the farm on the other side of our hill. Life to him was a round of laughter. In the hottest, most tiring moments of threshing, when muscles strained, and the dust made us long for teatime, Jason pulled his face into ridiculous shapes behind the old men's backs and kept me boiling with laughter. For many months I raced home from school so that I could be with Jason when he took the ferrets out. He had been charged with bringing to an end the plague of rabbits that turned the hill we shared with his employer into a veritable Hamelin. A large part of our arable land spread over the hill and it was sown with wheat. But although the land was in good heart and the weather perfect, it was never reaped—at least not by humans. The usual fawn rabbit combined with an equal force of black ones, in destroying the wheat. Beautifully marked piebalds, the half-caste and quadroon offspring of the parent tribes, frisked about the hedges and scurried in and out of the wheat shoots.

Gradually the crop vanished. At first the fields looked mangy and then quite naked as though visited by locusts. The whole countryside talked of it, for never had such devastation been seen, nor on such a scale. Jason's employer kept him hard at it with dogs and ferrets, though little progress showed. I was equally happy as Jason to take part in the massacre, for I received a share of the profits. Meat was rationed and scarce, and since British and American troops had many big camps around, coney flesh was at a premium.

The alliance of destroyers, however, was soon itself to be destroyed. Jason lost his job, and I lost his friendship. Unable to remain serious for long, Jason found rabbit hunting too dull. One afternoon when surveying the hill with the farmer for whom he worked, Jason pointed excitedly to a rabbit. But the old man could not see it, and so Jason went through the antics again, not daring to speak for fear of warning their prey. The farmer handed over his gun and that was my friend's undoing. 'Hands up,' he cried, turning the muzzle on the startled old man. Laughing fit to burst, Jason declared that there was no rabbit and never had been, and now the old man would have to obey *his* orders. The farmer dare not refuse, Jason's passions as well as his pranks were well known. Since he was encumbered with a wooden leg, he could only raise one hand above his head. With his stick in the other, the poor old thing stumped on his peg leg round the field commanded sergeant-major fashion by Jason. 'Left turn!' 'Right turn!' 'Halt!' 'Quick march!' All the time the rifle was trained at the limping, sweating figure. The timely appearance of another farmhand saved the situation, and with tears of laughter running down his cheeks, Jason handed over the gun, and never went back to the farm again.

Mostly by hearsay, but partly from experience, I shared Jason's dislike of his father. I met him only once. On a bitter winter night I set out for a wake on one of the lake islands. Nesbutt senior was going too and we arrived together at the home-made pier just in time to step aboard the little cot. Others made room for us, and as soon as the cot pushed off, Jason's father, who was quite drunk, fell asleep, his brick-red face hanging back, mouth agape. A wind like a knife cut across the water. One of the men slipped the whiskey bottle from old Nesbutt's pocket, took a swig and passed it round. After every-one had had some, only two inches remained, but topped up with lake water it looked as good as new. When the sleeper stirred, his hand went to the bottle. With the first mouthful he knew what had happened and went into a drunken rage, and was not quietened until someone was tipped out into the icy water.

Wakes held a fascination for most people in the district but for Jason's father they were irresistible. He went miles to them, whether he knew the family or not. At one he saw a cat jump up and walk over the corpse. With one blow of his stick he killed the cat, saying that the beast had no right to carry the deceased's complaint to mourners. By contrast to the un-invited, Christy was often asked especially to attend wakes, for he was the most popular person in the neighbourhood for helping to draft wills or act as executor. His fame started when he won four crossword puzzles in the national newspapers, but besides this obvious cleverness his quiet discreet manner in-spired confidence.

Of all the strange stories he had of this activity was one of an old herdsman who bought a coffin for himself long before he died. He argued that since it would be the only piece of furni-ture to accompany him to the grave, why should it not also be used during his life. 'Isn't it the grand place for storing calf meal against the rats?' he asked his visitors, and of course it had to be admitted there was some point to his idea. Having no family or relations to lay out a funeral spread of hams and whiskey and other customary wake festivities, he bequeathed a sum of money for the mourners to have a drink on the way to the graveyard with him. Since he lived in a bog, he had to be carried all the way, and at the pub was lodged on the hedge bank while the mourners went in for a drink. Christy had gone on ahead to attend to arrangements at the church. When they did not appear, he pacified the rector and went in search of them. A great deal of persuasion was needed to tear the mourners away from the bar, and to bring them into the frame of mind usually associated with last rites.

Unfortunately there was not a great number of wakes that year, as our part of the county was thinly populated, and by people who seemed to cling tenaciously to life long after the span allowed by the Bible. The nearest thing for excitement was poking about in derelict houses. This craze of mine was instigated by a thatcher, who, called in to recondition a neglected roof, found two tins full of gold sovereigns in the rotten thatch. But when Jason Nesbutt went away my life became very quiet, and before the war was over he was to enlist and die in some outlandish desert, a mere boy of eighteen, his practical jokes ended for ever. After he went off laughing over the hill, Christy and I had to attack the rabbits. As soon as I got back from school we set out with our traps and snares, staying away until milking time.

Evening milking, a kind of benediction on my full days, was my favourite hour, especially in winter and spring, Maggie and I collected pails and hurricane lamp, and crushed oats for the newly calved cows. The byre's warmth struck us as we entered, a sweetness of steamy cows' breath and the stronger tang of dung, and the clean smell of freshly strewn rushes. Immediately the hot jets of milk struck the pail bottom with a metallic sound, the cats scurried in mewing for their supper. We worked in the subdued but pleasant light of the lamp, throwing absurd shadows on the whitewashed wall. Except for the occasional call of night birds, no sound drifted in from the darkened countryside. The soft splash of the milk stream purring into the frothy bucket, and the munching jaws of the beasts as they chewed the cud, seemed unnaturally loud. Sometimes we could hear the wind outside, blowing with faraway music, cold in winter, but in spring full of rich scents forgotten from one year to the next. Maggie and I leant our heads against the sleek flanks and sang, believing that singing charmed the animals and made the milk come more freely. The heavy fullness of their udders eased, the cows would turn to us with eyes of love as though we were the calves they had never licked. If our stock of ballads ran out, we turned to hymns, sometimes even preferring the sacred to the profane, for the cows undoubtedly loved the lofty soar of their melodies. The byre's cloistral calm often ended abruptly if a cow's warty teats were sore, or a tail flicked round, whisking away Maggie's glasses. The Kerry-blues had a habit of tossing hay up with their sweeping horns in order to search out favourite grasses. And when they had a feed of nuts, and the bucket fell out of the manger towards the next, they went down on their forelegs, as if to pray, and retrieved the delicacy with their tongues.

When the milk was strained we had our first supper, a good bowl of stirabout. Anyone who arrived for an early *ceili*, was offered some as well and a helping of milk still warm from the byre. Then the fire was built up and a space cleared for the farmers and their lads, and shop girls from the town, who cycled all the way out for a late session of dancing. Out came the melodeon to wheeze a lively jig. The player rocked to and fro as he pulled on the straps, making the pleated sides swell and collapse like a caterpillar crawling up a cabbage stalk. And Maggie sat in a corner with her fiddle, the plimsolled foot beating time and her fingers flitting more nimbly than the dancers themselves. No sign of the day's work showed about her now as she plied the bow.

I thought the dancing all right, and loved to see the old

people go white-faced during tales about ghosts told in the intervals. But I really waited for the ballad singing, the evening's best part for me. 'Give us a wee bleat, while I wet the tea' Maggie would announce, encouraging the shyest to sing while she made a snack. Hospitality, to the point of force, was a strong element in our lives, having the same importance as in Muslim countries. However poor or rich, no one ever dreamed of not giving guests the very best in the house, and to receive was just as blessed as to give. Such generosity was indivisible from the rest of life, and had its roots with superstitions and faith and all the dim past. Maggie would have spent her last penny in providing for visitors.

A lot of the songs that people sang round our fire, I had never heard before, but Maggie knew them all. Though some of them went on for a long time, she would remember if a particularly sad or comic verse had been omitted, and make the singer go back to the beginning again. The best singer among the women was an old crone whose repertoire was inexhaustible, and included many songs in Gaelic. Her popularity with many was not, alas, due to her ability as ballad-singer but to the fact that she only had two teeth badly fixed on to a denture plate. As she opened her mouth the teeth danced up and down, even falling out during sustained notes. Martin Calaum was our undisputed *Meistersinger*. He too had an endless stock of songs and he performed them in a powerful baritone. But he sang with a curious oriental inflection of the notes, full of turns and quarter-tones, and queer catchings of his breath. His music had an ancient ring about it, vibrant and full of emotion, but alarming at first hearing. I was certainly never to hear such singing anywhere else.

Maggie and I were always planning mischief. When we heard that some lads had come to work on the reafforestation, and intended making a *ceili* with us, Maggie's great idea occurred. It consisted in my dressing up as a girl, a real joke for Maggie as one of the boys was suspected of being the sex maniac up at the crossroads. When the young men arrived, they were told that Maggie had an English visitor up in the parlour—while I was being finished off with cochineal and cornflour on my face. I went into the kitchen then, behaving shyly, and giving timid handshakes. So impressed were the newcomers, that they removed their caps, a gesture usually reserved for meal times.

Maggie said in a coy voice that I had to be going, and perhaps one of the men would kindly see me past the bog-holes. There was a scramble for the privilege, and the big gruff woodman won. We went down the dark lane. I was not at all surprised to learn that the courtship pattern was exactly what we Belfast children had imagined took place in the night entries. Without mishap the woodman and I got as far as the bog-holes. Then becoming bolder he suggested we retraced our steps to the hayshed. Deftly I extricated myself from his arms, before he should discover the truth. One push was enough to send him sprawling into a bog-hole, while I ran back to the house screaming like an offended girl. But rough treatment suited him fine, for now his passions were unleashed. He climbed out of the hole in no time, gave chase and tripped me up in the heather. Fortunately Maggie could not bear to miss the fun, and having given away the secret to the others, had come out of the house. The woodman's workmates pulled him away, and told him I was only a cub. His anger sent Maggie into paroxysms of laughter, which burst out now and again during the whole evening.

Catholics came as freely as anyone in the evenings, and this surprised me at first, for though Maggie and Christy were staunch Protestants, bigotry formed no part of their life. In spite of the Orange Lodge's treasury chest being kept upstairs, and the dining-room walls being covered with the secret society's emblems, they would not stop anyone singing a Fenian song during a *ceili*. I was not too young to sense that subtle beauty haunted the rebel ballads, and a tragic mood far more moving than our own breezy Orange ones. Laments for those who went to the gallows 'for the cause' were the most recurrent theme, and longings for loved ones gone to 'the land of the stranger'. These gentle, lilting melodies probed deeply into Maggie's feelings, and everyone's present. When the singer stopped a mournful silence fell on us, and we were glad when the kettle boiled over, sending up clouds of peat ash, breaking the tension.

Unlike many of her neighbours, of both camps, few signs of belonging to either faith showed in Maggie's day-to-day routine. True she would not allow the beastings to cover silver, but apart from this I saw only one other clue as to difference in religion, and consequently politics. A nun sent Maggie an apron she had made which was decorated with the Free State tricolour. Maggie could not hurt the nun's feelings by not wearing it, but first she unpicked the offending tricolour border.

At night, all the roads round about were haunted by I.R.A. men, going about their activities, but still Christy and Maggie held open house, turning no one away. They would not even refuse a hen to serve up to the P.P.—the parish priest. The Catholic rector was always known as P.P. In fact, he enjoyed the status of canon, like our own rector, whom we called 'the Canon'. Every evening someone had a new story to tell of the P.P. or the Canon, crowding out whatever the news might be of stirrings on the border, or of the war, or the price of bullocks. The Canon, a strong Orangeman (a powerful Ribbonman as the Catholics would say) had once been heard to declare that he would rather 'go over to Rome' than become a Jehovah's Witness. And this statement allowed us some fellow-feeling with the Catholics over the encroaching evil of this persistent sect.

Much respected as a fine parson and a great tiller of his glebe, the Canon also commanded fear. In a tiny cottage by the main road lived a very unruly family. One of the daughters had already had a 'wee love bird', for which impropriety the Canon severely castigated her. But it happened again while she was away serving in a big farm. She went out into the hayshed, delivered herself of the child, and went straight in to serve up the dinner. Such goings on could not be hushed up and once again she and the Canon fought it out. Of course, she could not win. At the end of this second battle she was so prostrate that everyone fully expected her ways to mend. The war was not making resistance to temptation an easy thing, especially when large numbers of American troops descended on the district. After the third birth the young mother, remembering the Canon's searing sermon on the previous occasion, took fright when his stern voice was heard in the kitchen below. It was enquiring if she might be at home. He started to mount the ladder to her loft-bedroom above. Only one way of escape was left—through the skylight, down the roof and into the bog.

The depths of affection in Maggie's heart, out of which she could bring love for any creature, was not universal in the district. Broadmindedness at even a normal level was hard to find among some of the neighbours. I never forgot the shock and sense of being personally involved when a friend of mine was turned out of a dance on account of being a Catholic. I explained this hurt to Maggie and she told me of the old undying prejudices. She showed me the local newspaper and its announcements of dances. At the end of each was a notice 'All Loyalists Welcome' or 'God Save The King' to show that only Protestants would be admitted. It had not been too many years previously that I regarded Catholics as incarnate devils, and walked about Belfast fearful of going near the Catholic quarter. I realized how these views were changed by the friends I had made since, with people whom I afterwards discovered to be Catholics. Such stringent segregation did not seem to make sense any more. And Maggie's kindness to all and sundry confirmed my attitude.

Nevertheless, she and Christy were committed as supporters of the Orange cause, and so we went often to the dances held in the hall not far away. Sometimes Maggie was put on the 'social committee' for a dance, and this meant that on the afternoon she must go to the hall and sweep up, and get everything ready for the evening. When this was done she would teach me a new dance-step that I could use later on, if I had not already forgotten it by nightfall. What hours of wild dancing shook the wooden hall, where everyone around (Protestants only) came to throw themselves heart and soul into the fray. Despite her advancing years, poor Maggie let herself go with the best, swinging round as light as thistledown. On and on the jigs and reels went without mercy. At last the farm girls and boys, many of whom had come miles to be present, became so heated that they slipped out into the bogs and had a noggin of whiskey lying in the heather.

The evenings when Maggie was in charge of the big copper tea urn and the mountain of cakes, were not much fun for me, for I had to sit out in the little shed on guard. This was essential, for at a former dance some wag had gone unobserved into the shed and emptied certain powders into the urn. Before the dance finished everyone was rushing out in search of an unoccupied place in the hedge. The hall dances provided interest in our lives, but I really preferred our own kitchen dances, perhaps because Sophie, a Catholic maid from the local mansion-house, had become my favourite partner. Although her mother was the old singer with the two hopping teeth, Sophie herself was very much the beauty.

We were not entirely hedonists and not all our evenings were secular ones, though we enjoyed them equally. Farmhouse services conducted in the winter by the Methodists were our favourites. Everyone turned out in full numbers for these, tramping across the ice-crusted fields to sit in the warm, lamp-lit kitchens. The services were never dismal, and even the thundering evangelist one evening, had to stop his solemn appeal for souls and join in the laughter. On finding no vacant chair a late-comer had sat on a tea-chest near the open fire. Gradually it buckled beneath his weight. Unable to bear it any longer, the very polite woman of the house jumped up shouting 'Lord! my wee bull duck' as she tried to rescue an orphan drake from the bottom of the box. The same woman always went into raptures when talking about her brother in New Zealand, whom she called 'The Reverent Mister Willie, master of the arts, minister of God's word'.

Maggie enjoyed the farm services but refused to commit herself over being 'saved'. She laughed so much after one service that her false teeth put in to honour the occasion, came adrift and were almost lost when a crowd of us walked into a midden in the darkness. Those were the days when the muck-heap in the yard was still the gauge of a man's wealth. A good mound of fresh dung steaming quietly was there for all to judge the size of your stock. Vague hints of money in banks impressed nobody, for people still did not trust banks as they did the old crocks of sovereigns hidden under the turf stacks.

Whether we fell into such dire straits or not, laughter prevailed on the way back from the services. Maggie tried to get everyone to come into our house for it would only be nine o'clock, and who would be wantin' to get to their beds at that hour? Not one did. So out came fiddle and melodeon, clogs and hobnailed boots started the rounds, and midnight would be on us before the house was still again. Christy waited until the last torches flashed down the lane and then put on his Home Guard overcoat, a signal for our last round of the farm. We looked in at the cattle, and went on a tour of our traps. By resetting them it was possible to get two rabbits a night in each.

We walked for more than an hour through the bog heather,

into the fir plantations, down the dark haunted orchard, finally making the long climb up to the very top of the Fort. I never missed this nightly tour for I had quite a substantial financial interest in trapping. Three times a week I cycled off with scores of rabbits slung over the handlebars of Maggie's tall bicycle, with others piled behind on the carrier. The return journey was lighter though my pockets were heavier with the money stowed safely away. I kept the pound notes, half-crowns and florins in the innermost of my Japanese boxes, until I went in search of new treasures from the auctions.

Maggie waited up for our return from the traps. If the weather was cold she passed the time by soaking her bunions in paraffin oil before going to bed. Her first question when we came in was an anxious one, to know if any of her cats had been caught in the traps. All too often in the winter we had to give the affirmative, though the injuries were never fatal. When we had removed our boots and hung our socks along the crook, Maggie raked the fire by putting a few damp turfs into the embers and covering them with ashes, the nightly ceremony that kept the house alive through the decades.

Sometimes I would hear Maggie pause on the stairs as she went up to bed. Then I knew what was in her mind. Back she came, tiptoeing to my room to ask if I would like a 'tasty bit', knowing full well that I would, in spite of having at least three snacks ('bits in the hand' they were called) since supper. The 'tasty bit' usually consisted of bacon fried with heaps of onions, and eaten stealthily, as Christy did not care for such things and wished to be undisturbed. Like two conspirators we sat over the greasy dish in a very dim light.

We still had no blinds though the war had been on more than two years with its blackout regulations. But there was no fear of police coming to tell us of the offence. Friends on their way home from a dance or going off Home Guard duty might see the pale glimmer and think we were having a big spree, or sitting up for a cow calving. Then they would make a detour up the lane and come in for a long visit. Maggie would often be sleeping on her feet when these late-callers came. It was not surprising that she often put salt instead of sugar in the tea, or baking powder instead of salt into the porridge. And her glasses were always in need of wiping. The steam from pots on the fire clouded them but she did not notice, until the canisters had been mixed up and the guests were making wry faces.

The latest that anyone ever called in, was after two in the morning. And we did have to get up so early next day, to get the cows in and the milk away off to the creamery just the same.

Chapter Fourteen

Here Comes I . . .

Waiting for the thresher that winter was not the only thing that sent us up into the ancient Fort. We struggled up the steep hill, right to the top, in order to scan the distant roads. I even climbed into the fork of the 'lonely bush', to see if I could catch sight of the ghostly figures with their fiddles and flutes.

It was already the sixth day of Christmas and the mummers had not appeared. Maggie had never known them to be so late, and concluded that their creels were filled with coppers. This meant the remaining days would be spent on drinking until the time came for them to light their tar barrel and embark on the celebrated Straw Boy spree.

But Christmas would simply not be Christmas, without the seventeen mummers coming in their shrouding sheets and their heads covered in straw. A big bottle of Old Bushmills was ready for them as well as the best home-made cordials and wines. And under the stairs, which went over a corner of the kitchen, Maggie had her long rows of jars crammed with chocolate biscuits and fingers of shortbread.

To stock up for our Christmas celebrations, Maggie and I had been across the border into the Free State on several smuggling expeditions. Our booty was confined to rationed goods, chiefly sugar. Everyone indulged in smuggling to some degree, and we knew the minor roads where there were no British or Eirean customs controls. Little risk but great thrills attached for me to these trips. And as always with Maggie we had plenty of laughs on the way. It amused me immensely to see the thinnest and tiniest of women, like Maggie, pedalling hard back to the Fermanagh side in an acute dropsical condition from concealed supplies of food. The police got rather tired of the bolder methods, such as mock funerals with coffins loaded with loot. Luckily Maggie and I never met with the humiliation of being taken into the customs shed and being stripped, in spite of travelling the road regularly. What else could we do with so many people coming in to *ceili* and requiring hospitality? When no one came in of a night to gossip by the fire, we found life very empty. And to miss the mummers, and have nothing to offer them would have been the end.

At the eleventh hour before New Year, we heard a disturbance in the lane and knew the mummers had arrived. I went as wild as Carlo, who got so excited that he had to be locked in Maggie's bedroom. But through the floorboards came the strains of fiddles and the noise of the Straw Boys. Carlo thought the house was besieged and his master and mistress being attacked. He took a flying leap through the window, landing with fearful yelps in the hedge. Unhurt but still on the offensive he had to be put into the windowless boxroom, for he would have torn the seats from the mummers and much else beside.

> *Any admittance for Captain Mummer and his men?*
> *Christmas comes but once a year*
> *And when it comes it brings good cheer,*
> *Active young and active age*
> *The like was never acted on the stage.*

And well we could believe it. The hefty farm labourers in their primitive garb, and heads lost in cones of straw, were horribly grotesque as they reeled in and out of the holes in our kitchen floor. Maggie passed from helpless laughter to hysterics as she recognized the performers by their movements or voices insufficiently disguised. This was the first time I had ever seen the mummers, and after looking forward for so many weeks to their visit, I determined to enjoy every minute of it. But the theme of their play bewildered me and I could make neither head nor tail out of their rhymes.

I distinguished Martin Calaum under his sheet. There could be no mistaking his sonorous voice, raised as if he were shouting to his brother to say his prayers in the bog. Martin made a very weird Doctor Bighead indeed, gyrating like a jungle witchdoctor but with surprising results in the curing of various feigned ailments.

> *What can I cure?*
> *I can cure the wee plague, the big plague,*
> *The plague within and the plague without,*
> *The pip, the palsy and the gout.*
> *I've a wee bottle called Sally the Pain,*
> *Rise up dead man and fight again.*
>
> *A ram's feather mixed with a pig's bladder*
> *Nine times before day,*
> *And if that doesn't cure 'em*
> *I'll ask no pay.*
> *If you don't believe in what I say,*
> *Enter in. . . .*

The mummers had been out for hours going round the whole countryside, being entertained at each farm, and now were quite drunk. But this made them spin all the harder, their straw tops knocking again and again against the old bell from Lisgoole Abbey. It swung to and fro on the ceiling clanging in the New Year, with as good a ringing as ever it had in a long existence. In the boxroom above, Carlo heard it and began a frantic scratching at the floor boards, trying to get through so that he could drop down and devour the fiddles and flutes that went on with incessant energy. There were little rude dramas where the biggest, most oafish country bumpkin played the female role with gross exaggeration. His strident, falsetto voice alarmed poor Carlo more.

Included in the performance was a historical play of Oliver Cromwell:

> *Here comes I Oliver Cromwell;*
> *As you may suppose*
> *I conquered many nations*
> *With my long copper nose.*
> *I made the Spanish quake*
> *And bait the Jolly Dutchman*
> *Until he couldn't speak.*
> *If you don't believe in all I say,*
> *Enter in Devil Doubt*
> *And clear the way.*

With this pronouncement we knew the mummers were nearly done, and got our pile of coppers ready. On the weight of coins in the two ass panniers depended the season's success, and the quality of the mummers' final orgy. Perhaps for two days or more after their tour was over the drink would flow. Then the straw hats would be burned, a sign that mumming was over for another year.

> *Here come I*
> *Little Devil Doubt,*
> *If you don't give me money*
> *I'll sweep you all out.*
> *Money I want, and money I crave,*
> *And if I don't get money*
> *I'll blow you to your grave.*

Here Comes I . . .

Money, mail, brass or tow,
Pay the mummers before we go.

For weeks after it was all over, we talked of nothing but the Straw Boys. We found out all we could about their reception at other farms. The mummers were not welcome everywhere. At some houses of strong evangelical persuasion, dogs were set on the mummers not merely for being drunken and rowdy, but for trying to bring the remnants of medieval witchcraft near the sacred hearths.

They need not have bothered their righteous heads, for the following year's performance proved to be the last. The constant changes and movements of wartime broke up the group, and there was nobody to replace them. But the war did more than scatter the particular mummers we knew personally—it broke a tradition centuries old, a half-magical tradition that stretched away back beyond the Middle Ages to no one knew what pagan days. Not that any of us were aware of such things at the time. Only later did I realize how, by the simplest means, the age-old custom was brought, sadly, to an end.

Martin Calaum was one of the last genuine mummers and what he had learnt from his father, came direct out of the distant past. When the mummers played no longer Martin told me all about his troupe, though he himself had never been Captain Mummer. His part had always been Doctor Bighead, as his father taught him. His brother had played Prince George, but when he died a younger brother took over, playing the part as Oliver Cromwell, with no change of words. None of them had the faintest idea what the words meant, the sense had been lost long ago, and they certainly had no idea as to who the Jolly Dutchman might be.

The mummers' advent that year involved me in great personal mortification. My hair had grown far beyond its normal length and my regular time for having it cut was long past.

But with mummer excitement in the air, I could not cycle into town for the barber, fearing that the troupe would call in my absence, and I should miss them. Instead, I prevailed on Maggie's brother Freddy to come up with his clippers. His only claim to knowledge of the tonsorial art, was possession of the clippers, which, as it turned out, was not a sufficient qualification. He sat me in a chair and after a contemplation of my head attacked it as though it were a long-neglected hedge. Working strictly to a horizontal line round the back of my head from the very top of one ear to the top of the other, he removed every trace of hair below it. I never saw anything like it ever again until years afterwards when I watched the film of *Henry V* being made, and saw the actors with their medieval haircuts. Freddy did not seem unduly disturbed by his first measures. However, the rather startling appearance of my head may have struck him as being a little stark, and so his scissors went in on the higher part. The longest hair came out in clumps chopped at the roots. The result was a moth-eaten nightmare. Maggie stopped further depredations, hotly refusing Christy's suggestion that it ought to be shaved altogether. Unfortunately I had to go home to Belfast the week-end following, but I refused to take my cap off anywhere, and would not even go to church.

Now the worst spell of winter began, and I was glad when my hair sprouted again as added protection against the winds. At the back of our farm the cow-pass was almost knee-deep in mud. Poor Maggie arrived back from the well long overdue, having lost her one wellington over and over again in the oozy sockets. Hard frost set in, freezing the earth so that we could get about easier. Frosts glazed the cow-pass hoof-holes like pretty hand-mirrors, encrusting the elaborate patterns of mud round the edge, and stretching a delicate film of ice between them. The earth froze so hard and deep that even the soil covering of our traps was like iron. We dug them out and reset them, but every night was the same, and our bag of rabbits dropped. Maggie declared no warmer weather would come until snow fell.

We watched hopefully as the sky went smooth and heavy. Looking up from sawing logs one morning we felt the first flakes whirling down to melt on our hot faces. The dim hills, gloomy before in the winter light, now emerged again, their flanks resuming noble forms under the deepening snow. And next morning the land was changed, sparkling in a new, pure existence, its imperfections hidden, and the last memory of summer blotted from the fields that had rung so often with our voices. The trees bore fresh, crisp blossoms of snow that would catch the sunlight and be brighter than ever the May orchards would. And printed into the pristine plains, swept by the wind into beautiful curves against the hedges, was a hieroglyphic pattern of fresh spoors. Christy was certain then that sterner methods than trap and ferret must be used, if next year's crops were not to disappear also. We expected to find the rabbits' trails laid across the snow, but we were looking specially for those of the fox. Maggie's fowls had suffered heavy losses recently. And as though to mock our hunt for them, the vixen gave vent to uncanny screams and waited for her mate's answering yelp in the darkness. The night seemed to inflame passions which only a kill, another plump hen, would allay.

We could not allow the snow to interrupt our routine, though certain jobs had to be abandoned. Walking in the fields or up over the hill took much longer than usual and was far more tiring. I got into my boots and puttees to go over and fetch Sophie at the mansion-house, and bring her back as it was her afternoon off. I struck off in the direction of the gate-lodge, wading through deep drifts until I was exhausted. Away from our own house with not another in sight, I realized how deadened the country was, how frighteningly quiet under the blanket of snow. Though the mistlethrush might be called the snaw cock, even his exuberance was lost with the cold.

Dipper and wren and the various tits that usually filled the hedges and coppices with endless chatter had lapsed into silence. No insects buzzed in the sharp air or busied themselves in the crevices of the earth. The sounds had vanished of cattle tongues encircling and tearing up grass, and of sheep stampeding with fastidious hooves and breaking into the meadows. The work-noises of reapers, and the chugging of dusty threshers, of ploughmen cursing the horses for not pulling together, were banished from the folding curve of field and hill—leaving a void that ached to be filled. I thought perhaps the earth was sleeping at last, blissfully oblivious under the dazzling whiteness.

Maybe the Canon remembered an afternoon like this when he talked about the peace of God passing all understanding. Certainly I could imagine the soul's eye being bathed in this stainless salve of snow and silence, and its ears lulled in these low, loneliest notes of nature's year. The landscape's beauty was too austere, its chastity almost painful. And yet its glistening, at the same time, held promise of new birth, new seasons of dove cooings and redpoll twitterings in the bog, new nests in the hedgerows and still more new families in the burrows and setts.

Carried away by my thoughts I had flung myself on to a bank, and now had to break the sedative effect of the snow. I knew how dangerous its spell could be, how easily the lonely wanderer sat for a rest, but fell asleep, never to wake. Maggie had warned me, and when I felt the snow-drowsiness coming over me I remembered her words. Besides I had to plod on in order not to disappoint Sophie, who was coming down to the gate-lodge to pick me up. I was there before her and this time sat on the fence, making a verse, which later became:

> *When the snow came we were unready*
> *For the sudden rebirth,*

Here Comes I . . .

And woke to a bright morning
So new, untouched, and clean,
Without the soiled marks of day to day.

Wondering, we knew that this was not the first time
We had roused from dark dreams to such radiance.
And knew also that it was not yesterday,
Or a hundred years before,
Or even when beholding you,
Startled by the seeking in your eyes,
The white waves of my desire rushed inshore
To dash in joyous spume on the waiting rocks
Of your love.

But that it was when the world
Was still the molten gold of dreams
And you and I a single thought of passion
Flaring in the crucible.

To sit on fences and write was becoming not at all unusual
for me in those days. The hard work done for the scholarship
and my early love of jingles combined to produce this new
habit. And poetry was always around us in the school I now
went to. From my first years I had collected newspaper cuttings
of verse in a Black Magic chocolate box. These were mostly
sentimental lines from the deaths' column. But now for homework I had to write three or four verses on a given subject,
strictness of metre and rhyme being the great points of con-
struction. I found this a fascinating occupation and made up
hundreds of ridiculous verses about anything that came into
my mind.

Because the Canon had quoted 'The Destruction of Sen-
nacherib' we had been set to learn this poem. 'Drake's Drum',
'The Lady of Shalott' and the 'Ancient Mariner' were also
standard works in the repertoire. I much preferred their glow-

ing colours and the thrill of adventure in them to the terribly dreary phrases of *How we differ from Rome*. I gobbled up these verse stories, always on the lookout for more. But I had no idea that poets still lived and wrote. I thought they belonged only to the past and were a race as dead as dinosaurs. Tom Williams put me right about that.

He was a soldier stationed nearby. On my way home from school, I often stopped to drink at an old cattle well. And there, among the ferns, one day Tom lay, reading. He flipped his book shut and we talked, and then he accompanied me home, but was far too shy to come in. However, Maggie had spotted us through the window, and before Tom knew what had happened, he was sitting in front of the fire with a steaming cup of black tea in his hands. He stayed to supper.

The book he had been reading in the ferns was the *Selected Poems* of Louis MacNeice. Strange I had never heard of him along with Coleridge and Tennyson and the rest of them at school. Tom explained the reason why and that unlike others Louis MacNeice was not only not dead, but had been born in Belfast—my own town! At first this seemed impossible, but the truth of the matter slowly dawned on me. Poems were something for *now*. I listened agog as Tom read:

> *I was born in Belfast between the mountain and the gantries*
> *To the hooting of lost sirens and the clang of trams.*

Had I not myself been born on the dockside, facing the blue mountains of Antrim, with the clang of trams rushing by to the Queen's Bridge with the sad hooting of tugs in the oily waters below. Now I devoured *Selected Poems*. I could not recover from the excitement of discovering that poets were not *ipso facto* dead people. And as for this one who wrote about the things at home, I thought I must have actually seen him, for I was one of his father's diocesan orphans. During bygone years I had often called at his home with my collecting card. His father, *our* bishop, had been one of the first people to whom I showed my chocolate box collection of verse. And every change of billet I had made since coming to Fermanagh, had to be recorded in a humble little letter to his lordship, bearing the new address. Did the young poet (of course he *must* have ringlets and strange neckties, and be quite as romantic-looking as our engraving of Shelley in school) go into the hall and get the post? Perhaps he hunted through the letters, and recognized my scrappy little note, and took it to his father. I wondered if the bishop would read it over his breakfast boiled-egg, as Mrs. Morsett read the morning letters. But what sort of a demon would the poet think I was, to be always turned out of houses and writing so boldly about it. And what would he make of those notes:

Dear Lord Bishop of Down, Connor and Dromore,

They have sent me now to Carrickreagh on Mr. Saggart's farm. I think I shall be happy here. There is a river and lots of cows. I will have to walk three miles to Sunday School.

Your obedient servant,

ROBBIE.

Tom Williams came often after his first visit, and he remained the most regular of our soldier callers. The military camps round about had quite an effect on our lives. In hot weather the soldiers came over the hill to cool off in the river like cattle among the reeds, their bodies often surprisingly pale against the brick-red faces. In the evening the fiddle and melodeon lured them to the house. Friends brought friends and Maggie's hospitality earned quite a name. Some of the American forces thought the place was a farm restaurant, and when a little sergeant came in and ordered tea with fried eggs, asking how much it would cost him, Maggie was really hurt. All the soldiers left their names and addresses. It fell to me to write, for Maggie only found time once a year to send letters to her relations in Canada. But she followed the soldiers' careers closely and when we failed to hear from any of them, or my letters were returned unopened, she became depressed, fearing they had been killed. 'Och, he was only a lump of a cub himself, Robbie,' she would say, biting back the tears. 'I don't suppose he had a taste of the razor in all his life.'

Tom was a lone wolf and preferred to come when we had no other visitors. In the long sensuously warm days that alternated with our spells of summer rain, his favourite perch was up in the great maple tree by my window. Its roots were anchored beneath a high bank only a few yards from the house, and the magnificent crown of dense leaves helped to keep the dairy cool. We all thought of it as a serene guard never sleeping in its watch over the house. In the late afternoon when I came home from school I would run to see if Tom was up in the branches. He was, often, puffing his pipe, brows knit in the anxious tension of his thoughts, an expression seldom relaxed. He just sat, gazing at the perspective spread below him of house and steading, listening to the everyday noises of domestic stirrings, Maggie lilting a song as she scoured the churns, the hens idly pecking whitewash from the walls, the piglets worming pink snouts through holes in the sties. I found the maple's branches a comfortable enough loft for my long legs, but I could never spend the hours lodged up there that Tom did. Not until he had been posted abroad and the tree had to be felled, did we discover his initials carved deep in the highest limb where only the magpie and poking fingers of the storm could see.

Tom left me two legacies. One was his book of Louis MacNeice's poems, the key which had opened the door of poetry to me. And the other was his cigarette holder. How I had envied the elegance of that whistle-like gadget. Tom knew how much I loved it, for I was always wanting to use it in the bog. When he pushed it shyly into my hands with the book, before going away, my vanity was without bounds. Now I could look as lordly as Tom had done with the holder and a fag in his mouth.

To raise war funds, a flying-boat was moored on the lake near Enniskillen and opened for the public. This, I decided, would provide me with a splendid opportunity to show-off my new acquisition, an even better chance for display than wearing Portora clothes. What a disappointment awaited me when I went up the gang plank and was told 'No smoking here, sonny'. The loss of dignity at being called 'sonny' set me back slightly. But I recovered quickly when I got to the Diamond. Here, in the centre of the town, I lit up and thought myself such a dandy. I paraded past the shop where the Fenhill daughter worked, so that she might see how high I had risen, and carry the news back to the horrible 'gentry'.

Then I caught the Canon's eye, as he went pedalling by on his bicycle. I raced away from him, dodging in and out of the crowd. By the Town Hall, I dived into the public lavatory—I was sure he would not follow me there. For the first time in my life I squandered a real penny to operate the lock, and sat down until I was sure the cross old parson was well on his way back to the rectory.

Cutting down the maple, or 'Tom's tree' as Maggie called it, caused me much sorrow. It seemed to symbolize the happiness I had found in Christy's and Maggie's home. From my very first night in the little room, the wind had played music among its web of twigs and branches. Through the months after I heard every variation from soft serenades of mere rustlings to sonorous roarings as Atlantic gales swept inland agitating the maple into a wild thing. And at the coming of autumn the tree had turned into the most magnificent spectacle on the whole farm. The leaves turned to ruby and russet, mustard and emerald, blazing yellow like Van Gogh's cornfields, glinting bronze like Gauguin's bodies. They seemed not to belong to the grey fissured bark of the branches, writhing like elephants' trunks. The maple shimmering and glowing in its October glory was like a pagan idol, plated with the thinnest sheets of beaten gold all a-flutter in the breezes. Even the neighbours valued the tree. Those whose eyes saw only the practical use of things. They came for the maple saplings that had sprung up round the great parent, for maples were not common. Then the axe of fate was swung, and with a rending and tearing terrible to hear, its autumnal radiance was a mere memory.

None of us liked cutting the tree, not even Maggie and Christy, for it had stood there as long as they could remember. But the reason for doing so could not be avoided, unless Maggie was to spend sleepless hours from a conscience stricken with the guilt of selfishness. Maggie had dreamt about a farmhouse on fire. She told me about it the morning after, as she heaped my plate with 'burnt bread', as toast was called. There was nothing unusual in hearing the details of her nocturnal fantasies, for she was a great dreamer. I forgot about this particular dream until two days later. The homeward journey from school was delayed when I came to a newly burnt-out thatched farmhouse at the roadside. Maggie's brother Freddy was there scurrying in and out of the black shell, salvaging odds and ends. Many things had been rescued, and already a hen had become familiar enough with the parlour harmonium, now standing in the road, to lay an egg inside the open lid.

Having satisfied my curiosity, I ran helter-skelter home to break the news to Maggie. She wept at the tragedy and remembered her dream. I was the tall person in it who would bring the awful tidings. Christy gave a cluck of irritation at this dream-talk, he was thinking out ways to repair the damage, and saw no object in turning over events once they were finished. He went round the farm sizing up trees that would provide the best building materials, as the unfortunate farmer had no timber on his land, and the neighbours were ready to help with the new house already. Though he hesitated, Christy knew the maple was superior to anything else he possessed, especially for doors and tables. So he made the decision and my beautiful maple was cut down, and carted away to the mill.

Ghosts and 'little people' were not realities for Maggie, but charms and dreams were very much so. Like many in the district she set great store by dreams. The fascination of having my tea-leaves read was replaced by the daily interpretation at breakfast of my own dreams. Perhaps because I had such dread of evil omens like a bull or a black sheep chasing me in my sleep, or finding myself in a storm with lightning revealing the presence of badgers, these things really did appear occasionally. But Maggie was not the finest interpreter, and difficult dreams had to be kept until evening when greater authorities coming in to *ceili* could unravel them. Martin Calaum basked in fame of this kind. He always sat in the same place by the fire, his deep-sunken eyes shining under their shaggy brows as the dream was recited to him. He nodded sagely, stroked his nose with his finger, and said 'Ah' as though the dream struck chords in his esoteric knowledge. 'That,' he would add, warming to his art, 'that sounds a bit like a dream one of Lord Belmore's old gamekeepers had just before The Rising. Boys adear, that was a dream and a half, that was.' His methods of interpretation were like charms and the mummer's rhymes—handed down by word of mouth, father to son, for countless generations.

I was not at all convinced of the reliability of such interpretations, and held them in the same suspicion as I did charms. In any case, I had a shrewd idea that in some way, this morbid concern with dreams was connected with mental instability. Martin may have been the great seer, but he spent occasional periods in the asylum, and four of his brothers and sisters had either died in it or had been in for the 'head rest'. And that winter a wave of insanity swept over the neighbourhood, confirming my doubts. Those most concerned with garbled versions of the supernatural always seemed to end in the asylum. First the farmer with the burnt house went, and then a widow who lived in a cottage near us with her son. The big woodman for whom I dressed as a girl, was taken away, to die in the asylum still a strapping young man. A friend only two years older than myself, whose mother died, had to take the cure for a year. Of the twenty or so houses in our townland, at least half had an inmate down at Omagh.

And with ironic justice the epidemic not only touched Catholics and the more superstitious of the Protestants, but our 'saved' neighbours too. In repugnant self-confidence they generally regarded themselves as proof against evils which beset unsaved mankind. Lacking tolerance and common sympathy, they were never surprised or sorry when a Catholic was taken down to Omagh. Being half-way to the devil, in their view, it was not to be wondered that he came to claim his own. And over insane Protestants they shrugged their shoulders declaring it must be a punishment. None of them imagined for a moment that one of their own congregation would be smitten. Yet one morning, as Christy was leaving the churns out for the creamery lorry, a fellow-farmer came hurrying across the hill. The Lord had appeared to him in the night, he said, and had told him that He was coming again to earth on December 19th. The farmer implored Christy to get 'saved' there and then. For a month the man covered miles and miles, neglecting his farm, and proclaiming the news of his sacred dream. But on December 19th no Lord came, and the farmer was found next day with his throat cut, razor in hand.

The tide of insanity began to worry me terribly. For ever haunting me was the memory that my own father had died in an asylum, though admittedly because he had fallen and a railing spike had pierced his brain. But the fact remained. And I had been called a 'dafty' on a number of occasions. At the Lyttes' cottage I had been observed wandering in the woods declaiming *As you Like It*. And at Maggie's someone had seen me more than once rolling over and over in the thick bed of beech leaves imagining myself to be a real badger cub. And at the far end of our farm, grew a tunnel of ancient oaks. They leaned with age over the barely-noticeable grass-grown avenue that once led up to the castle before it fell into ruin. Along this way I sometimes went to brood. After the snow melted, torrents dashed with urgent splashings into the bole-fringed pools. Under the stark cloister of naked boughs I wandered up and down, looking like a monk in an old brown coat of Maggie's, possessed in a sad happiness. Some expression had to be given to my feelings and so I began shouting a Psalm learnt by heart many years before:

> *I will lift up mine eyes unto the hills,*
> *From whence cometh my help.*

The wind laughing in great gusts among the oaks blew the words back in my face. And my help came, not from the hills, but from some herdsmen who heard my cries, and thought I was in difficulties. Unknown to myself they came into the avenue, saw my arms waving and concluded that yet another local person had fallen to the head-sickness.

About a week later, my fears for my own sanity came to a climax. A boy of my own age at school told me of the theory (backed up, according to him, by doctors and clergymen) that masturbation brought on madness. Now there could be no doubt about what was happening to me! My secret sessions in the hayshed, the summer nights in the bog heather, stabbed my soul with guilt and accusation. My sins would surely find me out, and everyone would know when I was carried off to Omagh.

About this time I started going every evening to visit the boy whose mother had recently been 'sent away'. Their cottage was picturesque enough outside, lodged on a hillside just above the road in a flourishing garden. But inside a spooky atmosphere lessened its attraction. Half the rooms were boarded up with the owner's possessions inside. The woman worked as a matron in an American hospital and my friend's mother only rented the house from her. Strong mystery lurked about the locked rooms and my friend and I spent hours trying to see under the doors and through slits in the rotten curtains. We expected at the very least that a corpse lay in one of the rooms with a knife in its back or a strangler's silk stocking round its neck.

By the time I left to walk home I had ghosts thoroughly in my mind. On the fateful night when the gathered storm-clouds of my worries burst, I saw a tinker slipping along the road close to the hedge. Midnight had long gone, and not a light showed from any of the scattered houses. He seemed to be following me and I thought of the menace of the locked rooms. Obviously the tinker could be up to no good at that hour. With beating heart I began to run, increasing my pace until reaching our lane. The melted snows gurgled eerily through the drains and bogs, and when I stopped for breath the sound was like the voices of people waiting in ambush for me. I was still a long way from the house. Then I heard the tinker's footsteps turn into the lane also.

Seriously frightened, I thought another sound had begun. This was the place where our postman swore that he often saw a headless horseman riding a white charger, and now in my fear of the tinker and my head full of imagining about corpses in my friend's cottage, I heard the sound of galloping hooves. My paralysis left me and I stumbled blindly, frantically towards the house. The overfull brook on the other side of the hedge, which ran into the cherry orchard, kept pace with me and its gurglings belonged in my terror to the steps of the murderous tinker catching me up. Crying out from a dry throat I saw the house come into view. The dreadful nightmares, in which I had been chased by a nameless horror but could not escape because my leaden legs refused to run fast enough, were now reality. I screamed and Maggie, hearing me, rushed to the door where I fainted at her feet.

As I lay in bed the delirium returned, and I could see the tinker heaving himself through my window. Not even Christy standing beside me with his rifle could allay my fear, and I spent the night upstairs.

Next day Christy went about roofing a new henhouse. It was the kind of constructional work I loved and it took thoughts off other things. We worked all day and Christy made no reference to the previous night's events. When darkness fell and we had set our traps, he took me down the lane. We stopped at the place of the phantom horseman. Before Christy spoke I realized my overwrought mind had caused it all, the tinker had never followed me, the hooves had never sounded across the fields. But Christy laid his hand on my arm and bade me listen. Water from a thousand swollen runnels still coursed away with un-abated chatter. What sounds could *not* be heard in that multiple rippling and dripping and gushing, I wondered. A whole ghostly army of horsemen dashing up to the Fort or the castle ruins might make such a noise. But I knew then there were none. And when Christy pointed to the field that ran to the site of the old penny-schoolhouse, I saw the moon catching the white tails of rabbits as they bobbed away. It slid its beams into the bogholes, pouring pools of quicksilver that flashed from their black depths. Except for ourselves, no one walked the meadows.

At midnight we made our usual last round of the animals. Christy went into the byre and asked me casually to throw the out-wintering bullocks an arm of hay. I knew what he meant. Going into the hayshed I loaded up, closing my mind to the fact that someone might well be asleep up in the mountain of hay above me. Instead as I built my bundle I tried to think what good clean hay it was, in first-class condition in spite of all the rain. In the far corner of the meadow where the schoolhouse had stood, we had put up a thatched shed for the bullocks. The moon had now risen to its fullness and it was so clear that the holes in the calves' ears, made as a mark of subsidy received, could be seen. And across the field I spotted an unwary rabbit sitting on the burial mound of a cow that had died recently.

Putting the hay in the shed where the bullocks could get it, I walked through the bog, right out to the road, and back through the cherry orchard. The tumbling brooks and choked drains still filled the moon-white valley with melody. But I heard no hooves or running tinkers.

Chapter Fifteen

The Linnet of Boho

The wild world of sally and giant hemlock, stretching from our long bank to Maguire's orchard, was typical of Fermanagh's bogs. Whiter than the lace caps of hemlock, was the cotton grass. Its snowy beards spread over the June bogs, as though January had whirled its flakes down again. And before the heather and ling of autumn blazed above the cotton grass's withered remains, the spades of thirty families sliced into the spongy peat.

In all, the bog did not extend more than twenty acres, but people thankfully owned a few precious roods of it and did not complain though they might live five miles away. We were lucky in owning a part that directly adjoined our farm. In addition to the traditional holding in the communal acreage, Christy had two fine banks higher up. The west's greater rainfall had formed this extra layer, waterlogging the slope and laying strata of rotten vegetation on a much older seam of decomposition. Such a thing as an Ireland without bogs was not conceivable. Yet aeons before, the poor drainage and high humidity had commenced their work. Long, long before James the Fleeing and the Wild Geese had gone to France. Tuan Mac Cairill had not even changed into a salmon, or the Black Pig's Dyke been made, when the relentless rains had swollen and burst the streams and gurgled through the forests that fell to die, and yet strangely to live on as bright flames on our hearths.

The land in which Christy decided to put early potatoes, had been buried under eight feet of turf. No one had tilled that soil since at least the Bronze Age. Yet our spades went in the brown earth as if it had been turned only last season.

Cutting the turf began early that year, for after the vengeance of winter, spring was steeped in sunshine, as though high summer had come immediately, bringing a sun good enough for winning the harvest. From far and near, neighbours and comparative strangers, husbands and wives, dried-up old men and laughing hussies, came to the bog by ass and cart, jennet and trap. Hard work waited for them in those miniature, man-made cliffs cut out of the meadows. But being all together in the bog was 'great sport', and, so far as anyone could tell, had been from immemorial time. The Old Kent Road going down to pick hops had nothing on our peat-cutting.

While working at the various stepped levels of excavated turf, slicing new layers with our spades, the jokes and leg-pulling flew fast. But we watched each other's progress along the bank's face to see what marks our neighbours' spades were leaving. For though a man might tell us this or that about himself or boast about his farm, in the bog there could be no lies. The spades left the imprint of truth. As surely as a mason leaves an imprint of his skill in the stone, so the turf-cutters made a picture of themselves in the wall of decayed plants.

The whole of the little valley between the drumlins was cut into two levels, but no two banks bore the same pattern. When the heather and thin grass were cleared away, the year's requirement of turf was marked out, and then the spade with its side wing was fetched from the cart. The hardest work was at the top, which had dried from exposure since last year's cutting. But once below this level, the slicing became easier when the soft, wetter material was reached. As our spades moved along, levering out the brick-shaped turfs, the pattern on the bank gradually emerged. A good worker left a regular, unvarying texture of spade-strokes, all lying in the same plane, all of the same depth. But the careless or lazy man's danced a jig of shapes so that his neighbours, when they gathered to chat or share a can of buttermilk, laughed at his pock-marked bank.

On my first morning of the cutting week, I discovered how much skill was necessary. I was longing to use the fancy spade with the cow-horn handle. Carefully, precisely, I went along the row, stepping back to admire it at the end. It looked fine. Then I began a second row, but alas, though perfect in itself it did not match the first. And none of mine would match, however hard I tried. Since my handiwork would remain on the bog-face plain for all to see during a whole year, Christy took over the drier top layers to improve the situation. In the lower, wetter layers I resumed again, finding the peat as easy to slice as cheese. But in the oozy bottom layers another difficulty arose. My spade slipped on the flaggons and clumps of reeds from ancient lakes, their tough leaves perfectly preserved through thousands of years. Twigs from the primeval trees, still unbroken and unchanged in shape, and seeds or tiny grains of pollen, were constantly coming once again into the light as though in resurrection, and I paused to examine them all.

Our bog-face remained badly disfigured that year in spite of Christy's efforts, for we struck a really big oak trunk, perfectly preserved like the twigs. We two alone could not shift it and so everybody came to lend a hand with ropes. The centuries fled away as we worked the giant from the prehistoric forest to and fro, slowly extracting it from its grave. Bog oaks were not uncommon and trunks and the larger limbs of the buried trees were kept for building. They long outlived planks made from the living timber above ground. Its discovery thrilled me, and I had all our neighbours alerted and on the lookout for other treasures. But I found no gold or bronze, discs or rings, or even that other golden treasure of bygone ages, sometimes found perfectly preserved in the bog—butter. Because I had helped Freddy in his turf-cutting by wheeling the turf amongst the heather to dry, he presented me with a grubby coin he had once discovered. But it lacked the wonder of lifting up the spade and unearthing the marvel for myself. Over a lifetime Christy, too, had made many finds. The best was two shawl pins found on an island in the lake nearby, which he sold to the National Museum in Dublin.

Disappointment over relics of the past were more than compensated by the 'sport of the bog'. The springtime summer-sun drenched us and around midday became unbearable, so we threw off our clothes and jumped into the liquid mud of the bog-holes. The water stimulated and revived tired muscles, drawing new vigour from unknown sources in our bodies. But it was hardly a polite affair, and I never knew the like again until I saw submerged water-buffaloes do precisely the same thing in the far hotter plains of India. Those turf-cutters who came long distances to claim their yearly heritage of peat, lit fires to cook, and every day without fail, a stray spark would catch the heather alight, adding one more excitement to our work.

Old Charlie McGurty was there to provide us with non-stop entertainment. He lodged with a woman of whom he stood in great fear. So ancient and bent was he, that people said he moved no faster than a 'courting snail'. This only went to prove, they thought, the failure of the crude crosses made of hazel which he carried in the pockets of his frock-coat, now green with age. The crossed twigs were meant to ward off the 'little people' who shot at him with poisoned darts of rheumatism. Protestant laughter at his superstition was all very well, but without his crosses perhaps the old man might not have walked at all!

Charlie's conversation was geared in speed to his gait, and for him conversation was considerably simplified by the use of

only one gender. 'A good day for the meadow, Charlie,' someone might say, and be rewarded with, 'Ah, she's none so bad.'
If his pipe went out, he would mutter resignedly, 'Ah, she's as
cold as the grave'. The feminine charms of his pipe were useful
at other times too, for he only had his old age pension to put
towards his keep, and out of this the landlady allowed him one
ounce of tobacco a week. Of course, it had gone long before
Friday came round again, and so old Charlie stopped everyone
he met, pushed the pipe under their nose and pleaded, 'Ah, she
needs a bit o' baccy'. His stick, a bicycle, a cake of bread, in fact
one and all were 'she'. And, of course, so was the cow.

The winter might hold the land in a vice, and the bitter
north winds freeze by a mere touch, but even on such a day you
could always be sure of meeting Charlie McGurty on the road.
The landlady had only a tiny garden at her cottage, and cold or
no, poor Charlie had to take the cow and graze it by the roadside. It was the boniest old cow ever, though blessed with an
udder like a set of bagpipes. And it never went a day without
breaking into the bog. Lush titbits could be got there, that no
other cattle were allowed to graze because of the dangerous
bog-holes. Charlie's oaths and cries coming across the heather
after the beast, had to be heard to be believed. I was one of
those who willingly stopped work to run over and drive the
cow back to the road. But nothing could compare with the tiny
figure stooping over its sticks, trying to keep pace with the
animal, while scolding and shouting after it, as though the poor
thing were his wife. But it was sadly true that the cow and the
pipe were Charlie's entire world.

Then one day I fell far from his favour bought previously
with a lump of tobacco. I was jumping and leaping over the
bog-holes and banks going home, flinging myself with great
force from each springy level to the other. But the old man was
on the farther side of one, attending to a call of nature. Over he
sprawled in a good fright as I went flying above his head. From

that day he regarded me as his first enemy, and ever after brandished his stick, calling after me, 'Ya clatty Orange bastard'.

Cutting of the turf provided an excuse, if any were required, for much singing. When the soda farls had been eaten and the last of the tea drained away, we crowded together like a tinker's *ceili* and had concerts in the heather. I heard the same kind of music that Martin Calaum and his friends sang round our fire at night, but seldom the same songs. We had many ballads from each barony, and the strangers gave us their own selection. Some of them sang like Martin in the odd five-note scale, sharpening and flattening the notes by a primitive musical instinct.

A song I learnt that spring in the bog heather was the finest I had heard until then. It reached into the tenderest part of my life in Fermanagh. I felt that all the love I had found in the west was embraced in its graceful tune and desperately sad, beautiful words:

> *When I was young my heart was glad*
> *Round Scillies' groves and stream,*
> *Each moment was a sparkling joy*
> *And every day a dream.*
> *For many's and many's the hour I spent*
> *While yet the sun was low,*
> *Listening to the linnet green*
> *That wakes the groves of Boho.*

The singer was Desmond MacClaughey, who lodged in the same cottage as old Charlie. Desmond only came out to the bog in the evening when he left off his job in the forest. He always worked in his bare feet, with his trouser-legs rolled up. At first sight he was not prepossessing. But he was sensitive and intelligent and by some unknown magic worked himself into my affection. Delaying as long as possible, listening to songs in the bog, before fleeing home to supper, I would implore Desmond to sing the 'Linnet of Boho'. There were many verses, mentioning by name the bird songsters of the very ploughlands in Fermanagh where I had been billeted. As Desmond perched singing on the bank, his bare feet dangling over the clean-cut edge of the bog, I learnt each verse. Every wonderful moment lived again—His-self and me at the Scillies after bream with boiled corn—the blackbirds at Strathore, and the dark caves I had wandered in, among the groves of Boho.

But Desmond was to lead me into deeper experiences of life. He had been a 'wee love bird' and homeless for most of his life. At the cottage lodgings he was very unhappy, and lived only for the day when he would kindle the everlasting fire on his own hearth. His girl was called Pauline and they had already been engaged for a number of years, but must still wait to get married for reasons I never discovered. Pauline lived some miles away, and after Mass on Sundays Desmond cycled over to see her. He always brought me back news of her—what a sight of turf she had spread in a week, or I would be told that she had rucked eight acres of meadow by herself. I so wanted Desmond and Pauline to get married and be happy, and I promised them all sorts of plates and cups from my collection of 'posh'. I lent Desmond my camera to catch the freckled face of his love. But before even the film was used up, the great tragedy fell on us.

Sunday came again and Desmond rode off to the lane where Pauline always met him. But that morning she did not come. He learnt that she had been out with an American soldier from the camp. The ways of these wealthy strangers appealed to her and she wanted to see more of them. Desmond's heart broke. He did not come home that night, and old Charlie had to tie up the cow and go in search of him. But the good Sunday suit, with the rosary in the pocket, had already been found by the lake shore, and Desmond's soul was far from the groves of Boho.

The news shocked everyone. Even the most prejudiced of the Methodists and Pilgrims were thankful when the P.P. promised a Christian burial, and said they would attend. Christy and I also went to the funeral. I had peeped into Catholic churches before to blow out their popish candles. But this was different. The church was as packed as a preaching-house harvest thanksgiving. I was so proud to see all the people come to do Desmond honour. To me it was as though an elder brother lay inside the box in the aisle among the flaming pinnacles of Death's unbleached wax. But even my love for the lost Desmond could not clear away a feeling of guilt at being in a Catholic church, for I was a boy from Sandy Row and could never forget that my forefathers had made the Catholics 'fly like chaff before the wind'.

Yet Freddy and Christy were Orangemen, and many of their fellow Lodge brethren were at the funeral too. Even stranger was it when the priest came out and asked for offerings. Up went old Charlie with his precious shilling, at which the priest called out, 'Charlie McGurty—one shilling. God bless you.' Already, others were filing out to queue by Desmond, where he lay in his coffin with a large red heart pierced by an arrow, nailed on the lid. Then I could hardly believe my eyes, for there was Freddy going up to give half a crown. I realized all these offerings were to be used for pulling Desmond out of Purgatory—the place we all knew did *not* exist because of our *How we differ from Rome* and the Orange songs. But I was pleased Freddy had done it, so pleased that I wanted to give something myself. But I was in too great a state of nerves, thinking of Desmond's brown legs that dangled in the bog, now lying stiff in the horrible box. And were the arms so paralysed that they would never recapture even one of a thousand nights of love? It seemed too hard, too bitter to think that even if Pauline herself were to come in, as I half-expected her to, and fling herself on the coffin, then not a sign would poor Desmond make.

Had his shrouders, I wondered, taken off the leather strap he wore round his wrist in lieu of a watch. The strap was black and shiny with sweat, and soaked with the redolence of forest dust from old beeches and the essence of young pines. I wanted to go up past the coffin, just to touch it. The money grew warm in my hand. But I couldn't dare file up with the others— what would my family in Belfast say if they heard that I had given money for a soul in Purgatory?

Then the priest began to sprinkle the holy water, and I watched this very closely. I had been told that two brushes were used for this. One was the normal big one, disliked by the Orangemen for it got holy (or from their view *un*holy) water on their Protestant clothes. The other brush was a very bald one with only a few straggling hairs. But it was this mangy affair that the priest was using now. And I was glad, for the hair was said to have come from the tail of the ass on which Christ rode into Jerusalem, and I knew that would have pleased Desmond.

When at last we got to the graveside and the service continued there, I saw my chance. Most of Desmond's friends had made offerings and so I wanted to express my feelings. I stood on the group's fringe and going back to help carry some wreaths, I saw the box with the money. Quick as lightning I dropped in all the coins I had, and dashed out. But I had not reckoned with old Charlie. In recent months he had only hurled abuse at me. Now he tottered towards me, the candle in his hand dripping over the floor. 'Who will tie up my boots for me now?' he wailed despairingly. Who indeed? And who would sing for me 'The Linnet of Boho' and find me acorns for my pet pig?

Perhaps because of the sad loneliness of his death I could not forget Desmond. Nor could I forgive Pauline. From talking about her so much in the bog, it seemed as though I knew her well, yet in fact I had never seen her. How had the tragedy affected her, I wondered. Would she now dress in black, or wear a black diamond on her sleeve? Her hair may have turned white overnight, like Mrs. Montgomery's was said to have done in the First War, when they brought news that her son had been killed. Or Pauline's teeth may have fallen out, the beautiful teeth of which Desmond spoke and which had left such animal marks on his brown neck. A compulsion seized me—I had to see Pauline for myself.

It must have been on the Sunday immediately following the funeral, that I got on Maggie's bicycle, and made off through the green, singing lanes. I had no eye that day for the flax fields turning into a sea of blue with millions of lint-bells, nor ear for the linnets and the hunger calls of first, second, and even third broods of the nesting season. My heart pounded with the urgent business of vengeance. I stopped several times to ask the way and went down to the lake shore where the clothes had been found neatly placed with the cycle-clips on top.

Every American soldier walking innocently under the trees, appeared as a potential enemy. At last I reached the fateful lane leading to Pauline's farm, and where Desmond had gone to meet her. But I could not summon enough courage to go up and ask for Pauline. It would be difficult to give her a piece of my mind if the family were there. Only if we met on the road could I pour out all the accusation that had filled me since Desmond's death. And I would tell her of things other people had said of her wickedness. Cycling slowly to and fro past the end of the lane, I waited. But Pauline did not come out. Then I rode up to the farm for a view of the house and steading, but the dogs rushed out barking, and so I hurried away again.

On the third Sunday of my search I was luckier. A plantation ran beside the road, bordered by their lane. I bowled by just in time to see an American lift a girl down the steep ditch separating the young trees from the road. Obviously it must be Pauline for the strange copper-beech mane curtained a long oval face, white and freckled like a nightjar's egg. Allowing them time to settle, I rode on, then doubled back to the bank. I crept to the edge and found them just below, in the green shallows. I could see and hear everything. The soldier was black-haired and oily-looking, like a baked potato with butter melted over it. He might have been more like a film star than Desmond, but he could not compare with the gentleness of my rugged woodman friend. I thought the American's manner very cissy, for he got up from an embrace to refold his jacket, thrown down carelessly in the first excitement. Desmond would never have done that, not even with the Sunday suit. He would have thought it an honour to have it crumpled by Pauline, or to lose the creases in his trousers as he raced to trip her in the hayshed.

I was getting into a rage, but was impotent. Had I been a man I would have jumped the bank, laid Desmond's tragedy at their feet, and fought his rival to the death if necessary.

When the lovers settled again, like willing prisoners bound with flesh, I decided to make some protest. A sudden shower of water would give them the greatest shock, and we did not always have to find a well, to fill a few tufts of moss. Getting my bicycle ready for flight, I hurled the nasty missiles over the bank, stayed long enough to hear the screams, and then jumped on. The tight spring inside me was suddenly unwound. The pall of gloom that had clouded my happy summer began to lift.

This victory, a blow struck on poor Desmond's behalf, led me to further efforts, for the balls of wet moss were inadequate for the wrong done. Around our fire at night I had heard tales of people who had received threatening letters written in human blood, during the Bad Times, and there was the possibility of sending Pauline a dead rat through the post with such a missive. But there were practical difficulties to this, and besides Maggie might be grieved by it if she knew. So Pauline was spared. When I went to a dance a better scheme came to me.

The hall was near Pauline's farm, but being a Catholic, she could not attend. Waiting until I felt sure she and the family would be in bed, I left the dancing and went silently up the farm lane. When the buildings loomed in the darkness, I collected a dozen good-sized stones in a heap. Flung high in the air, they landed on the steading's galvanized iron roofs with a resounding twang, and rattled down with a noise of machine-gun fire. The startled dogs went mad, barking and pulling at their chains. Lights appeared at the upper windows, the peace of first sleep broken, no doubt they imagined by bombing, or German parachute invaders. A good thing too, I thought, slashing at leaves with a stick as I ran down the lane.

After that I only saw Pauline once. Driving calves back from the fair one day, a whip cracked behind me. There was the girl with the copper-beech hair, taking a pony-cart home from the creamery. Our calves scattered, galloping in a panic to the hedges. She laughed and edged the cart forward. Her smile was turned on me then, the bright clear reflection of a sweet nature. I had not expected to see her at such close range, and was shocked to find no lines of evil scored into her face. The parted lips showed strong, even teeth that gleamed. Were these the love-hungry fangs that had bitten Desmond's neck? Fine teeth were unusual amongst local girls, and a smile like this one took me by surprise. I had to admit it thrilled me. No wonder the lonely Desmond fell captive.

We spoke no word.

And then, before she got free of our calves, the Angelus rang. Some of the other farmers coming from the fair crossed themselves at the sound—but not the girl in the cart.

An astounding idea occurred that this might not be Pauline after all. Could this lovely, carefree creature be the girl who rucked the eight-acre field and who had lost her green willow by the shores of Erne?

Chapter Sixteen

No Longer a Cub

Day of days in the city corner-boy's life crept in with
first light.

My fourteenth birthday!

I was, overnight, a man. Every Belfast boy knew what the
coming of this day in his life meant. No longer would the
school-inspector's shadow fall with dread into the dark passage
way, nor would the wearing of a trilby and a white silk muff-
ler be refused. He could smoke openly and swear as an equal
with the men. It was the glimmer of hope at the end of long
childhood, a golden gateway to the adult world, bringing
sanction to play in billiard halls, to click the girls in public.
It was the day on which to devour the whole leaven cake of
rights.

As I lay in my little white-painted bed at the farm, the sun
streamed into the room. I waited for Maggie to come down the
wooden stairs and put her stockings on, before making a move
to get up. The postman would soon call, I knew, and I was
anxious as always on my birthday for that vital contact with
home. Yet this year I dreaded it also. The great day had
seemed so far away when I was a child and had sat by the railway lines in Belfast dreaming of the future. Now, unbelievably,
it had come. And the glorious dream was shorn of all its tinsel.
I feared the arrival of my mother's letter, knowing full well it

would be the summons home to the old ways, the grim city, and the commencement of my life in the noisy shipyard.

But there was no letter that day, only a postcard, marked at the bottom with kisses like a barbed-wire fence. Within a week, however, the news came, though it was good, marvellously good news. The firm to which I was to be apprenticed could not take me until July. Since government funds (and diocesan orphan ones also) would continue to support me until then, my mother had given in to my pleadings and would allow me to remain in Fermanagh. And the church, which had helped towards my upkeep from the age of six, wanted to see me confirmed before I left the country and in its full communion.

I could breathe again now, with three whole months of freedom ahead.

After my birthday breakfast, I trundled on Maggie's cycle into Enniskillen to be photographed in my new suit, bought with proceeds from the fox skins. I also wore my new shoes. They were the first pair of real man's shoes, for up to then I had owned nothing but boots for Sundays and plimsolls or sandals for everyday use. Maggie had organized a big party of us to go across the border into Blacklion for the shoes and other smuggled presents for my birthday. Sophie came too and bought me a pair of socks and made a wet cross on each of the shoes for luck.

Finished with the photographers I got home to find Maggie doing battle with the magpies. They were her arch-enemies as rabbits were Christy's and mine. They marauded her chicks in the fields, went into the henhouse after them or to suck the eggs. And the birds became so bold that they would swoop and carry off their catch even if anybody was near. Maggie's flocks diminished so seriously that at last she hired a retired wheelwright, with a reputation as marksman, who had nothing to occupy his time. She posted him, gun at the ready, in a snow-berry thicket, near the henhouse.

The pirates of course would not oblige by all coming to be shot at once, so to while away the hours, Maggie supplied the guard with a welter of newspapers. Neither she nor the old man cared in the least that most of them were last week's, month's, and in some cases, last year's. Reading papers was the wheelwright's one indulgence in life, and consequently his weakness. Coming back from the well later in the day, Maggie saw a magpie mounting the air with one of her chicks. She put the buckets down and ran as fast as her plimsoll, Wellington, and bunion would allow her, to the steading. Havoc had been wrought among her flock, magpies were everywhere. But all she could hear of the sentinel was a mumble as he read the papers to himself, bent low over them with a large magnifying-glass. So after this I was bribed to go hunting in trees and bushes for magpie nests. Every batch of bluish-green eggs I got had a reward in the form of a piece of Waterford for my collection, or a thick, fat salt-cellar from some old castle.

In his own way, Christy was my companion as much as Maggie though of the two she was the livelier and more talkative. Christy was certainly older than my remaining great-aunts, who had been museum-pieces all their lives, certainly in the years I had known them. Yet my regard for the little man had no connection with his age. Unlike the great-aunts, who were never young, Christy retained the simplicity and love I imagined he had as the shy boy who had planted the chestnut tree so many years before. Age had simply seasoned him like the fine timbers down in Red Hughie's mill-yard. He had acquired the natural wisdom of the countryman, but was not changed other-wise. Christy was of a serious turn of mind. His thoughts ran deep, fed by the beautifully tooled books rescued from abandoned mansions. And I knew that when he went to bed after our final night round of the cattle, he did not sleep straight away. Near the big patriarchal bed in his room a pile of books was placed beside the candle, by whose light he read until the small hours. The noisy dancing and singing which Maggie and I loved did not interest him.

Because I so admired him, and emulated his ways, I too began to peer into the heavy tomes of history or accounts of travel. The books effused a faint smell like a church Bible, a scent of bygone times which belonged very well with the author's ponderous style. The books were full of engravings and I never tired at the wonder of the thousands of fine lines scratched on copper, giving such odd impressions of the Matterhorn or Upper Austrian villages, or the market square in a German town.

A crowd of us just out of school met Christy as he collected the returned milk churns down by the road one afternoon. He spoke to the others who were joking about the headmaster's geniuses. These were the boys he would enter at the next examination for the Northern Ireland School Leaving Certificate. When we were alone, going up the lane, Christy remarked, 'I think you should go in for that, Rob'. I hated the thought of examinations, and recalled the previous hours wasted over the scholarship, that could have been spent down by the river. Yet Christy clearly wanted me to try, and that was enough. I would do anything, even that, for him.

Only three months were left of my life in Fermanagh, two of which would have to be sacrificed to studying. But there was no unwillingness or resentment in my heart when the books were opened at the point where I had closed them on leaving Mrs. Stokar's house. Outside, the summer evenings called with a strong voice, and I resisted temptation. But the sums and the dates and the grammar were no longer pliable in my mental fingers. As the two months wore on I grew convinced that failure was inevitable. I kept this a secret from Christy. Fail the examination I might, but fail him I could not. His concern may have been partly vicarious, perhaps he identified his boyhood opportunities with mine, and wanted me to do as well as he would have done. And whatever the result, a certain credit reflected already on Maggie and him, as I knew from comments the neighbours made—'He's the quare settled cub now. That wee Christy's had the great hand with him.'

I went to school on the exam morning feeling quite unprepared, knowing that I would not keep abreast of the other seniors. We went in a large party to Enniskillen where the exam took place. Not until the second English paper was given out, did my nerves quieten. There, on the list of essay subjects, was 'The life of a magpie'. I no longer saw the bald invigilator passing between the rows of desks like the *comite* on a galley. Instead, as clear as day, I saw the domed nest of mud and sticks and the brown speckled eggs that I had handled only yesterday. As though they fluttered in the room, I saw the birds' black livery glazed with blues and greens, made conspicuous by the snow-white scapulars and bellies, as they loitered in Maggie's lane.

Deadly silence in the examination hall enhanced the pens' urgent scratchings and the squeak, squeak, squeak of the invigilator's shoes as he paced out his dead march. But really the room rang with the harsh chatter of the magpies in our henhouse. I saw the fieldmice, the snails, the acorns, the pupae and larvae, and our helpless chicks, all falling victim to the strong bill. I became dimly aware that the other boys must have long finished with 'The life of a soldier', or 'The adventures of a shilling', while I had still reams to write about the spring mating and the slug feasts of September.

We went into the town for tea at Yannarelli's café and there my worst fears returned. From our blotting-paper, answers to the maths paper were compared. None of mine agreed with the others. There was general laughter among the boys, who were more than pleased to know that at least one had made a terrible mess of the exam. I left and cycled home, free for ever from the boredom and fruitless labour of school.

The calm of the farm engulfed me, and working at the turf and haymaking I forgot about the wasted day in town. Weeks later, a voice hailed us from the road as we moved slowly down the field with our rakes. It was the school van-driver shouting that I had passed the exam, and was the only one of the local boys to do so. I did not believe him. But Christy did, and would hear nothing to the contrary. He was right, for the certificate came, and Christy could not rest until the big scroll had been framed and hung on the parlour wall, to keep company with the mildewed prints of Queen Victoria, and the Catholic soldiers bleeding to death as King Billy crossed the Boyne.

As though it had waited for my birthday, a rash now appeared and covered my face with nasty pimples. Assurances that 'all boys have it' and that it would soon vanish, were of no comfort, and I became embarrassed and obsessed by it. What would Sophie think? In the splendour of May and June days I raced over the hill to fetch her on half-days off from 'service'. We would return to the Fort, and lie in the mysterious earth-mound under the 'lonely bushes'. I wondered if my rash would put her off, and she would find excuses to avoid me. But I need not have worried. We climbed the slope as usual. The heat and sensuous pungency of meadow and loaded hedgerow, drugged me into a waking sleep, in which I dozed but still heard Sophie's voice and the cry of birds overhead. Always practical, Sophie held my head in her lap, and worked on my unfortunate face. She had brought scented cream, borrowed from her lady's maid. After hunting pimples as though plucking quill-ends from a chicken in the mansion-house kitchen, she rubbed the cream smoothly in, stopping at intervals to plant a sweet, soft kiss on my forehead. We were very still, and the rabbits ventured cheekily out of their burrows again. They hopped so near that at the slightest movement of a kiss, they sat up, sensitive ears erect. Then we could see the sun straining through their ears, turning them into exotic pink seashells. And afterwards, holding hands, we ran breathlessly and laughing down the hill, wondering if Maggie had remembered to boil eggs with the tea, for we were ravenous.

Always on the horizon was my departure, and we cut the hay early, to get as many rucks up as possible before I went. Some of the soldiers came to help on their way back to camp after bathing. They talked of their farms in Pembroke, the piers at Brighton, and loves and hates of Paddington Green. But as the meadowsweet withered and was carried away, so we all sensed our lives were soon to be carried beyond the bridgehead of the brown Scillies. Such thoughts would never be expressed, but we all recognized the sad look that in an unguarded moment showed in our eyes. As we worked we felt an invisible hand waiting to snatch us from the hayfield. Our new friends would leave for the evening with a cheerful 'See you tomorrow', and walk off carrying their thick khaki jackets carelessly over their shoulders. But the next afternoon when they did not come, we guessed that their unit was going out to the fighting and that they were confined to barracks until the move was made. We seldom had the chance to say good-bye.

One boy swore he would return to our farm when the war ended, and forever tend the meadows and fill the turf. He had been in Dr. Barnardo's homes for years, and thought of Maggie and Christy as his real parents. He burned with such sincerity about coming back, that he left a lot of personal things with me until he bade farewell to uniforms and came back. But as I peppered them, wrapped them in brown paper, and laid them carefully in the parlour wall-cupboard, I knew that, somehow, life did not work out like that. What a shining hope in childhood the coming of my fourteenth birthday had been, but now sadness had tarnished even that.

Rain fell for an hour or so on several days. As we turned swathes in the new orchard, Maggie pointed out that the frogs which hopped from under the cut grass, had lost their bright yellow for a russet-black. She knew then that the sudden squalls presaged more prolonged rain and storms, and we set about lapping before they should creep up on us. Maggie's forecast was reliable, for a few days later sweeping curtains of rain shut Belmore from view and turned the cow-pass once more into a quagmire.

In a deluge, I set off for confirmation instruction. No other candidate had braved the flood and so I sat alone with the curate. He was well aware already, that I was mechanically versed in such matters as the outward and inward parts of the sacraments, and we talked about the glebe activities instead. Ensuing lessons fell on finer days and encouraged by Christy, I took them seriously. The pomps and vanities of this wicked world referred quite plainly, for me at least, to the pimples on my face and the cigarette holder. I had also to translate the meaning of the sinful lusts of the flesh. The ban on these became an even stronger reason than the fear of insanity, for giving up my secret visits to the hayshed. Card-playing had also been specially mentioned. I realized that I could not join up with the old gang again when I went back to Belfast, to spend my hours free of the shipyard along the railway banks, flipping out the clubs and diamonds. The laying on of hands would sound the knell of all my old pleasures.

Christy was out working in the bog as I passed down the lane on the tall bicycle on my way to the church, wearing my new suit. I had given my hair a hard brushing, but not its usual coating of cheap brilliantine, for I thought the bishop would not like to touch its glue or smell its too-sweet perfume, surely a sign of ungodliness.

As the battered machine shook and rattled over the ruts, I tried to think of the approaching sacrament and all it implied for me. Lost in grave thoughts I arrived and wheeled my cycle through the churchyard, under the yews. The pews were full, and I thought everyone was looking at my smart clothes. I felt extremely nervous and fingered my Prayer Book. It was new to me, but on the flyleaf, I could see by an attenuated copper-plate script that it had been given to Isabella Diana Denham of Fairwood Park in 1829, at her confirmation. In all the years it had remained as almost new. Now it was Maggie's confirmation present to me. While the organist's improvisation and the shuffle of latecomers being squeezed in, struggled for supremacy, I thought of the young Isabella Diana.

Had she held the book in her white-gloved hand, as the horses of her carriage brought her to receive the sacrament? Was it she who had underlined so many verses in the *Benedicite*? Had she still been a young girl, or had the mature woman emphasized the praise of Dews and Frosts, Green Things upon the Earth, Lightnings and Clouds, the Wells and Seas and Floods? Or, when she was an old woman and confined to her bed at Lisgoole Abbey, had she repeated the canticle 'O ye Winds of God, bless ye the Lord: praise him, and magnify him for ever', moving her lips silently as she rang her bell and waited for Maggie's mother to hurry through the dark wood? By then, her only son, 'the good Master Obins' would have been dead, and her great family fortune already bequeathed, in her will, to the support of Protestant orphans—boys like myself.

Then the clergy filed in and I forgot Isabella Diana. It helped me considerably to see that the curate, who had given me my 'private talk', was looking nervous too. He walked in front of the magnificent bishop with a crozier that shone like a seraph. For a moment a grin drove out my seriousness. The bishop had a black patch over one eye, as though under the episcopal robes a pirate was playing the part, or as if he were the ancient Balor of the Blows, the one-eyed King of the Fomorians, after whose wife Enniskillen was named. But as he took the crozier in his hand and moved serenely towards the

239

candidates he seemed to create a mystical atmosphere which absorbed my attention.

> *Behold us, Lord, before Thee met*
> *Whom each bright angel serves and fears,*
> *Who on Thy throne rememberest yet*
> *Thy spotless Boyhood's quiet years;*
> *Whose feet the hills of Nazareth trod,*
> *Who art true Man and perfect God.*

The singing lustier than usual on account of the bishop's presence, faded away, and through the open door the birds' passionate song flowed in. In mounting tension we bowed our heads at the rail, and the consecrating hands moved towards us. I stole a glance at the curate but he stood stiffly, a non-committal expression hiding his thoughts. Then I noticed that the boy in front of me had a skin complaint and that his hair had fallen out in patches. I was worried, for I did not want the bishop to touch it and carry the germs to me on his hands. My terror dissolved when I knelt before him, and the solemn pronouncement was made. When the climax passed, I rose from my knees and went back to the pew. And after that I was aware of nothing more until we poured out into the sunshine. Picking up the cycle from the wall where I had leant it, I rode home, hardly noticing the jolts.

The days were numbered now.

Our hay lay wet or in laps, waiting for a good wind to dry it out. But the rains still came up in sudden gusts, darkening the land, and driving the forlorn flocks of chickens to shelter under the snowberry bushes. On Thursday I was to leave. Before being allowed into the docks of Belfast on Monday morning, a police interview was necessary to get the official war-time permit. On Wednesday the strip of seaweed hung in the hall dried out so crisp that we thought it just possible to save the hay that had turned as black as the frogs. Sure enough, during the day, the clouds melted away leaving a good drying wind. The damp atmosphere and the lingering smell of wet foliage cleared away by the afternoon when benign summer smiled over the fields and hills.

Tomorrow's beginning of another hot spell might be the last chance that Christy and Maggie would have of getting all their hay rucked. I could not desert them and staying to help would postpone the terrible moment of parting. My mother would have to be informed. A telegram was out of the question. Only once in our lives had the boy with the red bicycle stopped at our house, and that had been (so long ago it seemed now) to bring the dread telegram about my father's death. I could not risk giving her another shock. So before the cows were milked I went up to the mill and telephoned the woman who kept the babywear shop on the main road. She promised to run round and tell my mother that I would not be home until late on Friday.

I did not care what results this would have. Lying blissfully in front were another twenty-four hours in the Fermanagh valley. As many rucks as hours, with assistance from the soldiers, could be put up in this time. Nothing of the days and years ahead mattered at all, they had no substance in my mind. My sole concern was that Jenny the ass, the white bullock I had bought as a dropped calf by the roadside, that the cows I had vetted, milked and loved, should have enough fodder for the next winter.

And the work went well. There was good help from the camp. As the sun went down, clouds of midges circled our heads, and we lit cigarettes to drive them off by smoke. Then we forced Maggie to try a cigarette, but after the first few draws she spluttered and coughed, and thought herself very fast because Jamie Frazer driving his cattle home on the distant hills might see her.

We had never worked so late as on my last night at the farm.

The moon ran high, and the stars stalked abroad as the soldiers put on their singlets and tunics after the heat of haymaking. Maggie's nerves were on edge for she feared that I would not be able to get up early enough for my long journey. To her it was as though I would be travelling to the earth's end. Though near in spirit, Belfast was as far away for her as Timbuktu.

But I was fully awake when I heard the familiar pattern on the stairs. From my little window I could see a gentle breeze disturbing the trees. The sunlight of another beautiful day was already slanting through the leaves. When it had set, I would not be there, and the usurping moon would fall on no figure lying under my white counterpane.

In the kitchen I took my socks from the crook and pulled them on slowly, and set about getting ready. Christy had got me two tin trunks from an auction sale, for all my pottery and china. Maggie had found a Victorian carpet-bag for my clothes. My precious blue vase was wrapped in woollen vests and put in a leather box shaped like the top-hat it had once held for the young Master Obins of the Abbey. In spite of the sunshine and the hay that still wanted winning, Christy had no second thoughts about giving up a valuable day's work in the meadows and taking me in to Enniskillen station in the ass and cart.

After it was harnessed, Maggie stood by the donkey's head, while Christy and I carried out the luggage and the trunks with the 'posh'. When we got up and started off down the lane, she ran beside us, one hand on the cart, through the hedges that needed cutting, past the cherry orchard, the bogs, the old oak with a bulging stomach like a Chinese Buddha, the enormous twin poplars that nodded and swayed like the two nuns who always came collecting money.

And then Maggie was gone.

The donkey trotted towards town. Christy and I did not speak much. We passed many people I knew, farmers or women going in search of cattle or to fetch water. They all waved good-bye and shouted things I did not hear. When the trunks had been put on the platform, and the little white-headed man got up into the ass-cart again, I thought my heart would break.

I felt like a man already as the train gathered speed. For ever a part of me now were the things left behind. The countryside through the carriage window changed into fields and woods I did not recognize, and I thought that nothing would be so dear, so beautiful as what was gone, and I no longer the Cub—Our Cub.

> *Derrygonnelly, good-bye. Fair days are done,*
> *Of springing heifers, yapping dogs,*
> *And cutties running the lanes*
> *Bare legs red-branded by heather.*
>
> *Lisbellaw, you gave me tweed*
> *Upon my back, but do not wait,*
> *I shall never come again for Orange sprees*
> *Or your weaver's daughter for good measure.*
>
> *Silent splendour of my Scillies, flow on.*
> *Days of dreaming for humble perch*
> *And the dancing flies of red serving-boys*
> *In King Meilghe's lake, are gone.*
>
> *Farewell Pauline of the spring-cart*
> *Take home the milk cheque.*
> *I leave you, and the far hill of the badgers*
> *Where Desmond lies with his Sacred Heart.*
>
> *Good-bye hallowed barn and best trap*
> *And sound of axe in solemn woods.*
> *Angelus, ring for Hail Marys*
> *And Protestant dinners, not for me.*

No Longer a Cub

To winter nights and voices round the fire,
Smiles and frowns, charmers and Pilgrim wives
To singing flames and shadows that fell
Into my waiting arms, good-bye.

Farewell Maggie, Christy, love,
Wisdom of seasons I shall not know again.
And Carlo cock no ears for my call
In soft rains, by 'lonely bush' or spring-well.

Magnet sights and sounds I leave,
Byre incense for city smoke.
The train's hard pulse stirs now the vibrant string,
My song of Erne falls dying on the air.